5⁹⁵
Rel

FOUNDERS OF LIVING RELIGIONS

D1100495

FOUNDERS
OF
LIVING
RELIGIONS

by
Herbert Stroup

THE WESTMINSTER PRESS
Philadelphia

Copyright © 1974 The Westminster Press

All rights reserved—no part of this book may be
reproduced in any form without permission in writing
from the publisher, except by a reviewer who wishes
to quote brief passages in connection with a review
in magazine or newspaper.

Book Design by Dorothy Alden Smith

Published by The Westminster Press®
Philadelphia, Pennsylvania

PRINTED IN THE UNITED STATES OF AMERICA

Library of Congress Cataloging in Publication Data

Stroup, Herbert Hewitt, 1916–
  Founders of living religions.

  Bibliography: p.
  1. Religions—Biography. 2. Religions. I. Title.
BL72.S8   200'.92'2 [B]   74–10934
ISBN 0–664–24994–9

ALICE TYLER STROUP
AND
TIMOTHY DIENER STROUP

Tendebantque manus ripae ulterioris amore.
Virgil, *Aeneid* 6.314

CONTENTS

PREFACE

The eight founders of religions that are portrayed in this book are the founders of the religions that bear their names or with which they are associated as prime innovators in the religious and cultural sphere. Three other major religions (Hinduism, Shinto, and Judaism) have no known historic personages who can be identified as founders and so are not included. In each case, the eight have reflected the historical and cultural situation into which they were born. But they also achieved some degree of fresh and decisive insight into the ultimate nature of man, society, and the universe. Combining their past and their genius of insight, they have formulated religions that have appealed to countless numbers of persons. Their followers have modified the founders' doctrines, cultic practices, and communal forms, but even in doing so they have sought to be faithful to the original formulation of religion provided by the founders. Thus, the lives of the eight founders are pivotal points in history. These men have reshaped and redirected the past. They have set large segments of world society off into new modes of personal and social existence. Their sense of what is holy has widely and deeply influenced such social realities as the family, economic relations, social stratification, political and legal forms, and individualism. They are indeed heroes of faith.

The primary aim of this book is to provide a relatively brief, uncomplicated biography of each of the eight founders of the living religions. Being introductory, it is intended for the uninformed beginner. Each of the lives involves vast problems of historical and literary scholarship, but this volume does not consist of a series of critical studies of the founders' lives. Yet it seeks to be faithful to what modern scholarship has contributed. Admittedly, various scholars hold varying views on many of the details of the founders' lives, even the dates of their births and deaths. Although this scholarship is taken into account, the eight biographies are here constructed in straightforward, simple delineation. The interested reader will have to turn to other books to secure a critical understanding.

The presentation of the lives follows a common pattern. *First,* the religion is located in time and space. That is, each religion is characterized as to its kind or type. Its relationship to other religions is indicated. The country of its birth, its founding date, and its size are also given. *Second,* the general cultural situation at the time of the religion's founding is described briefly. Each religion derives from a distinctive cultural inheritance, a knowledge of which is indispensable to an understanding of its motives and nature. *Third,* a short account is given of the literary sources from which a life of the founder may be obtained. *Fourth,* the life of the founder is portrayed. This is the basic focus of each chapter, and in this section information is arranged to show the birth of the founder, his family connections, his early life experiences, including his education and vocation. Then his calling to found a new religion is described, his gathering of disciples, his fortune in winning converts, his journeys to promulgate the new faith, and his final years leading to his death. Reliable information is not evenly available for all the founders on each of these points. *Fifth,* some evaluation of the life of the founder is given, along with his later veneration. *Sixth,* a short summary of the founder's teachings closes each chapter.

The common pattern precludes attention to several other subjects that are related to the religions. For example, no effort is made to outline the history of each religion beyond the founder's lifetime. Again, a systematic theological presentation of each religion is not attempted, because the basic aim is biographical rather than theological or philosophical. A number of questions of a literary, sociological, and psychological nature are touched upon, but they are not here developed. Similarly, the lives of a number of other spiritual heroes within each tradition are not dealt with in any detail. Finally, each life is not exhaustive; it is representative. This means, for example, that where a long series of miracles were said to have been performed by the founder, not all the miracles will be related; some will be recounted to show representatively how the founder acted.

A minimum of technical terms have been included and where they appear they have been explained in simple English. Many of the terms are spelled in various ways by competent scholars. The chief virtue of the spelling used in this book may be merely that of consistency. Similarly, all diacritical marks have been eliminated in the belief that the beginning reader will merely find them obstructive. Consistently, too, references to the gods of the eight religions, and others, are given in lower case. This practice is not meant to disparage the weighty claims that such references intend; it is intended to show a measure of objectivity toward all the religions.

The bibliography at the end of the book is primarily for the general reader. Many technically competent studies have been made of the founders of the living religions, but the books that have been selected for the bibliography have in the main avoided a depth and detail that might be overwhelming to those persons with little or no knowledge of the subjects. Also, the index includes within it a glossary in simple form which may be used by those who wish to make a quick reference or a student's review.

I am indebted to my friend, Professor Henry Clay Niles of Westminster College, Fulton, Missouri, for a careful and critical reading of the manuscript. He brings special competencies to this task.

I have dedicated this book to my son, Timothy, and his wife, Alice, and to their dedication to the intellectual life in the service of humankind.

Although I am indebted to many persons, now both dead and living, in the preparation of this book, I as author remain responsible for the substance of the work.

1
INTRODUCTION

The founders of religions are highly significant shapers of the course of history. They stand with a scarce number of secular heroes who also have led mankind in the conservation and destruction, the reforming and renewal, of intellectual, social, and emotional forms through which history secures whatever meaning it may have. Karl Marx, for example, through the impact of his innovative thought set into action a wide variety of social consequences that have gone far to mold a large part of the modern world. Marxism as a social movement has contributed to the ways in which many people think about themselves and their world. It has instituted actions by which whole governments and societies have been reorganized. It has established a new and different mood for the emotional expressions of countless thousands of persons. Marx, of course, is merely an example of the way in which history has been changed by heroic leaders.

The founders of religions are in their own way also heroic leaders. They too have been pivotal personalities in rechanneling history, in the process of reemphasizing traditional values and asserting the appeal of new values, and in pointing men and women to fresh visions of the ideal.

In traditional societies especially, religion may be viewed as representing the core meaning of these societies. It is that set of values which mainly characterize both personal and collective life. Or, to say it another way, culture is the form that religion takes. Thus the view that religion and culture are separate elements, only more or less related, is not historically substantiated. Religion and culture, as history attests, are intertwined. Each depends upon the other. Each gives the other its form and meaning. Because religion and culture are traditionally inseparable, the founders of religions must be considered as history's heroes who have had profound influence upon the shaping of culture.

Religion has a threefold effect upon culture. First, religion contributes intellectual expressions. It seeks to grapple with questions of meaning. It takes to itself such inquiries as: How did the universe come to be? Does human life have a purpose? What is the nature of the good? Does life really end with death? Its answers to such questions often take poetic and mythological forms. These forms, however, may stimulate more rational efforts, as in philosophy and science. Religion's intellectual quest usually is termed theology. Its specific teachings are called doctrines.

Second, religion contributes to action. What religion affirms to be the nature of reality is not merely accepted, it is celebrated. In fact, the intellectual expressions of religion are affirmed through celebrative action. Such action is usually called worship. The truths that religion affirms are not considered to be ordinary or casual. They pertain to the most real and respectful aspects of human experience. The use of religious language, especially as expressed through symbols, is one mode of worship. Ritual or liturgy is another. The word "liturgy" comes from the Greek and refers to a thing that is done. It is solemnly intentioned action which in dramatic form sustains conceptions of that which is deemed to be holy. Sacraments are ritual practices by which the especially mysterious aspects of human and divine experience are celebrated. Sacrifices are things done or objects offered to appease and restore relations with that which is considered to be ruling in the human experience of the divine. Religiously inspired action in personal and social life is also a form of worship.

Third, religion contributes to social relationships. Persons who hold intellectual expressions in common and who worship together form a community. The idea that religion is what a man does in his solitariness seems to be false. What men do together is the substance of religion. Religion does support some forms of individualism, but such individualism develops from an even more basic sense of belongingness.

The founders of religions have been leaders in this threefold contribution of religion. First, they have proposed truths by which the nature of reality is more clearly and accurately perceived. Second, they have advocated actions toward reality by which reality is affirmed and celebrated. Third, they have called persons into distinctive social relationships. This is what it means to found a religion, for this is what religion means.

To say that religion makes three major contributions to culture is not to say that there is such a thing as generic religion. Religion exists just about everywhere that human beings are found. People everywhere are characterized by religion. As has been said, religion expresses the core values of culture and culture is a human requirement. But religion is always found in a specific religious form. There is no single and universal form of religion; there are only the discrete religions, the specific religions of specific peoples. So far as the founders of religions are concerned, they are the founders of particular religions. Both the founders and their religions are in every case historically unique. They simply are themselves. The founders and their religions are part and parcel of the particular cultures in which they exist. The founders, as has been said, cannot be separated from the culture that they have inherited and that they to some degree have changed.

Strangely enough, then, it is not possible to name a founder for each and every religion that has been created. In fact, there are relatively few known founders of religions. To understand this situation it is necessary to consider three broad categories of religions: dead, primitive, and living. Many religions have been born with their accompanying societies, have grown and flourished, and as their supporting and supported societies have lost vitality and died, so these religions have died. One thinks immediately of the religions of ancient Greece, Rome,

Egypt, and Babylonia, although there are many others. The Old Testament describes how the ancient Israelites were in constant conflict and competition with the surrounding peoples and their religions. Reading these accounts today is somewhat tedious, for in the main all these peoples and their religions have died. Only Judaism has survived. Similarly Christianity at the time of its origin was faced with a variety of competitive religions, most of which today are not live options.

If the so-called dead religions had particular, individual founders, they are surely not known now. It may be argued theoretically that all religions, since they are innovative cultural expressions, must necessarily have been founded by a particularly creative individual. Thus the religions that appear to have no founder did in fact have founders. Certainly they had priests and teachers and others who gave leadership to them in the course of their histories. But it is not possible to point with any certitude to specific persons as having the status of founders.

Primitive religions also appear not to have founders that are known. Primitive religions are the religions of primitive peoples. These peoples are characterized by small populations, geographical restrictions, and highly homogeneous cultures in which such factors as economics and politics are relatively simple in themselves and undifferentiated. Generally they are preliterate and evidence little change. In these ways they differ from so-called advanced societies and advanced religions. Yet when one reviews them from the time of Cro-Magnon man to the present, one is hard put to find specific individuals who may be claimed as the founders of their religions. As with the dead religions, primitive religions may have had their particular founders, but if they did, they are not now known. Taking the dead and the primitive religions together, it is possible to say that the largest number of religions in history have no identifiable founders.

The living religions comprise the third category. The three categories, however, should not be viewed as exclusive. Obviously many religions of primitive peoples are alive today. Then, too, the religions of bygone peoples, although formally dead, live on in other religions that have been influenced by them and that survive at the present time. But there are a number, a limited number, of religions which by almost any account are living. Four of the major living religions originated in India: Hinduism, Jainism, Buddhism, and Sikhism. Hinduism, Jainism, and Sikhism are today largely confined to India. Buddhism has gone beyond the national boundaries and has become a widely held religion throughout Asia. China has been the location for the origination of two of the living religions: Confucianism and Taoism. These religions historically have been largely confined to China. At the present time, however, it is difficult to know to what extent they are vital forces in Chinese culture in the light of the domination of Marx-Mao thought and organization. Japan has given birth to one religion: Shinto. Buddhism also is a feature of Chinese and Japanese life. Iran is the home grounds for yet another living religion: Zoroastrianism. Finally, the Fertile Crescent, as it was called, gave rise to three living religions: Judaism, Christianity, and Islam. These eleven living religions are widely accepted as the major forms of extant, advanced religions in our time. Hardly anyone would deny that the eleven are truly living religions, but some persons would add to the list those newer religious expressions which have come into being in relatively recent times. In most instances these seem to be variants of already existing religions. At any rate, it is the founders of these eleven religions, where founders can be designated, that the present inquiry will portray.

Three of the religions bear the names of their founders in their titles: Confucianism, Muhammadanism, and Zoroastrianism. Muhammadanism, however, is less used today to refer to that religion, the more common appellation being Islam. Several of the religions carry the honorific title given to their founders. Jainism, for example, was founded by Vardhamana, who popularly is often called Mahavira. Jainism, however, refers to an attribute of Vardhamana. A Jain is a conqueror;

Vardhamana was a spiritual conqueror. Again, Gautama, the founder of Buddhism, achieved a very distinctive state of being a *buddha,* or an enlightened one. So Buddhism is not a religion that has been named for the name of its founder. It refers to a state that the founder accomplished and that is the goal of all true followers of the founder. The third example is Christianity. Obviously the name of the founder of this religion is Jesus. But Jesus was deemed by his followers to have been the Anointed One, or the Christ. Christ, then, is a title given to the founder rather than an actual name of the founder.

Several of the religions bear names that highlight a principal teaching of the religions. Taoism, for example, which had a founder, Lao-tzu, is not named for the founder or for an attribute of the founder. Rather, Taoism refers to the Way, the Divine Path. This title refers to a teaching of the religion. Shinto did not have a founder. But the title refers to the Way of the Gods, emphasizing a basic teaching of the faith. Islam, which is sometimes called Muhammadanism, stresses a key characteristic of the religion's teaching: submission, especially submission to the transcendent deity, Allah. Sikhism, which was founded by Nanak, takes its title from the idea of discipleship. Sikhs are Nanak's disciples. Hinduism as a name for a religion was not known in India until the conquest of the Muslims, or followers of Islam. The Muslims began their invasion of India in the eighth century A.D. and by the eleventh century were in firm control of much of the country. They began to designate the indigenous peoples of India as Hindus. The religion of the Hindus became known as Hinduism. But originally the term Hindu was used by the Muslims to refer to all the native peoples of India, regardless of their faith. So originally both Jains and Buddhists were included. Later and dominantly today, Hinduism refers to a complex, historical religion of great diversity which is acknowledged to be a separate religion from the other faiths that have come into being in India. Hinduism has no known founder. Judaism refers to the religion of the Jews. Yet it is a title that is not found in its sacred scriptures. The word occurs in Gal. 1:13 in the New Testament and also in II Macc. 2:21; 8:1. But in the main it seems to be a designation that non-Jews originally gave to the religion of the Jews.

In the cases of two of the eleven living religions it is clear that they had no known founders. These are Hinduism and Shinto. Hinduism is a very old religion and its origins are relatively obscure. Probably it dates from about 1500 B.C., the time when the Aryans invaded India from the northwest and gradually conquered the native people, the Dravidians. The resulting religion is described in the four Vedas or books of knowledge. The religion at that time was notably nature worship, although there are signs of belief in a number of "high" gods and the development of a religiously inspired social organization which later became the Indian caste system. The hymns of the Rig Veda, the earliest of the Vedas, for example, are ascribed to *rishis*, or inspired sages. These were holy men of great imagination and poetic-mythological capacity, but they can scarcely be termed founders of Hinduism. Obviously there were a sizable number of *rishis* and no one of them has been singled out as a founder of the whole religion by the Hindus themselves. Hinduism grew and changed after the time of the Vedas and various persons made contributions to its development, but no one can be accurately called a founder.

Shinto is the second religion that clearly has no known founder. It is the agelong religion of the Japanese people. It teaches that the islands and the people of Japan were the first of all creation. No historical dating of the creation is acknowledged. Precise details of the creation of the land, the people, and the religion of Shinto are not stated. So no historical moment when the religion came into being is known to the tradition. Similarly no known founder is celebrated in the Shinto tradition. The assumption is that Shinto had no founder.

Judaism is a doubtful case of a personally founded religion. Traditionally Abraham is designated as Judaism's founder. Yet so little is accurately known about Abraham that some scholars even doubt there was such a historic person. Probably he was a tribal leader of the ancient Hebrews whose personal religious experience and the turmoil about his people led him and his people to migrate to Palestine, which then was inhabited by the Canaanites. He believed that he was called by a deity, an El, who was greater in presence and power than the animistic deities worshiped by the surrounding peoples. Later Abraham and his faithful followers migrated to the south and settled in the fertile valley of the Nile. His leadership was replaced in time by his son, Isaac, and his grandson, Jacob. Abraham undoubtedly was a personage of remarkable social leadership who significantly advanced the religion that became Judaism.

Moses also made a highly important contribution to the development of Judaism. To some, he may be considered its founder. The story of his birth in Egypt, his rise within Egyptian society, his slaying of an Egyptian who had abused one of his fellow Hebrews, his flight from Egypt and his return to lead his people to the "land flowing with milk and honey" after a period of receiving the commandments and the Torah, or law, at Sinai or at Horeb, as the case may be, is familiar to many. Moses, then, may be considered along with Abraham as a great social leader, guiding his people to freedom in a new land, and a contributor of a high order to the religious development of the Jews. It is commonly said that the worship of Yahweh, the name of Israel's god, began at the time of Moses. This form of worship was distinctly more complex and advanced than that previously practiced. The idea of the Jews as a covenanted people who bear a special relationship to Yahweh is another singular contribution if not of Moses himself then of his period. Because of his significant contributions socially and religiously, Moses has been held in high esteem by all three of the Semitic religions: Judaism, Christianity, and Islam. Yet there is reason to be hesitant in ascribing to Moses the founding of Judaism. For one thing, such a designation tends to overlook or minimize the important contributions of Abraham and his successors. Again, it seems clear that Moses did not think of himself as a founder of a religion. Rather, he was a teacher and a leader. He presumably explicated a religion that already was in existence, although perhaps not in so highly a developed form. He also gave enduring definition to a people, the Jews.

A third turning point in the development of Judaism as a religion has been suggested. It is the period of the prophets: Elijah, Elisha, Amos, Hosea, Isaiah, and others. The claim is that it was not until the rise of the prophets that Judaism became its fullest and finest self. The prophets proclaimed a truly single, transcendent deity, Yahweh, who for himself and his people required the highest ethical standards of personal and group behavior. This claim has some validity, although it appears largely to indicate a major step in the life of a developing religion and not its point of origination. Obviously, too, there is no one person or prophet of that period who is designated as the founder of Judaism. Few persons would consider any of the prophets to be genuine founders of the religion of Judaism.

For these reasons the foundership of the religion of Judaism seems to be in doubt. Probably if any one person may be viewed as the founder it would be Abraham.

Not one of the founders of the world's living religions was a woman.

Little is known historically about would-be founders who failed. The sheer fact of their failure exempts them from consideration, for their failure indicates that they were unable to establish a religion to which detailed reference may be made. An outstanding case of a person who wished to establish a new religion and who failed is Akhenaton (1372-1354 B.C.). Akhenaton of Egypt was the son of Amenhotep III and the husband of the renowned Nefertiti. As ruler he sought to break the power of the priesthood of Amun by replacing the chief deity of the traditional religion, Amun, with a selection of his own, Aton. He proceeded in stages by changing his own name from Amenhotep to Akhenaton and building a new capital called by his name. He sought to eliminate completely all references to Amun, even on monuments, and to establish other elements of a complete culture, including art, which would give recognition to his proposed new religion. But despite his efforts, he failed. The priests devoted to Amun were not defeated; rather, they succeeded in having their religion prevail over that of their ruler. Akhenaton also antagonized the army in his lack of devotion to nonreligious matters of state. His successor, Tut-Ankh-Amon, seeing that the cause of Aton was lost, made his peace with the priesthood and reestablished Thebes as the country's capital. Akhenaton's name became anathema and evidences of him were eliminated by official decree. Although he sought to introduce a new religion to Egypt, he failed.

The account of Akhenaton illustrates some of the difficulties that exist in seeking to define the nature of a founder. In certain respects Akhenaton appears to be a reformer rather than a founder. In the cases of the others who founded religions, they may also be viewed as reformers, for all the founders established their religions out of an existing religious past. In religion, as elsewhere, there is no possibility of creating something out of nothing. In every instance the founder of a religion utilized elements from one or more religions that were part and parcel of the culture of his time. In addition, the role of the founder commonly has not been that of a leader who claims a completely new vision of reality. More often than not, the founder calls his followers to a reformed version of one or more existing religions. Or, his appeal may be to a selected strand of an existing religion, coupled with fresh insights regarding the ancient truths, and embodied within a distinctive consciousness. What marks the founder of a religion from all other types of religious leaders, including that of the reformer, is that the founder succeeded in establishing what has been ascribed by others who have followed him as a distinctly new religion. Contrariwise, the reformer is essentially marked off from other religious types by his failure to establish an autonomously new form of religion. The reformer does his work within a traditional context of a religion and is satisfied to purify the religion without breaking fundamentally with it. Perhaps another way of saying the same thing is to indicate that reformers and founders are rather alike, except that reformers are not as innovative, tradition-shattering, and capable of establishing new sociological forms. Various religious leaders introduce changes in their traditional religions, but only the founder is looked back upon as an originator of a religion. All the other leaders are viewed for what they have been: reformers, priests, prophets, seers, diviners, saints, and so forth, but not as founders.

The founders of religions did not all view themselves in similar fashion. Confucius and Lao-tzu, for example, thought of themselves as they were thought of by others, essentially as teachers or social philosophers. The resulting religions reflect this self-concept. On the other hand, Muhammad clearly thought of himself as a prophet who stood very much in the tradition of the prophets of ancient Judaism, and such he was. The relations of the founders to the world around them also differed. Vardhamana and Gautama, for example, were characterized by a clear sense of withdrawal from worldly activities. Hardly may they be viewed as social philosophers with a positive message of how better to organize society. Confucius, on the other hand, was a teacher of social responsibility. He sought in large measure to indicate how the good society might be attained. The founders differed in other regards, but what makes it possible to classify them as founders is the single fact that they are so looked upon by others, their followers especially. Founders may be conceived, then, as quantitatively different from other kinds of religious leaders in that they have actually established sociologically new forms of religion. They also may be viewed as qualitatively different in that they succeeded in introducing changes within their religious traditions which caused others to attribute to them the highest qualities of innovative leadership. These qualities are assumed to exceed those possessed by any other types of religious leaders.

The founder of a religion does not stand alone in his creative endeavors. He is a part, albeit the leading part, in the founding of a religion. But he also is dependent upon a sociological process in which others are involved before a genuinely new religion comes into being. The founder usually responds to a "call" or to a mystically experienced event of communion with ultimate reality which forms the basis of his religious activities. This call is not always related to a personal deity. In the cases of Vardhamana of Jainism and Gautama of Buddhism, the existence of a deity is not assumed by the founders. But the founders do claim to have experienced an event, which may consist of successive stages, in which they have been seized by a higher reality or truth than that which has been known. For them this experience is central to a true understanding of self, society, and the universe. Through later developments the experience forms the core values of the new faith.

Religions, however, need followers as well as founders. So, while a founder is indispensable, a religion also must depend on an ever-widening circle of adherents in order to be a success. Usually the relatively small band of initial followers are called disciples. They are characterized, for one thing, by being a small group. After he announces his calling, the founder is able to gather only a small number of adherents at the start. Some of these are attracted to the man and his message, but others may be called into the inner circle by the founder himself. Commonly the disciples are a varied and diverse group. They often represent different backgrounds of education, occupation, moral standards, devotion to the founder, and temperament. For example, in regard to temperament, some may be emotionally demanding and prone to quick responses. Others may be philosophically or mystically inclined. Still others may be of practical bent, caring for such matters as eating, housing, and public relations. Disciples usually possess a composite of human foibles, talents, and aspirations.

Disciples also have other characteristics. They show their devotion to the founder by leaving their ordinary pursuits to give full time to the work of the new religion. They leave whatever work engaged them, making their activities in support of the founder their main responsibility. Their break may also call for them to leave their friends and even their families. In some instances a break with family is deemed to be the final and most decisive sign of their acceptance of the new faith. Often, to be disciples they must engage in forms of self-denial beyond the foreswearing of friends and family. They must be prepared to face hardships of various sorts, including persecution from those who oppose the new religion. Discipleship, almost by definition, means facing hardships that might have been avoided. Discipleship sometimes leads to martyrdom.

But discipleship also has its peculiar rewards. There is the sense of being engaged with the founder in a most important enterprise. The disciple counts himself to be fortunate, even in the face of hardships, to be a participant in the communication of a new vision of ultimate reality. Also, the disciple shares an intimate relation to the founder. The founder is by designation a charismatic personality. He attracts others to himself and to his message. The disciple revels, at least at times, in his direct, immediate approach to the founder himself. His is no second-hand relationship. The band of disciples, moreover, are characterized by having a strong sense of belonging to a privileged group. They have a keen sense of social solidarity. This does not mean that the disciples are always a harmonious group. They have their quarrels among themselves. One of the persistent bases for disagreements is the desire for primal recognition by the founder. Some disciples want to be preeminent in his eyes. Similarly, disciples may have disputes of an emotional nature over the essential message of the founder, each one tending to color the message through his own personality. Different parts of the founder's message appeal differently to the several disciples. But beyond such disagreements there is commonly a strong sense of togetherness. Disciples have deep social bonds. Despite differences, they are one. This oneness is due to intimate personal relationships with one another and with the founder. Disciples are not usually highly organized.

There are few divisions of labor. Authority for action and belief comes from the founder. In all things he is supreme.

A personally founded religion, then, is more than the founder as a solitary individual. Disciples are necessary and play an important part in the launching of a new faith. But disciples alone are not enough. A successful religion must appeal to a larger circle of adherents. A community of believers becomes necessary. As increasingly large numbers of persons come to share the vision of reality offered by the founder a religious community comes into existence. Another factor of great importance is the death of the founder. While the founder is alive, there is a clear basis for belief, action, and belonging. The founder's authority is paramount. But after the founder has died, the basic responsibility for the maintenance of the new religion rests upon the disciples. Their divisions at such a time may be more accentuated than in the past. The disciples tend to develop their own followers. The original unity is strained. The charismatic nature of the disciples cannot equal that of the founder. Slowly it is perceived that some form of organization is essential to the continuance of the new faith. The simple and direct relationships between the founder and his disciples yield to more routinized forms of ritual and structure. Theology is on its way in the sense that the organizing faith without the leadership of its founder must struggle with intellectual formulations of what the founder meant in his teachings. The survival of the religion in this period calls for rationalization of all aspects of the movement. The new religion is taking form.

This stage of the religious community, however, is not final. Despite the need for formalization in the period of the religious community, informality marks its passage. The disciples do have their own authority and charismatic appeal. But either in the later years of the disciples' lifetimes or certainly following their deaths, a new stage of development occurs. An ecclesiastical body is required and is born. The tendencies of the prior period are magnified. There is an even greater need for self-definition of the new religion. As the religion spreads geographically there is the need for a social organization by which the various segments of the new religion may be brought together and maintained as a single whole. Orders of authority within the leadership and followership are required. The religion in this stage must work harder at defining proper belief. As a religious movement spreads geographically, there is a tendency for local interpretations of the faith to appear, reflecting at times local constituencies and customs. The followers of the disciples with their at times partisan perspectives on what the founder taught and was like require a countervailing principle by which a general unity is established. Intellectual formulations of the new faith become more theologically astute. Creeds may come into being and even in their variety indicate the effort to establish orthodoxy. In the period of the ecclesiastical body, moreover, there is the need for the systematization of forms of worship. The practice of worship during the time of the founder and his disciples, and even in the period of the religious community, is relatively spontaneous and unsystematized. But a large and enduring religious movement is difficult to manage on such a basis. In time, standardized forms of ritual observance come into being as fundamental attributes of the religion. Furthermore, as a religious movement succeeds it is called upon to differentiate itself from the surrounding culture. If the surrounding culture is unsympathetic to the new faith, an added incentive is given to the need for the clarification of the bases of the religion. The ecclesiastical body, therefore, is necessary as a means of developing the self-definition of the religion. The ecclesiastical body addresses three fundamental questions: What is it necessary to believe in order that one be considered a member? How is it necessary for a follower to act, including worship, in order to be distinguished as a member of the religion? What is the desirable social form which individual adherents should recognize and participate in in order to be identified as members of the religious community?

The founder of a religion, then, does not stand alone. A new religion cannot be accounted for simply on the basis of one

man's experience. Without that one man, of course, a religion
cannot come into being. But the founder of a religion is aided
by a social process in which other persons, actually many others, share. Simply put, a religion develops from the founder to
a group of disciples, from disciples to a broader religious community, and from such a community to an ecclesiastical body.

This description of the manner in which a religion comes
into being, however, is proposed as a broad sociological generalization. While the generalization may be taken as true from
a certain level of abstraction, it is not possible to assert that
each and every founded religion fits the pattern in every detail. Each founder is a distinct individual. Yet he may be understood only in relation to the society and culture in which
he lived. His message, as well as the distinctive forms of worship and religious community which he advocated, is his own.
The course of each religion's history also is unique in its details.

From a sociological and historical perspective, the founders
of religions are thoroughly and inescapably human. It is true
that they cannot be considered as ordinary human beings, for
not every ordinary human being initiates such striking and
massive changes in historical development. Nevertheless, they
are human beings. From a religious perspective, however, the
founders of religions cannot be fully understood and appreciated on this assumption. Religiously the founders participate
in several ways in the divine. The followers of the founded religions usually do not consider their founders to be only
human. They are thought in various ways to be super-human
or divine. Thoughtful followers of the religions find themselves standing within both the sociological and the religious
perspectives. They affirm the paradox that the founder is both
human and divine. They are not always able to define their
founders as including both elements, but they make the
affirmation in the belief that it proclaims a higher truth than
either assertion by itself. At one time or another in the course
of a religion's growth one emphasis may gain ascendancy to

the virtual exclusion of the other. But over the long course of religious development both assumptions are held.

The religious perspective generally proposes six major factors that affirm the divine character of the founder. First, the founder is assumed to have had divine antecedents. Religions with founders seek to place their founders in a divine, preexistent scheme. They may be claimed to have existed eternally with the deity. The import of their lives may have been foretold in prophecies. They may have had earthly precursors who announced their coming. But, by whatever means, the assumption is made that the founder had divine origins.

Second, the founder is assumed to be an incarnation of the divine. The founder is viewed, despite his human existence, as an expression of divinity itself, a god in human form. Sometimes it is difficult for the followers of a religion in its early stages to account for the dichotomy of the human-divine person of the founder. The virgin birth of the founder, denying a human father, has been employed in more than one religion. Despite the difficulties inherent in this view, the followers of religions commonly consider their founders to be gods in human forms.

Third, the founder is assumed to have a divinely inspired calling. The calling to special religious leadership is not viewed as a product of merely human generation. The founder undergoes personal illumination with mystical overtones which are thought to be the sign of divine inspiration. The founder is assumed to be in personal and direct communion with the divine and it is from this relationship that the call is provided. Such illumination overcomes any historic condition of the founder, whether he is a humble carpenter or a palace prince.

Fourth, the founder is assumed to possess special powers. The lives of the founders are often characterized by miracles. They are able to accomplish that which is denied to ordinary mortals. They are able to heal the sick. They bring salvation to the alienated.

Fifth, the founder is assumed to speak a divine message. Founders claim to have a saving message. This message is thought not to be the result of merely reflective, scientific, or other means of generation. It is revelation. Revelation signifies that the message has divine origins. Revelation connotes the breaking through of ordinary experience and thought by initiatives that come from beyond the human.

Finally, the founder is assumed to be divine through the process of deification. It is true that the founders of religions have refrained from claiming their own divinity. At times they have specifically asserted that they are thoroughly human. They have even denied the claim of their disciples that they are exceptional, saying that only god is good. But their followers do not accept their views. The followers traditionally respond to the heroic lives and the noble teachings of their founders by worshiping them as gods. Even those founders who denied the existence of the gods or god end up becoming gods. From the religious perspective, then, the founders cannot be fully understood or appreciated through sociological and historical means. They are truly divine.

2

VARDHAMANA
AND
JAINISM

Of the four living religions that
originated in India, Hinduism is the oldest and has no known
founder. The other three, Jainism, Buddhism, and Sikhism,
each had founders and each developed out of an attempt to
reform and purify Hinduism, although in time they turned out
to be independent religions. Sikhism is the latest of the three
efforts at reformation; probably Nanak lived from A.D. 1469
to 1539. The two other founders, however, lived at approximately the same time, the sixth century B.C. Scholars differ in
their dating of the lives of Vardhamana and Gautama, but a
number say that Vardhamana may well have been the older.
If so, Nataputta Vardhamana is the founder of the oldest personally founded religion in India.

It is striking to note that both Vardhamana and Gautama
lived and accomplished their great works at the time of widespread religious and philosophic creativity in several parts of
the world. The sixth century B.C. also is the time location for
three other religious innovators whose activities established
three other religions. Both Confucius and Lao-tzu lived in
sixth-century China, while Zoroaster in the same century was
creating a religion in what is now known as Iran. This period
also saw great leaders within Judaism, such as Jeremiah, Ezekiel, and the Isaiah of the exile. In philosophy in Greece this
was the time of such figures as Anaximander, Pythagoras, and
Heraclitus. While there is no historical indication that all these
heroes of thought and faith were related in the development

of their creativity, it is a remarkable coincidence that they all lived at about the same time.

Jainism, like Buddhism, was a reaction against the pre-vailing Hinduism of the day. It can be understood largely in terms of its opposition to the teachings and practices of the Hinduism that regarded the Vedas and the Brahmanas as scripture. In that period, Hinduism was characterized by a number of features, a few of which may be mentioned. It taught nature worship for the most part, reveling in its recog-nition of a large number of animistic deities as well as in a few "high" gods. Polytheism was the rule of the day. Again, the Hinduism of that period gave rise to the caste system in which rather rigid hereditary social distinctions separated the believ-ers into four major castes and many subcastes. Priestly reli-gion, which stressed the power of the priests to regulate life through legal prescriptions, sacrifices, devotional exercises, and in other ways, also predominated.

In time, however, a number of reactions against this kind of religion took place. Two of the chief ones were primarily phil-osophical: the Upanishads, and the *nastika* thinkers. The Upan-ishads developed as lectures on the part of astute philoso-phers who sought a more coherent and intellectually defensible system of religion than that which was flourishing. They sought to explore the nature of ultimate reality. Al-though their teachings do not present a single doctrine, in the main they concluded that the final, ultimate, unknowable, transcendent reality in the universe is Brahma and that this re-ality is also found within man as his *atman,* or soul. Thus the starry reaches of the heavens and the inner life of persons were connected. The effect of the Upanishads was to elevate religion from its prior condition, add intellectual elements not then known, and to threaten the control of the priestly caste. But the Upanishadic thinkers did not break away from Hin-duism. They reformed it to a considerable extent, but they re-mained loyal to the historic faith, even basing their ideas upon aspects of the prior scriptural tradition.

Another philosophic effort to reform Hinduism is found in

the *nastika* thinkers. At approximately the same time as the Upanishads, the *nastikas* reacted by denying the basic claims of the historic faith. *Nastika* means "denier." One of these teachers was Brihaspati, who denied the existence of the gods, including Brahma, the efficacy of the priests' sacrifices, the validity of moral codes, and the necessity of political authority. The *nastikas* were essentially materialists, believing that the only knowledge which could be respected is that of the senses. While the Upanishadic thinkers may be said to have sought a positive way out of the morass of priestly Hinduism, the *nastika* philosophers were vehemently negative.

Two other reactions to priestly Hinduism took place in the sixth century B.C. and these led to the formation of new religions. These are the reformation by Vardhamana which issued in Jainism, and the reaction of Gautama which led to the formation of Buddhism. Although there are clear historical differences between Vardhamana and Gautama and the religions that they founded, it is important to note that both their lives and their resulting religions bear many similarities. The key element which explains them both is the fact that they are reactions against the Hinduism of their time.

Jainism and Buddhism, however, differ in a number of important aspects. It may be noted that Jainism has never left the land of its birth, India. While Buddhism has become an international religion and is found in a large part of Asia, Jainism has remained within India. And within India it is found mainly in the south and west, especially around Bombay. Gandhi, who was reared in Bombay for part of his life, was attracted to some of the teachings of Jainism, notably *ahimsa*, or nonviolence, which later he took as a cardinal conviction in his fight for India's independence from Great Britain and as a feature of his domestic policy. Jainism also is a nonmissionary religion. Originally the founder, Vardhamana, was called upon to propagate a religion that would be a blessing to all creatures. But the original impulse was lost and for centuries Jains have been content to be a relatively self-centered religious community.

Jainism, moreover, has only a relatively small number of adherents. There seems to be no certain way of determining the actual number. A current estimate is two and one half million persons. Their number also seems to be decreasing. Yet this relatively small number of adherents have wealth and social importance in India that is far out of proportion to their numbers.

The total information available on the life of Vardhamana is noticeably scant. It is difficult, therefore, to speak with any certitude about his life. Much of the available information comes from the religion's sacred scriptures. The scriptures are known as the Agamas, meaning precepts, or Siddantas, meaning treatises. Even the composition of the canon is in dispute among the two main sects within Jainism. The Sthanakvasi sect acknowledges thirty-three sections, while the Svetambara recognizes forty-five. It is in the thirty-seventh that there is some biographical information about the founder, although twice in this section it is indicated that Vardhamana had died 980 years earlier. None of the sacred scriptures of the Jains can be dated prior to about two hundred years after the founder's death. All of this means that there is very little sure data on which to build a biographical sketch.

A further problem in any effort to portray the life of Vardhamana lies in the fact that much of the available information is clearly in mythological form. Only the most devoted Jains would care to claim that such information is historically reliable. Yet the mythological material is of interest and even of importance, for it consists of stories that have been told about Vardhamana, his birth, life, and death. They indicate the influence the founder has had over the lives of his followers. Such stories tell less about what Vardhamana was really like than what his followers believed about him.

His real name was Nataputta Vardhamana. Scholars debate the date of his birth, although many would say that it was in 599 B.C. That would put his death at 527 B.C. The name Vardhamana means "increasing," a quality that reflects his spiritual growth. But he is more popularly known as Mahavira. This signifies that he was a "great hero." Vardhamana's followers call themselves Jaina, which signifies that they are adherents of the Jina, which is another title for Vardhamana, their "victor" or "conqueror."

The Jain tradition, as is true for the traditions regarding other founders, does not assume that Vardhamana's life began at his physical birth. It recognizes at least three major antecedents which support later views that prior to his birth the founder was indeed a divine personage. First, Jain tradition teaches that Vardhamana underwent a number of incarnations before he was born as the founder of Jainism. The stories vary, but a chief one tells that in a previous life Vardhamana had been incarnated as Nayasara, the carpenter. Working his trade in the jungle, he one day met some weary *sadhus,* or holy men. Nayasara took pity on them, eased their burdens and fed them. In turn they preached to him the Jain faith, which he received gladly. Later Nayasara met his death when a branch of a tree fell on him. He was then reborn as the grandson of the first *tirthankara,* or "ford-finder," of Vardhamana. Other stories tell that in previous lives he was gods, kings, and priests. These stories attempt to show that the earthly life of Vardhamana did not fully account for his greatness or divinity.

Second, Jain tradition teaches that Vardhamana's life was preceded by twenty-three other *tirthankaras,* or "ford-finders." As ford-finders these personages, practically all of whom are mythological, are held in the highest regard by the Jains, who believe that they have appeared in human history to show men the passage through the dark waters of life. They too can be called *jinas,* or conquerors. Vardhamana as the last of the series is also considered as a *tirthankara.* Jainism claims that there have been twenty-four *tirthankaras* of the current cycle of history and that each has had a slightly shorter life than his predecessor and has been slightly shorter in height. Each one was a member of the *kshatriya,* or warrior caste, as was Vardhamana, and the mother of each had a series of fourteen dreams at the start of her pregnancy, giving birth in accompaniment to celestial signs and events. So, by way of the *tirthankaras* the earthly life of Vardhamana is perceived in a broader historical and even divine context.

Third, Jain tradition teaches that Vardhamana's birth was surrounded by a number of auspicious events of more than natural significance. The time of the birth itself, for example, according to the Jain calendar, was most auspicious. It took place on the thirteenth day of the bright half of the moon in the month of Caitra. Another important portent were the fourteen dreams which Trisala, Vardhamana's mother, had prior to his birth. Each of these dreams is cherished by believing Jains, who see in them the hand of a divine designer. In one dream, the third, for example, Trisala learned that she would give birth to one who would be able to overcome all his enemies. Spiritualized, this signified his capacity to break out of the bonds of *karma*, the law of moral causality as taught in Hinduism. In the dream she saw a great white lion who leaped from the sky toward her face. The eyes of the lion were like pure lightning and his tongue extended from his mouth as a shoot of beauty. This part of the dream informed Trisala that her son would be the "lion of houseless monks." The lion is Vardhamana's symbol. So, in one dream after another the divine meaning of the son was depicted. Vardhamana's birth, then, was not that of a mere mortal; it was presaged by accounts and events which indicated that his coming was part of a divine plan.

Vardhamana was born in Vaisali, which is near modern Bihar. Vaisali was probably administered as a kind of oligarchic republic. The government of the place was vested in a sort of senate. The several heads of the *kshatriya* clans composed the senate. The head of the senate was one of the clan leaders who was considered the *raja*, or ruler. Apparently Trisala was the daughter of the *raja*. Her husband was the chief of one of the *kshatriya* clans, perhaps the Nata or Naya clan. His name was Siddhartha. Thus, it was from a *kshatriya*, or warrior family with significant governmental responsibilities, that the future apostle of *ahimsa*, or nonviolence, was born. He was a second son of the family.

The usual Indian customs were observed at the birth of Vardhamana. The birth of a male child calls for communal rejoicing with presents given, prisoners released, and a general festival atmosphere. In the first days of the child's life certain rites were practiced. The child was shown the sun and the moon on the third day, a vigil was held on the sixth, the mother was given a ceremonial bath on the tenth, and the child was named on the twelfth, after a family feast. But Vardhamana was not named by his father's sister, as was the custom. Rather, he was given his name by his parents. The parents noted that since the child had been conceived, the family had greatly increased in wealth, which was assumed to be a sign of divine grace.

The childhood of Vardhamana was filled with luxury. He had every means to have his wants met. For example, it is indicated that he was attended in his early years by five nurses: a wet nurse, a nurse to keep him clean, one to dress him, one to play with him, and one to carry him about. Obviously the social station of his parents made all of this possible.

According to legend, the child also showed great ability. In one legend it is said that one day the children of his father's ministers of government had come to play with Vardhamana in the family's gardens. Without warning, a mad elephant charged the group of playing children, scattering them. Vardhamana, however, was not afraid. He went up to the elephant, seized it by the trunk, climbed up on its back, and escaped harm by riding on it.

Another legend tells that on another day he was playing with his friends when a god appeared and put him on his shoulders and took him high into the sky. Again, Vardhamana was not afraid. Riding high in the sky, he hit the god and pulled his hair so hard that the god was intimidated into bringing the child to the earth safely. The story also says that the other gods were so impressed with the boy's courage that they called him Mahavira.

In time, boyhood turned into manhood and Vardhamana faced the prospect of marriage. Although the traditions vary, it is assumed that he married Yasoda, the daughter of another princely family. To them was born a daughter named Anuja. Anuja in time married another *kshatriya*, Jamali, who became one of Vardhamana's followers, but who later broke with his leader.

Vardhamana, however, was not content with the princely life. He sought a satisfaction that the senses could not provide. He was probably familiar with the ascetic Parsva and his followers who stayed in a park outside of Vaisali. Parsva is reckoned to be the twenty-third *tirthankara*, those who were the precursors of the last *tirthankara*, Vardhamana. While it must be assumed that most of the *tirthankaras* were legendary beings, Parsva probably was a historical person. It is said that at the age of thirty he adopted the ascetic life after seeing a picture of Nemi, the prior *tirthankara*. Feeling a call to be a *tirthankara* himself, he gave away his belongings, assumed a state of homelessness, pulled out his hair, and entered a hermitage. Being seated under a holy tree and after meditating for eighty-three days, Parsva attained full knowledge. He began to gather a small band of followers about him, including some women who composed an order of nuns. Parsva taught four vows, which obviously had great influence upon Jainism's teachings. These were: *ahimsa*, or non-injury; *sunrita*, or truth-telling; *asteya*, or non-stealing; and *brahmacharya*, or sexual continence. Parsva and his followers adopted white clothing, which is the color later adopted by some of Vardhamana's followers. Parsva believed in the earthly and heavenly conflict between good and evil, another influence upon the later Jainism. A story says that Parsva died of voluntary starvation at the age of one hundred on a hill that later became known as Parasnath.

Some sources suggest that the parents of Vardhamana may have been followers of Parsva. More probably it was Vardhamana who found in Parsva and his teachings the kind of satisfaction that he was denied in his palace life. It so happens that Vardhamana's parents also chose to die of voluntary starvation. Such a practice, while very infrequent, indicated a desire to break the chain of rebirth. At his parents' death, Vardhamana indicated a desire to renounce his worldly life, including his wife and daughter, in order to follow the life set forth by Parsva. His older brother was the heir to the kingdom, so Vardhamana had some degree of freedom. But his brother urged him not to leave the royal household for a period of a year lest others think that they had quarreled. During the final year in the palace Vardhamana planned his future ascetic life. He gave away his possessions, his gold and silver, his valuable treasures, and his troops and chariots. Probably the amount of his assumed largess has been exaggerated by his loyal followers. He was about thirty years of age.

Within the community of the monks who followed Parsva, Vardhamana adopted the life of an ascetic. He gave away all his ornaments and kept only a robe that was marked by a flamingo design. Also he proceeded to pull out all his hair in five tufts. A shaven head has been the sign of the ascetic, but the ability of the initiate to pull out his own hair by the roots was taken to be a special sign of austerity. Vardhamana, according to the tradition, performed this ceremony. He adopted, moreover, the four vows of the teachings of Parsva. Believing that the body is the source of evil, he pledged to neglect it and to abandon any care of it.

But the satisfaction that Vardhamana sought did not come to him within the company of Parsva and his companions. After a year or so of ascetic endeavor, Vardhamana left, and going out on his own for a period of about twelve years sought the final salvation of *nirvana,* that blissful state in which *karma* and the transmigration of souls are broken. Little is known of his activities in this period. But it is claimed that he was indifferent to both the smell of filth and the scent of sandalwood, to straw and to jewels, to dust and to gold, to pleasure and to pain, desiring neither life nor death. Usually he would stay no more than one night in a village or five nights in a town. Perhaps this was so that he would not be a burden upon those who took some responsibility for him, but it also may be due to his desire not to develop any regular attachments to others. During the rainy season, which usually lasted about four months, he remained in one place because in that period the land was teeming with creatures. Vardhamana's vow of *ahimsa* forbade him to kill any living thing. Commonly he would walk about, looking closely where he was going so that he would not inadvertently step on a living thing. In fact, so devoted to the principle of *ahimsa* was the founder of Jainism that he did not bother to scratch off of his body those creatures which crawled about him, causing him pain. It was also his practice when walking about to carry a small broom to sweep away any insects that might be in his way. He strained water through a cloth so that he would not drink anything that was living in the water. He did not eat raw food, but only that which had been prepared by others and offered to him as leftovers. He would examine the offered food carefully to see if any living creature had gotten into it.

When Vardhamana left Parsva's company he also gave up wearing clothes of any kind. It is assumed that as an ascetic he felt that he should give up all worldly attachments, including clothes. Thus he conquered all emotions, including shame. Much later, Jains came into conflict over the wearing of clothes. The more populous sect within Jainism, the White-clad or Svetambara, believed that it was proper to wear white garments. They were mainly in the north of India. But a group of Jains in about the eighth decade of the Christian era felt that to be an orthodox Jain meant that they too should live without clothes. They migrated to the southern part of India, where they went about naked until the time of the Muslim invaders, when they were required to wear loincloths.

Vardhamana, also according to tradition, put up with all sorts of indignities and injuries. In his search for purity he refrained from talking to others. When he did not speak or salute those who approached him he sometimes was beaten with sticks. It is said that once when he sat motionless he was attacked by his tormentors, who cut his body, tore his hair, and covered him with dust. On another occasion when he sat motionless in meditation, angry villagers lighted a fire between his legs to see if he would move, and they drove nails into his ears; but, if the story is to be believed, he remained without response. He was seeking *moksha,* or salvation, and he did not permit anything either from himself or from others to deter him from his ascetic self-discipline.

Finally Vardhamana reached the blessed state that he had been seeking. In the thirteenth year of his search, after having left Parsva, while in a squatting position with his head low, in the deepest meditation, he achieved *nirvana.* His attainment was reached in the field of the householder Samaga outside the town of Grimbhikagrama, which is on the northern bank of the river Rigupalika, in a northeastern direction from an old temple and not far from a *sal* tree.

Having achieved *nirvana,* Vardhamana proceeded in the last thirty years of his life to become an advocate of his way of life. He had achieved *kevala,* or omniscience, and possessed perfect control over himself. He was a conqueror, a *jina.* Many were repelled by him and his teachings, but others were strangely attracted to this severe ascetic. He won disciples. They in turn helped him to convert other followers. Gautama Indrabhuti was one of his *ganadharas,* or chief disciples. Legend has it that Gautama, no relation to the founder of Buddhism, was invited by a rich brahmin in the city of Apapa to be present with his ten brothers at a great animal sacrifice in the custom of the Hinduism of the time. He and his brothers, however, heard that Vardhamana also was present in the city and was denouncing the intended sacrifice. Gautama and his brothers were indignant, but they felt that they should go to hear what Vardhamana was saying and to expose him for his heresy. They heard the preacher tell about the requirement of *ahimsa.* They noted the gentle mien of the advocate, and were convinced of his rightness. So they joined the master as early and important disciples. Gautama became a leader of one of the important Jain communities of believers.

Not all of Vardhamana's disciples succeeded as did Gautama. Gosala is one that did not. He appears to have been the head of a group of unclothed ascetics who were a part of the

Ajivikas. The Ajivikas were a strictly deterministic *nastika*, or non-believing, sect. They believed that there is no ultimate cause for anything, that *karma* is false, and that all of life is conditioned by *niyati*, or the principle of fatalism. They held an atomic theory of reality which is a form of materialism. What was the basis for the mutual attraction of Vardhamana and Gosala can only be imagined. Some of their views did coincide: the recognition of the material, the denial of Hinduism's gods, and their asceticism. But they also held widely differing views. Gosala was a disciple of Vardhamana for about six years. In this time their mutual interests made them an effective team. But then Gosala and Vardhamana separated. The cause of this separation is not entirely clear, although several legends seek to supply an answer. In one account, Vardhamana said to Gosala as they were walking down a road that a certain plant would bear seven flowers upon their return. In order to prove the Jain saint wrong, Gosala pulled up the plant and threw it away. When the two returned later to the spot the plant was found with seven blooms. Having been proven the weaker, Gosala left.

But more probably Gosala left the discipleship for more mundane reasons. Another account points to the possibility that Gosala had not kept himself chaste sexually. This seems to be true, for Vardhamana added the vow of chastity to the original four vows of Parsva sometime after his association with Gosala. Also the Jain scriptures lay stress upon the evil of those who do not practice chastity. The moral nihilism of the Ajivika belief may have led Gosala to hold chastity and other teachings of Vardhamana in less than absolute regard. At any rate, the two men came to a parting of their ways. It is said that after Gosala left Vardhamana he and his followers lived in open disabuse of ascetic principles.

As Vardhamana went about preaching and teaching his radical form of asceticism his message became increasingly clear and systematic. It took the form of the Five Great Vows. Some of these obviously were derived from his association with the religious movement of Parsva, and a few persons think that

Parsva may be considered the originator of Jainism while Vardhamana was its organizer and propagator. This view, however, does not seem to do enough justice to the widespread and successful religious movement which Vardhamana himself created and which in time became an independent faith, while Parsva is looked upon largely as a precursor of the founder of Jainism. A striking facet of the Five Great Vows, moreover, is their ethical import. While Jainism has laid some stress upon theological and philosophical analyses, it is chiefly an ethical religion. The Five Great Vows distinguish the Jain from those who do not accept the religion.

The first vow renounces the killing of all living things, whether movable or unmovable. This is the principle of *ahimsa*, or non-violence. It calls for believers not to kill anything, not to cause others to kill, and not to consent to killing by others. In its greater detail the first vow requires that the faithful Jain follow explicitly the manner of life of the founder.

The second vow renounces all vices of lying speech. Lying may arise from anger, greed, fear, or mirth. Again, as with the first vow, the practitioner promises not only to control his own behavior but also so to act that others will not commit offense.

The third vow renounces stealing. Stealing means taking anything that is not freely given, whether the object is great or small, living or lifeless, and no matter where the object may be found. Stealing is a form of greed.

The fourth vow renounces all sexual pleasure. The loyal Jain is not to give way to sensuality and is so to act that no one else is tempted. From the beginning Jainism stressed sexual chastity. But probably after the experience with Gosala the ban became even more severe.

The fifth vow renounces all attachments. The follower must not form attachments to anything, whether large or small, living or lifeless, little or much. This vow signifies that the attractions of the senses must be avoided. That which gives pleasure and that which gives pain constitute forms of attachment. Importantly, it is understood that both love and hate indicate attachments and therefore should be scrupulously shunned. This last vow is seemingly the most strict and demanding, for in some ways it includes all the others. It illustrates the very radical character of Jainism; it constitutes one of the most thoroughgoing forms of asceticism known in human history, a form that has appealed to fairly large numbers of people over a long period of time.

These five vows constituted the ground rules for Vardhamana and his closest followers. They were ascetics, who are called monks. But the great bulk of the followers of Jainism could not maintain so strict a code of behavior. For the laymen, then, a similar but less severe moral system was enjoined. For the laymen there were twelve vows. They reflect the sentiments of the Five Great Vows, but they are in some ways less demanding. They are: (1) maintain *ahimsa;* (2) do not lie; (3) do not steal; (4) do not be unchaste; (5) check greed by limiting wealth and giving generously to others; (6) avoid temptations to sin, such as in engaging in excessive travel; (7) lead a materially simple life; (8) guard against those evils which can be avoided; (9) meditate at planned times; (10) observe special periods of self-denial; (11) occasionally spend time as a monk, being devoted to the higher order of behavior; and (12) be generous in almsgiving, especially to the monks. The first of the laymen's vows has meant economically that Jains have not engaged in India in those occupations that involve the taking of life, such as tilling the soil, fishing, butchering, and even brewing. This vow has directed Jains into such occupations as banking, the professions, and various commercial enterprises. Coupling this injunction with the others, many Jains have become wealthy and philanthropically inclined. The fourth vow, it should be noted, requires that married Jains be faithful to each other and that they refrain from impure thoughts and deeds.

Obviously the social organization of Jainism consisted of monks and laymen. The monks were held to a stricter code of behavior. In addition, however, Jainism also developed an order of nuns. The establishment of this order stands as a paradox within the movement, since Vardhamana did not hold women in high regard. He looked upon them as the causes of all sinful acts in the world. They clearly indicated the true and evil nature of ordinary experience. He spoke of them as being the greatest temptation in the world and called upon his followers not to look at them, nor to speak to them. Yet he admitted women into a separate religious order. Similarly laymen and laywomen were viewed as separate bodies. In the main they were both held to the laymen's code of behavior, but socially they were distinct. It is significant that the order of monks, the original order, was called the *sangha*. It was a kind of democratic congregation in which each of the members was the equal socially of the others. The formation of the *sangha* was a radical innovation in Hindu India which maintained the rigidly enforced caste system. As disciples and followers came into the Jain movement, however, they dropped their caste within the *sangha*. Much later, however, the remarkable inclusiveness and absorptiveness of Hinduism influenced Jains to some resumption of caste distinctions.

While Vardhamana broke with the traditional caste system of Hinduism and India, he accepted the notion of *karma*, although he modified even this doctrine. *Karma* signifies that every human action has its inevitable effect which is recorded for all time in the soul. Present and former existences tend to encrust the soul with as many as five sheaths which impede the soul's quest for purity. Living in the present involves purification efforts to wear out these sheaths. In this view, contrary to the exalted monism taught in the Upanishads, both matter and mind are separate and eternal existences. Jainism teaches a dualism of ultimate reality. Matter or lifeless things are termed *ajiva*; soul or living things are *jiva*. The object of the moral life is to subdue the various forms of matter in order that the pure spirit of man may be enabled to reach the perfect state of *nirvana*.

Vardhamana also preached against the many gods of Hinduism. He suggested that it was unprofitable to pray to any deity, a usual source of help to followers of religions. He stated that man is his own friend and that he needs no friend beyond himself either on earth or in heaven. Thus, Jainism originally taught self-salvation. It placed the central task of redemption from *karma*-matter and the attainment of ultimate purity upon the inescapable, direct actions of persons themselves. In contrast to the animism and polytheism of the Hinduism of his time, Vardhamana may be said to have been an atheist. He even denied the logical necessity for a supreme creator of the universe. Yet this seemingly extreme position was modified in later times. A realm of secondary deities was recognized, although it was claimed that they have no real power over human lives. Again, Vardhamana, impressing his followers with his achievement of *nirvana*, was himself deified. Others who followed his way and who also attained *nirvana* became figures in the divine panoply. So, in due time the Jains came to consider themselves not as *nastikas*, or non-believers. They think of themselves as strong believers, yet within the special context of their own historical movement in religion. Historically the Jains have been characterized by their opposition to all forms of absoluteness. This has meant that they have tried to look at all sides of a question and to reconcile differences of opinion. Even their sectarian differences have not been created and sustained with the degree of bitterness that sometimes has characterized such partisan movements in other religions.

Vardhamana's teachings, moreover, are essentially directed toward an ethical form of behavior which leads to individual emancipation. It is true that these teachings have had many and varied social consequences. Yet Jainism originally and later did not initiate and elaborate a systematic outlook on society. It has been relatively unconcerned with questions of social policy. It is not socially accepting or approving of the way in which Indian society has been organized. It is not concerned with questions of public policy. Rather, Jainism calls for withdrawal from the world. It holds that the true condition of social life is evil. Only the individual may achieve salvation and that salvation is surely not easy. Societies apparently can look for no salvation in and through themselves. While Hinduism, for example, may be termed a world-affirming religion, Jainism, as well as Buddhism, may be defined essentially as world-denying.

Fundamentally, moreover, Jainism is an ethical religion for the individual. The moral life is its chief concern. Jainism does have a developed set of beliefs. These may be called its theology, although perhaps these beliefs may more properly be termed philosophy. But it is not solely or largely confined to its intellectual expressions. Similarly, Jainism is not basically a ritualistic religion, calling upon its followers only to perform religious acts in a holy setting. Characteristically it relates these and other elements of religion to the ethical conduct of an individual's behavior. It is clearly an ethical religion for the person as a person.

Vardhamana apparently died in his seventy-second year. Various stories tell of his death. They vary greatly among themselves. One says that having completed his earthly mission he died by the rite of *sallakhana,* or self-starvation, as did his parents before him. Another account tells that he spent his last rainy season in a small village in the present Patna region, Pavapuri. This village is still held to be a sacred place to Jains, who make pilgrimages to it. Temples of the two major sects within Jainism may be found there. The main temple is said to have the impress of the foot of the founder. According to this story, Hastipala was the *raja,* or ruler, of Pavapuri and a patron of Vardhamana. Before dying, Vardhamana in a proper position delivered fifty-five lectures on the subject of *karma* and recited thirty-six unasked questions that later formed a basic *sutra,* or set of writings. Then, after another lecture, he peacefully died.

But his death did not complete the record. His followers were so deeply impressed by the life and teachings of the quiet, moral, perceptive founder of Jainism that in time they came to believe that he was no mere mortal. They accepted the claim that his life was sinless and that he had attained the much-sought-for *nirvana*. They were impressed with his al-most absolute ethical discipline. They believed that he was omniscient. They believed that he had a life preexistent to his earthly life and that he was an incarnation of the divine. Thus, Vardhamana, who denied the reality of the gods, be-came in time a god himself.

3
GAUTAMA AND BUDDHISM

Siddhartha Gautama is the name of the founder of Buddhism, the second personally founded religion in India's history. Vardhamana, the founder of Jainism, discussed in the previous chapter, was probably born in 599 B.C. Gautama was quite possibly born in 563 B.C. Although their lives overlapped, there is no knowledge that the two ever met, but it seems clear that Gautama was influenced at one stage of his life by the extreme asceticism that characterizes Jainism. The path to salvation that was found by Gautama, however, denied the validity of such extreme asceticism. It advocated the course of moderation, the middle path between all extremes.

Buddhism as a religion within the Indian tradition also differs from Jainism in a number of particulars. Jainism has always remained an Indian religion. It has never traveled beyond the boundaries of India to become the faith of non-Indian peoples. Although it originally maintained some hope of being a religion for all peoples, it never achieved such a status. By contrast, Buddhism has become an international religion. Sometime after its birth Buddhism began to extend its influence beyond the national borders. Persons who might be termed "missionaries" took the message of the founder to other places, such as Sri Lanka, which formerly was called Ceylon. Later the religion expanded its influence to other parts of Asia. In fact, today Buddhism is not found to an appreciable extent within the land of its birth. In India, Buddhism is a minor religious expression. But the largest number of its adherents are found throughout the rest of Asia, from north to south.

Buddhism is one of the three living religions that are international in scope. The other two are Christianity and Islam. Both Christianity and Islam are sometimes termed "universal religions," and in a limited sense they are. It is obvious that neither religion is found in absolutely every location throughout the world. But they differ somewhat in this regard from Buddhism in that they have sought over the centuries to be actively the religions of all people. In Christianity, for example, the worldwide missionary movement has been one of its prime characteristics. Buddhism, however, is not essentially a missionary religion in the same way that Christianity and even Islam may be said to be. Buddhism has never featured an organized effort to convert the whole world to Buddhism. Its spread beyond India has taken place by a more subtle and informal movement. It does, in fact, lack the centers of missionary effort that have been a feature, say, of Christianity. Moreover, Buddhism is predominantly a religion of Asia. Unlike Christianity it has not spread to the several continents of the world.

Unlike Jainism, too, Buddhism has many adherents. Whereas Jainism is one of the smallest religions, Buddhism appeals currently to many millions of followers. It is difficult to know precisely how many Buddhists there are in the world. Some estimates suggest that there are at least one hundred million. (Some persons estimate that there may be as many as five hundred million.) In making such estimates, one must consider how one defines membership. Admittedly in some instances whole populations in Asia are included without discrimination. Again, membership in Buddhism differs in meaning from membership in Christianity. The sheer immensity of the task of gaining a set of reliable statistics in Asia comprises another kind of limitation. But by whatever calculation, Buddhism is a major religion in terms of the number of its adherents.

Buddhism, moreover, is more diverse in its expressions than

is Jainism. Like the other living religions Jainism is far from a monolith; its expressions are indeed varied, as was seen in the last chapter. But the degree of diversity is surely greater within Buddhism. In Asia there are two main branches of Buddhism today. One is called Hinayana Buddhism, or the Lesser Vehicle, which is found in southern Asia and claims to be loyal to the original teachings of Gautama. It maintains that he was chiefly a human teacher who sought escape from the miseries of this life. The other, found in China, Japan, and elsewhere, is called Mahayana Buddhism, or the Greater Vehicle. It has developed certain theological doctrines during the course of history, claiming that Gautama was no mere human teacher of salvation but a divine being. In addition, as Buddhism expanded throughout large portions of Asia, it has tended to adopt the cultural features of the places where it found acceptance. Thus there are many diverse forms of Buddhism, even within its two main branches.

Jainism and Buddhism, despite their differences, do hold a number of features in common. They both arose in India in the sixth century B.C. They arose, moreover, as reactions against Hinduism, the mother religion of India. They both opposed the dominance of the brahmin priesthood as the controllers of religious destiny. As they developed, both Jainism and Buddhism founded religious orders, the *sangha*, in which caste distinctions were effectively overcome. Both religions also opposed the authority of the Vedas, the revealed scriptures of Hinduism. Both religions developed philosophical and practical expressions that denied the validity of the Vedas. And both, moreover, denied the importance that Hinduism placed upon the saving role of ritual. Hinduism asserted that by the faithful practice of ritual the gods could be controlled and life could become satisfying. Jainism and Buddhism pointed those seeking salvation away from outwardly ritualistic forms toward the inner life in which personal discipline was the prerequisite of gaining the good life. In the original forms of both Jainism and Buddhism there were no acceptances of personal deities, prayer, worship, or other practices that had been fundamental in the Hindu tradition. In their original forms the two religions may be said to be basically skeptical, agnostic, or even atheistic. Some scholars go so far as to doubt that these religions in their earliest beginnings may be classified as religions, although that depends upon how religion is defined.

Certainly both Jainism and Buddhism, in contrast to much of Hinduism, are similar in that they are world-denying in their outlook. They do not look upon the created order as a positive force for enabling persons to find salvation. They tend to think of the world as fundamentally evil, to be avoided wherever possible. They view the reality of the social realm as a set of circumstances that do not support the quest for the good life. That reality stands in opposition to the good life. Rather, they believe that persons may achieve salvation only as they discipline themselves to attain levels of personhood that transcend the ordinary. Salvation is found through withdrawal from the practical life rather than through immersion in it. The two religions, however, differ in their conception of the precise way in which salvation may be achieved. Though Jainism advocated extreme asceticism Buddhism claimed that the path of moderation is necessary to success. In this and in other ways Jainism and Buddhism may be viewed as not only alike but unalike.

Another kind of similarity is shown in the lives of the founders of the two religions. Both Vardhamana and Gautama were born of *kshatriya,* or ruling caste families. Both were born in northeast India (though not near each other). Both lived a relatively luxurious family life with parents who sought to do all they could for their children. Despite such home surroundings, both were unhappy with life as they knew it. Both were married and each had one child. Both rejected living the lives of princes as being unsatisfying, and became mendicants searching for life's deepest meaning. They both rejected the traditional forms of Hinduism, including even the stress upon the monistic idealism to which they initially were attracted. Both denied the validity of the Vedas and the power of the rituals. They called upon no deity for help, and even failed to pray to a divine being. They both founded religious communities that disregarded caste as a basis for membership. Both, despite their disavowal of the gods, ended up by being considered gods themselves as their religions came into bloom.

It must not be thought that they were identical in their lives or their teachings. They were distinct personalities who discovered and taught quite different ways of gaining individual salvation. Perhaps their similarities may be attributed chiefly to the times in which they lived, the kinds of religious expressions that had been tried and found wanting, the traditional forms of revolt from Hinduism that were apparent among others in their day, and to other cultural factors. Initially neither considered himself the founder of a new religion. Both sought within the Indian tradition to establish reformed versions of the path to salvation. But instead of being effective reformers of Hinduism they became, in time, the founders of two acknowledged religions.

Buddhism as the name of the religion is not derived from the actual name of the founder. It refers to a state of personal existence or the nature of a finally self-realized person. Such a person is called a *buddha*—one who has attained buddhahood, one who has become enlightened. He is a wise person. In fact, Buddhism is a term that Westerners apply to the religion. Followers of the faith in Asia commonly speak of it as *Dharma*, the teachings or doctrine. In this regard the meaning of this Sanskrit term is the same as in Hinduism, except that Buddhists mean by *dharma* those teachings which are associated with Gautama, the Buddha. Gautama, moreover, did not refer to himself as the Buddha. He thought of himself as the *Tathagata*, or truth-finder. Having pioneered the path that led him to the truth, he called upon his disciples to take the same path on their own and similarly to find the truth.

Information regarding the life of Gautama appears to combine fact with fancy. Actually the chief source of biographical information on the founder of Buddhism comes from the reli-

gion's sacred scriptures, the Tripitaka, the three baskets of
wisdom. First is the Vinaya Pitaka, or discipline basket, which
contains rules for the monks. Second is the Sutta Pitaka, or
teaching basket, which contains the discourses of Gautama.
Third is the Abhidhamma Pitaka, or metaphysical basket,
which contains analyses of matters that are often of an abstruse nature. Together, the three comprise the Tripitaka,
from which some knowledge of the life of the founder may be
obtained. But the Tripitaka is not an ideal source for Gautama's biography. For example, it is far from complete. Although the scriptures do contain information on some aspects
of his life, they fail to include information about many other
facets of the life of Gautama concerning which many would
like to know. Also, the scriptures were carried for several centuries in the oral tradition. During that period, embellishments
quite possibly modified the original accounts. Finally, in giving their account of the life of Gautama the scriptures at many
points engage in stories of a supernatural nature as though
they were factual. Obviously it is next to impossible to provide
a factually accurate version of Gautama's life. The life that
may be told, on the other hand, indicates what his followers
thought about him. It reflects the impressions that he made
upon them and their efforts to tell of their response to his life
and teachings.

There is uncertainty regarding Gautama's birth date. Commonly it is given as 563 B.C., although other suggested dates
are 566 B.C. and 560 B.C. Siddhartha is the Sanskrit form of his
given name; Siddhattha is the Pali version, Pali being the vernacular in which Gautama taught. Pali is the dialect of the
common people in north-central India. Gautama is the Sanskrit form of the family name. In Pali his name is Gotama.

Gautama was born in a city called Kapilavastu, which lies
about one hundred miles north of the traditionally holy city of
Benares, which today is called Varanasi. His birthplace is
close to the modern Nepal-India border at a point where the
fertile valley of the Ganges gives way to the rising hills
beyond which tower the snow-clad Himalayas. The people of

the area were dominated by the Sakya clan. The Sakyas were Hindus in religion and derived from the Aryans who many centuries previously had successfully invaded India. The clan was composed of a number of families over whom there was a ruler who, far from being autocratic, managed their affairs through assemblies that provided guidance to him. Gautama's father was the ruler of the clan. His name was Suddhodhana Gautama, and his wife was Maya. The father's name means pure rice and the mother's name signifies illusion.

Buddhist accounts of Gautama's life do not begin with his physical birth. They portray a rich and varied existence long before he was born into this world. In keeping with the Hindu doctrine of the transmigration of souls, Gautama is pictured as having had a large number of existences prior to his earthly one. Those previous existences have been traced back millions of years by his faithful followers. In these he took many different forms—from an ant to a god.

The supernatural surrounds the conception of Gautama. The scriptures tell that his mother, Maya, was an admirable person with gifts of piety and intelligence. But she was not able to have a child. She visited temples to pray that a son and heir might be given to her. One summer she took part for seven days in the Festival of the Full Moon along with the people of Kapilavastu, singing and dancing in the streets, garlanding the sacred cows that crowded the streets. On the seventh day Maya arose early in the morning and bathed in scented water. Later she went through the city giving thousands of gold pieces to the poor. Upon her return she lay down on her bed, tired, and went to sleep. While sleeping she dreamed that the four kings of the four quarters of the compass came and stood at the four corners of her bed. They raised up her bed and took it as though it were a flying carpet to a Himalayan hideout. Four queens were awaiting her beside a sacred lake. They washed Maya in the lake and anointed her with perfume, clothed her with special garments, and put garlands about her neck. Then they led her to a golden mansion, built on a silver mountain, where she lay

down upon a bed that looked out on the mountainside bathed
in a golden light. Maya suddenly saw a white elephant at the
summit which held in its trunk a white lotus. The elephant descended the mountain with great speed and characteristic
grace. It came straight for the queen. But the elephant did not
harm her. It went about her bed three times and halted. Then
it struck her once with its trunk on her right side and disappeared. Maya knew this was a sign that something had entered her womb.

Maya awoke from her dream, filled with vitality and happiness. Knowing that dreams are filled with meanings, she
gathered her ladies-in-waiting about her and went into the
palace gardens. There she asked a servant to summon the
king, Suddhodhana, to meet with her. Although the king was
busy sitting in a council of state, he left his councillors and
friends and came to the garden. Maya told him of the dream.
The king did the customary thing—he called his soothsayers,
brahmins versed in interpreting dreams. They reported that
the dream was a good omen, that Maya had conceived a son,
a royal heir, who would become a king for the whole of India
and even of the world. But, they said, if he did not choose to
be such a king, he would become a *buddha*, a wise man who
would gain the respect of men. Thus, although Maya was not
a virgin, the account of her conception indicates that the son
had no earthly father. It was an immaculate conception. Various versions of this story exist within traditional Buddhism.

Legend also abounds regarding the birth of the child. Apparently it did not take place in the palace at Kapilavastu, but
in the Lumbini park nearby. One tradition has it that Maya
was on her way to her parents' home when her labor pains
came upon her. The birth was accomplished, according to one
account, while she was standing up and holding onto a tree
with her right hand at the final moment. Traditions vary on a
number of points regarding the birth. Some say that the tree
was an *asoka*, the tree of "non-sorrow"; others that it was a
plaska, or fig; and others say that it was a *sal*, a common tree
of the area and one under which Gautama was said to have

died. In addition, at the time of the birth various cosmic signs were given. There were some thirty-two signs in all, each of which had an unusual consequence, such as enabling the blind to see.

Following his birth, the infant Gautama in one version was given a ceremonial bath, which indicates the purifying influence of various Hindu deities. The tradition also indicates that soon after birth the infant stood firmly on his feet and took seven steps toward the north. Shaded by a white parasol, he looked to each of the four quarters of the compass and proclaimed that he was the first, that he was the best among all beings.

The return to the palace of the infant and his mother, along with those who assisted them, was a triumphal procession involving complicated pageantry and several thousand divinities who hovered over the thousands of persons who made up the human aspect of the return. Later the infant was presented at the temple and was acknowledged to be wise beyond maturity, a veritable god himself.

The unusual character of the newborn Gautama was further indicated by the sage Asita, a *rishi*, or holy man, who lived as a hermit in a cave high in the Himalayas. One day while meditating, Asita was electrified by the sound of heavenly music and the outpouring of a great light. He realized immediately that these events were a sign of some notable event having taken place in the plains below. The light led him down the mountain and to the city of Kapilavastu, where in his tattered clothes he came to and knocked at the gates of the palace of Suddhodhana. As a holy man on a mission he was admitted to the presence of the *raja*, or ruler, who bowed low in the visitor's presence. After seating the holy man on a fine chair, the ruler brought his newborn son before his visitor. Asita was astonished by the beauty of the child and began to praise Gautama, much to the joy of the father. But then the holy man began to weep. In alarm Suddhodhana inquired as to the cause of the tears. Asita replied that he was not weeping for the prince, for he believed that no harm would come to the newborn child. Asita declared that Gautama would become one of the wisest persons ever to live. His wisdom would be perfect. He wept, he said, because he, Asita, was already an old man and would not live long enough to know Gautama in his full glory.

Maya, Gautama's mother, however, was not to know of the events of his early life, for she died within seven days of his birth. Her devoted sister, Pajapati, was given the care of the infant. But the baby did not suffer from inattention. Within the family there were ample sources of affection and aid. Throughout his early years and until he renounced his worldly life, Gautama was a privileged person. He remarks in the scriptures of Buddhism that he wore garments of silk and had attendants who held a white umbrella over him to shade him from the intense sun. While these accounts, formulated several centuries after his death, probably exaggerated the luxury and power of his family, there can be little doubt that he was privileged in terms of the time and the circumstances of his life. Thus, probably in exaggerated form, it is noted that he was provided with no fewer than thirty-two nurses in his early life. The custom of the times, however, called for a person such as Gautama to be cared for by four nurses. Even four nurses were a sign of privilege.

The child also had other advantages in his upbringing. The accounts are full of stories about his formal education, which was accomplished within the palace through private tutors. Sixty-four subjects, including grammar, sports, fortune-telling, massage, music, and chess, were the boy's intellectual regimen. Apparently Gautama was very bright, for he entered into the various subjects with zest and with marked success to the point of astounding his teachers. Sometimes when he was in the company of other youths who were learning, he would show forth his eloquence and prior knowledge, making further instruction a dubious enterprise. His education was complex, including sports and various recreational activities. It called for training in horseback riding and in the art of riding elephants, for gaining skill in driving chariots, and for knowledge of the use of arms. In all aspects of education, Gautama exceeded expectations.

Despite the rigor of his early training, the young prince's life was not austere. Tradition tells of the many advantages that he had. He had couches of precious woods with fine rugs, he wore garlands with sweet perfumes, his foods were rich and varied, he was protected by a corps of guards, he possessed various means of transportation—including horses, elephants, barges, chariots, and litters—and other luxuries. His father wished his son to have every advantage and he planned Gautama's life so that one day in fulfillment of prophecy he might become the ruler of all India, perhaps even of the world. Suddhodhana even built three palaces just for Gautama, making them a present to his son on his sixteenth birthday. The three palaces were for residence in the winter, in the summer, and in the rainy season. The father, moreover, provided five kinds of sensual gratification for his son. These were: dancing, singing, musical solos of wind and string instruments, orchestral music, and women. All five were presumably a systematic feature of Gautama's parentally directed education. One source claims that some eighty-four thousand women were involved in the fulfillment of his sensual gratification, although here too the art of exaggeration certainly has exceeded even the possibilities of factual belief.

In his sixteenth year—although some say nineteenth—the question of marriage was faced. The ruler broached the subject to his councillors, and each offered a daughter. But Suddhodhana remarked that his son should be asked about the qualities that he would wish in a wife. Gautama said that he would give his answer in seven days. His response called for perfection. He indicated that his bride should excel in all moral qualities. In addition, she should be the perfect daughter-in-law to his father and the perfect mistress to her slaves; she should not be given to excesses in drink, parties, and public displays; she should be beautiful yet modest; she should be the first up in the morning and the last to retire at night, and so forth. His father, interestingly, remarked after the list was provided that he was somewhat doubtful that such a person could be found.

Suddhodhana resolved the problem by calling those with eligible daughters to bring them to the palace with suitable dowries. He also assembled a great collection of jewels—gold, silver, and lapis lazuli. The tray of jewels was placed at Gautama's side, and as each candidate approached him, he spoke briefly with her and gave her a jewel. Councillors waited in a secluded place to observe the expression on the prince's face in order to see whether one of the princesses especially appealed to him. They waited in vain. Finally the last girl appeared, the daughter of Mahanaman, a noble of the Sakya clan. For this last girl, Yasodhara by name, the young prince had no jewels left. The latecomer teased the prince, saying that she wondered what she had done to displease him, since he had no jewel for her. The protesting Gautama declared that he did not despise her, and so saying he took off his finely jeweled necklace and gave it to her. She modestly said that she was not worthy of such a great gift. In response he proceeded to give her all the jewels that he was wearing, thus declaring his love for her.

The story, however, did not end happily at this moment. Suddhodhana was not pleased with his son's choice. The ruler indicated that Yasodhara's father had declared that he would not give his daughter in marriage except to one who was able to beat all suitors in athletic and intellectual contests. There followed an open competition involving the telling of jokes, swimming, dealing with elephants, answering riddles, explaining dreams, imitating birds, and other activities. In each and every one, Gautama showed that he was the very best. For example, in dealing with elephants, one suitor killed an elephant with one blow. Another took up an elephant by his tail and threw him outside the gates of Kapilavastu. But Gautama merely took his toe and lifted an elephant, throwing him to the other side of the mountain. So it went. Siddhartha Gautama, with proper pomp and circumstance, was married to Yasodhara.

One might have supposed that Gautama was most happy. Seemingly he had everything that a person of his status could desire. He was held in high esteem by those around him, within his family and beyond. He was well educated and had an alert mind. His athletic prowess belied his years. He was handsome and was able to charm those who knew him. No wonder, then, that his father thought his son might indeed become ruler, perhaps even of the whole of India and beyond. But Gautama was not happy. He was not satisfied. All the benefits that had been showered upon him left him with a sense of inner void.

One illustration among several from his boyhood shows his discontent. As a part of the spring festival, Suddhodhana as ruler led a ceremony involving plowing and sowing. The *raja* went through a field with a jeweled plow. Gautama, like others, watched. But he was not impressed by the rich garments his father wore or the jeweled plow. His attention was directed to the insects and worms and other creatures that had been turned up by the plow. He was saddened that the birds descended and ate the tiny creatures. This incident taught him the harshness of nature, the fact that greater creatures devoured the smaller. In this incident he perceived the pain and suffering that characterized the world of physical and biological nature.

Increasingly Gautama became a brooding, restless, and unsatisfied prince. The artificiality of the palace's pleasures began to cloy. He struggled to formulate a basis for life that would transcend the five sensual gratifications provided by his father. Something was missing and he was given striking insight into the causes and the cure of his unhappiness by what the Buddhist tradition calls the four signs. Each of these had a decisive effect upon his life and ultimately led him to his great renunciation of palace life. It was his custom to travel about to his palaces and to local parks. But his father decreed that during his travels outside the palace he should not be allowed to see anything unpleasant. He had grown up without a direct knowledge of the true nature of the human condition.

On one occasion, however, he left the palace by the east gate in the company of his charioteer, Channa. This time the gods made it possible for him to see with his own eyes that which had been denied him in his upbringing. He found himself facing an old man with white hair, without teeth, wrinkled, and supported by a stick. Gautama asked Channa whether this condition was peculiar to the man and his family. He was told that all persons grow old in much the same way. Despite his groom's protests, Gautama had no heart for enjoying the pleasures of the park and went back to the palace.

In the second sign, Gautama and Channa went out the south gate and there found a diseased man. He was dried up, overcome with fever, weak, with his body immersed in his own filth, helpless, and breathing with difficulty. Inquiring again of Channa, he was told that this state of affairs comes to all men.

The third sign occurred when the pair left by the western gate and encountered a funeral procession. In Indian fashion the corpse was wrapped in a shroud and was being carried aloft on a stretcher, followed by weeping relatives and friends. Again, Channa affirmed that death is the common fate.

On the fourth visit outside the palace Gautama and Channa confronted a mendicant monk. The plainly garbed monk held forth his bowl, eyes lowered but radiating a serenity that immediately caught the attention of the young prince. This fourth sign indicated to Gautama that peace of mind was possible. It was possible through the kind of life that was epitomized by the possessionless monk.

Before returning to the palace Gautama went into a garden by a riverside to assess what he would need to do in order to secure the ascetic's inner peace. He decided that he had found the answer to the world's pain and suffering. He knew the course that his life would have to take. He perceived in these four signs the full meaning of human existence. The path was clear. He realized that in order to achieve his goal he would have to give up all he possessed. His material advantages as well as his family and friends were impediments in his path of personal salvation. He would have to engage in what later Buddhists called the great renunciation.

Gautama's break with his past life caused heartaches for family and friends. Suddhodhana was distraught, for he had such high hopes for his son. The father promised that he would give his son anything he wished if only he would remain prince and heir. Gautama responded that he would willingly remain if his father would guarantee that he would not be prone to the evils he had discovered through the four signs. His father, of course, could not meet that promise. So, after considerable discussion and pleading, Suddhodhana agreed to the parting with regret and yet with understanding and even with some appreciation.

Gautama's leave-taking from his wife, Yasodhara, was another matter. For many years the couple had not been blessed with a child. Some say that they waited for ten years before their firstborn, Rahula, blessed their marriage. Gautama faced the necessity of seeing his wife and son before taking leave of the palace. He went to the residence of his wife and opened the door to her room. By the light burning in the room he saw Yasodhara and Rahula asleep on a flower-strewn bed. The mother's hand rested on the child's head. Gautama wished to pick up his son and hold him for a time in his arms, but he realized that if he raised his wife's hand he well might awaken her, and that he did not wish to do. So he refrained from holding his son and from awakening his wife. In order to save Yasodhara from pain, he left the room and prepared for his journey from the palace.

The die had been cast. Despite the legendary resistances to his leaving, Gautama and his groom went forth to the open country, Gautama riding on a great white steed. They traveled until their horses were exhausted, believing they had gotten beyond the recall by any emissaries his father might have sent. Gautama then proceeded to change his appearance as his entrance into his new way of life. He shaved off his beard and hair, gave his princely ornaments to his groom so that they might be taken back to the palace, and dressed in the coarse

yellow robe of a monk. Pausing only a brief time to say fare-
well to Channa, and giving messages for family and friends
back home, Gautama broke his bonds with the world. He
plunged into the nearby forest and began his long quest for
relief from the burdens of his inner life that had brought him
to this decisive moment.

In the next six years, before his great enlightenment, Gautama strenuously sought personal salvation. He went first to
Rajagaha, the kingly city of the province of Magadha. There
he began to explore the meaning of the Brahmanical Hinduism. This was a kind of religion that offered salvation
through philosophic meditation and the practice of self-
discipline provided by yoga. The ascetic Alara Kalama, living
in a cave, was Gautama's first teacher. Essentially his message
was that a person could attain a state of nothingness if he per-
sisted in advancing himself through successive stages of meditation. But Gautama found this path to salvation wanting. It
was clearly too abstract, too intellectually grounded. What
Gautama sought was something more concrete and personally
useful.

He went on to a second teacher, Uddaka Ramaputta, also
an ascetic, who similarly taught the possibility of arriving at a
state in which the assertion and the denial of ideas simultane-
ously would bring peace to the person. This approach also did
not appeal to the seeker. By these two explorations, Gautama
was showing evidence of his willingness to seek out the more
abstruse aspects of the traditional religion of India, namely,
Hinduism. By rejecting the approach of intellectual sophistica-
tion, Gautama was also rejecting Hinduism and its proffered
salvation.

After leaving the Hindu ascetics and their essentially
intellectual versions of the nature of religion, Gautama entered a grove at Uruvela through which a clear river flowed.
Nearby was a village from whose inhabitants he might beg for
food. In the grove he began a five-year effort to win his salvation through extreme asceticism. Now asceticism of this sort
was widely prevalent at the time. In the previous chapter the

story was told of how Vardhamana and his followers found salvation through the practice of extreme self-denial. But the extreme asceticism of Jainism was only one of the possibilities that confronted Gautama. Other sectarian groups flourished at the same time through similar teachings and practices.

Gautama gave extreme asceticism a long and strenuous try. He reasoned that as the body is severely disciplined the mind becomes clearer and is more able to grasp the ultimate meaning of personal salvation. Gautama reasoned that the indulged self is like a green, sappy stick that is lying in the water. One would find it difficult if not impossible to ignite such a stick. In this analogy the life of pleasure moistens the body to the point that the fire of the spirit is not able to set it ablaze. In order to set the stick afire, it is first necessary to dry it out. So it is with the person. Extreme self-discipline dries out the soul and prepares it for the illumination of the spirit.

With this outlook in mind, Gautama proceeded for a long time to deny his body. He tried to restrain his breathing, a natural function, until his head roared and sharp pain almost made him unconscious. Yet he found no peace. He sought to press his teeth and tongue against his palate so that he might coerce the beats of his heart. Even though he did this until the sweat streamed from his armpits, he found no peace. He tried all manner of personal restraints: he ate his own excrement, sat on a couch of thorns, lay in a cemetery on burned bones and among rotting bodies, let dirt accumulate on his body until it fell off. He reduced his food intake to one hemp grain or a single grain of rice or one jujube fruit a day. He stood for days in one position, or squatted in one position for long periods of time, and dressed in tattered and chafing clothes. By these and similar means he sought to dry out his self. He became mere skin and bones. He said that when he felt his belly it was his backbone that he found within his grasp. Self-mortification had taken its toll. Yet he did not find the peace he had been seeking. He was troubled that with all this self-discipline he had no more insight regarding himself and the sought-for salvation than had any other mortal. All his efforts were in vain. The path of extreme asceticism was tried and found wanting.

While practicing his severe asceticism, Gautama was joined by five other ascetics. One day Gautama arose to enter the nearby river. There in his weakened condition he fainted. The five were puzzled by the incident, thinking that the motionless Gautama had possibly entered into *nirvana,* the blessed state of existence and non-existence. They thought also that perhaps he had died. But in time the water revived Gautama both in body and in spirit. In his refreshment he came to the conclusion that the path of extreme asceticism had not brought him to the desired-for salvation. He resolved that he well might now take food and drink, and taking his begging bowl he became again a *paribbajaka,* or a wandering, begging monk. The five ascetics were angry with him, believing that he had turned his back on the way that they and he had been practicing. They took off for Benares, the most holy of Indian cities.

Gautama, however, had not yet found the peace he was seeking. Even his new life was not satisfying. But his health was being restored and he began to look at life with renewed vigor. Leaving Uruvela, he wandered about until he came to a place that is called Bodh-gaya. There, entering a grove, he sat down under a fig tree. Later this type of tree became known as the Bodhi-tree, or the knowledge tree; sometimes it is named the Bo-tree. Now he was determined to win salvation. He promised himself that he would not move from the spot until he had found his life's peace. He reviewed his past life and the several efforts that he had made toward self-fulfillment. He meditated in a somewhat relaxed way, entering into successively deeper levels of meaning, conquering his emotions as he went.

During this time he underwent a great temptation from Mara, the Oriental Satan. Actually Mara knew that Gautama was getting very close to finding his salvation. This was Mara's last opportunity to win him back to his former life at Kapilavastu. Mara tempted Gautama with all sorts of worldly pleasures: rich palaces, fine gardens, great treasure, and parading armies keeping perfect step before him. But Gautama was not moved. Then Mara brought forth his daughters, and giving them the best of the world's beauty, commanded them to wile Gautama away from his quest. They showed their white teeth, dropped their saris from their shoulders, tightened their clothing to show their slim waists, danced, sang, blushed, and in every way tried to claim his attention. But Gautama was not moved. The daughters kissed Gautama's feet and returned to Mara saying that Mara was on the wrong side of the conflict. They testified to Gautama's disinterest and to his purity.

Mara, however, was not finished with Gautama. Mara then called for his creatures, the sins, and one by one they came before the meditating one and sought to entice him. They were: hate, selfishness, greed, ambition, pride, ignorance, and lust. But Gautama simply stared at them as they came to tempt him, and one by one they retreated. Mara now lifted up his sword and called for the forces of nature to combat Gautama. Mountains were torn from the earth, thunder and lightning were everywhere, floods of lava overflowed from the mountains. In these and other ways Mara threatened Gautama, but he was not moved. He knew that wisdom was superior to Mara and he clung to wisdom. He had confidence that he would be able to find his soul's salvation. Thus he pounded the earth with his right hand in support of his belief and the earth trembled, the ground opened up and swallowed the forces that had threatened him. He was the victor. Mara, in dejection, realizing that he had lost in this cosmically meaningful struggle, simply picked up a reed and wrote on the ground that Gautama had escaped his realm.

Continuing in meditation, Gautama began to undergo a tremendous, life-shaking experience. It was the basis for his enlightenment, his attainment of the perfect state which is called *nirvana*. No amount of psychological exploration will ever fully explain how Gautama received his enlightenment at the time and under the circumstances that he did. Yet he intuited the final goal of salvation. The end of his quest was comprised of several elements. He perceived that life is filled with pain and suffering. No one is able to live from birth to death without experiencing unhappiness. Certainly Gautama knew suffering. Yet he also knew that suffering is a universal feature of human existence. It is true that suffering within the Indian tradition of which Gautama was a part was said to derive from *karma* and the transmigration of souls. *Karma* signifies the law of moral consequence, that what a man sows morally he will inevitably reap. There is no escape from the consequences of one's actions. Good actions bring good results, but evil actions bring evil results. The self is rewarded according to merit, not alone in this life, but through lives that extend from all eternity to all eternity. The *atman*, or self, is eternally indestructible. Suffering, then, is the eternal lot of persons, unless a way be found for breaking the cycle of rebirth.

Suffering, according to the Gautama who was becoming enlightened, is due to ignorance. The person who suffers lacks the proper knowledge of how suffering comes to be. It is in ignorance that the person gives vent to his desires. Not knowing the true nature of things, the person foolishly craves all that will satisfy his desires. But since all desires are inherently insatiable, desiring leads inevitably to suffering. Thus, if suffering is to be avoided, desires must be suppressed. All suffering will cease only when all desires are suppressed. Such is the content of Gautama's enlightenment. This is his piercing analysis of the problem of life itself. It is a chain of causation. Ignorance leads to misconceptions about the nature of the human experience. Insatiable desires result from ignorance. By suppressing desires, the self may be realized and released from suffering. Yet to this sequence Gautama added another link. He declared that since the absolute suppression of all desire appeared to be impossible, then the person should live moderately. These insights, commonly known as the Four Noble Truths, were then supplemented by the Noble Eightfold Path which consisted of right belief, aspiration, speech, action, livelihood, endeavor, thought, and concentration.

The decisive spiritual experience that Gautama underwent as he sat under the Bo-tree caused him to think that he had found the final enlightenment. The Sanskrit word for enlightenment or wisdom is *bodhi*. It is this attainment, or state, that has been taken to be the title of the religion in later times. By his enlightenment Gautama became the *buddha*. He declared that he had received the full insight of that wisdom which is unsurpassed in the heavens or on the earth. He knew that he had won his salvation. He proclaimed that there would be no rebirth for him, for through the experience of enlightenment he had shattered the traditional claims of *karma* and the transmigration of souls. He had achieved the state of *nirvana*, the blessed state of being and non-being, which the words of human beings cannot describe.

A short time after his enlightenment, as he continued to sit under the tree resplendent in the aura of his newfound understanding, some merchants on their way to Benares were impressed by him. They gave him a new begging bowl and some rice and honey to eat. But Gautama was not yet ready for his ministry to others. He first had to grapple with the choice as to whether the path to salvation that he had found was one for himself only or whether he was called to proclaim the path to others. He asked himself whether he should be a *buddha* only for himself or whether he should be a *buddha* for others. He concluded that his enlightenment was sharable, that others also could attain it. He decided that he would be a *buddha* for others. He wondered where to begin. He thought of returning to his old teachers, for they would surely welcome him and his ideas. But they had died. He then remembered the five ascetics who had left him to go to Benares. He decided to seek them out. Within about four miles of Benares, he came to a deer park called Isipatana, which today is named Sarnath. The park was a haven for ascetics and religious philosophers and there Gautama found the five ascetics. They saw him as he approached and thought how fat and sleek he was. They told themselves that he had truly given up the search for salvation. At first they did not wish to acknowledge him. But, relenting, they gave him a seat and brought water so that he could wash his feet. They then engaged in conversation with Gautama, calling him a friend. But Gautama rejected the title of friend. He said he was the truth-finder and had found the path to salvation. Finding them somewhat skeptical, he asked that they might listen as he expounded the new *dharma*, or doctrine. They obliged him and Gautama preached his first sermon, the sermon of Deer Park. In it he told about his search for salvation. He related the Four Noble Truths and outlined the Noble Eightfold Path. He concluded by saying that there are two paths, two extremes, which the person who has given up the world should properly avoid. One is the life of pleasure. The other is the life of mortification. The life given to pleasure is degrading, vulgar, and ignoble. The life given to mortification is painful, vain, and profitless. Gautama then preached the knowledge of the Middle Path which leads to wisdom, insight, and calm. The Middle Path in this life leads to *nirvana*.

One by one the five ascetics were converted to the new *dharma*. Each asked to come under the leadership of Gautama and was accepted. They became the first members of the *sangha*, the Buddhist monastic order. The *sangha* later grew as more converts were made. Like the religious order in Jainism, it accepted persons from all castes and possessed a clearly democratizing influence within the historical development of Buddhism. Soon, as the word went out, the five original members of the *sangha* had increased to sixty. These in turn were ordained and sent out to bring the message to others. The circle widened to include many others. Then it became necessary for the new order to develop regularized procedures and rules for membership. Quite possibly some of the rules of the order arose after Gautama's lifetime. But in the main they were simple. They called for wearing the saffron, or yellow, robe; carrying the begging bowl; having the head shaven; practicing daily meditation; and taking a pledge that the *sangha* member would take refuge in the Buddha, in the *dharma*, and in the *sangha*.

The members also promised to obey the Ten Precepts. These are: to refrain from destroying life; not to take what is not given; to abstain from unchastity; neither to lie nor deceive; to abstain from intoxicants; to eat moderately and not after noon; not to look on dancing, singing, or dramatic events; not to use garlands, scents, unguents, or ornaments; not to use high or broad beds; and not to accept silver or gold. Obviously these precepts have much in common with the five requirements laid upon believing Jains, except that the vow to avoid all attachments, a very severe vow, is not included. The Ten Precepts represent the Middle Path, the course for human action that Gautama had found and endorsed for his followers. Of course, at times a monk violated one or more of the precepts. When he did he was required to go before the assembled *sangha* to confess and to seek forgiveness.

Not all the followers of Gautama, however, were expected to maintain the Ten Precepts. It was recognized that not everyone who wished to be a Buddhist was in a position to leave his family and worldly obligations and become a monk. The new movement, therefore, recognized a category of believers who were lay associates. These were expected to adhere to the first five of the Ten Precepts. The full ten were expected of those who devoted full time to the movement as monks.

As Gautama's message of salvation became more widely accepted, women also asked to belong to the movement. At first Gautama was reluctant to admit them. But in time an order of nuns became part of the movement. Gautama is said to have remarked that with the inclusion of only men the *sangha* would last for a thousand years, but that with the inclusion of women the order would last only for five hundred years. Yet for his times, the action of recognizing women as entirely worthy members of the new religion was indeed a forward-looking step of great consequence.

Early Buddhism was not a theologically oriented movement in the main. The Four Noble Truths may be said to be the product of reasoning. Yet they do not rest upon certain kinds of metaphysical assumptions. Obviously they do not include a doctrine of deity. Gautama did not call for the support of the gods. In fact, early Buddhism is striking for what it denied in the traditions of India. At no time apparently did Gautama call for the recognition of a supreme deity. He did not pray to a god, nor did he ask his disciples to do so. Gautama, moreover, did not engage, nor did his followers, in worship as it was understood in his time. It is true that meditation was a continuing obligation of the faithful, but it was not of a highly ritualized kind. Like Vardhamana, Gautama has been called an atheist who founded a religion. Gautama's religion is this-worldly. It taught that salvation is available in this life rather than in a state beyond death. It stressed the basic requirement that each person work out his own salvation for himself and without the aid of external influences. Also, the religion places less stress upon reasoning as a feature of religion and more emphasis upon understanding one's emotions, such as the nature of desire, and the importance of an ethical life. The Ten Precepts, for example, do not contain any element of a theological or philosophical nature; they all are directed toward the achievement of appropriate behavior.

Yet there are elements within Gautama's teachings that may be claimed to be essentially philosophic in nature. One of these, for example, is his teaching regarding the self. His second sermon at Deer Park expounded this view. Briefly his aim in this discourse was to show that the self does not exist. In asking about the presumed nature of the self, Gautama gave examples that showed the self to be non-existent. He declared that the body cannot be the self, for the body is impermanent, changing always, getting old and dying. The feelings are not the self, for one's feelings are ever changing. What one feels at one moment will not be felt at the next. One's thoughts are not the self, for these too are not permanent; they are not what was thought before and they will not be one's thoughts for the future. So, too, the soul is not unchanging; it grows, becoming better or worse with experience. In sum, there is no self. He called upon his hearers to stop thinking about themselves as selves. To do so, he averred, is to be liberated from the self. This discussion of the self, then, is an illustration of some attempt at philosophic inquiry. Similarly he avoided saying that the world is eternal or non-eternal, that the world is infinite or finite. These matters, he claimed, are not practical; above all else, the religion of Gautama the Buddha was intensely practical, calling primarily for action rather than metaphysical belief.

It is said that Gautama's great enlightenment took place when he was about thirty-five years of age. If so, his public ministry continued from that time until his death at age eighty. The years in between were a constant pilgrimage through the central basin of the Ganges. The area of India in which he traveled and preached was relatively small geographically, but the nature of his success was great. Everywhere the humble and the renowned heard his message, and many gladly received him as their truth-finder. He inspired those who believed in him to spread his message even beyond the area of his own preaching. In time, and especially after his death, the way of moderation had spread throughout much of India and indeed beyond India to other parts of Asia as well.

Leaving Deer Park, Gautama, the Buddha, came upon a sect of fire worshipers. They were directed by three brothers, the chief of whom was Kasyapa. Being of the brahmin caste, this order lived with their followers in huts built of branches. They meditated, practiced their sacrifices, and studied in austere ways. Gautama entered into a contest with Kasyapa particularly to affirm the wisdom of the new movement. Legend suggests that the contest was fierce. Gautama by one account had to work thirty-five hundred miracles to have his way. Another account says that Gautama gained permission to sleep in the hut where the sacrificial fire was kept. This place was inhabited by a wicked dragon. Inside the hut a huge struggle took place. Fire almost consumed the hut and smoke billowed from it as Gautama and the dragon fought. But finally Gautama was able to subdue the dragon and the victory was acknowledged by Kasyapa and his followers who accepted the new faith. It is said that not only the three leaders of the group but a thousand of the anchorites were also converted.

Gautama and his many followers then went to Rajagaha, the

place to which he fled after he renounced his palace life. It was there that he had sought his salvation through philosophical brahminism and by means of extreme asceticism. But this time he returned under different circumstances. He was now a person of some fame. His eager followers attested to his importance. As he stopped in the royal park just outside the walls of the city, he was greeted by King Bimbisara, the ruler of the province, and by the people of the city. This event was of singular significance, for traditionally a king would not go forth to greet a visitor. Gautama was invited to dinner on the next day, where he sat among the learned and the famous. He was fed well. The king himself offered both hard and soft foods to Gautama with his own hands. The discussion proved enlightening, for finally the king and many of his people were converted to the faith expounded by Gautama. King Bimbisara, moreover, made Gautama an excellent offer. He suggested that he would give his pleasure garden, usually called the Bamboo Grove, to Gautama and his followers. Gautama accepted and the king poured water from a gold vessel over Gautama's hands, confirming the passage of the property. Here for the first time since he left home Gautama had a place of his own where he could stay. He spent the next rainy season in the Bamboo Grove and returned there frequently. In time he was given similar places in a number of the large cities of his region of India.

It was in the Bamboo Grove that Gautama gained two great disciples who loom large among the early leaders of the new religious movement. They were Sariputra and Maudgalyayana. They had promised that should one attain *nirvana* he would immediately tell the other. As seekers, therefore, Sariputra one day came upon Assaji, one of the five ascetics who had formed the nascent *sangha*. Sariputra was very much impressed by the countenance of Assaji. Assaji's face glowed with the knowledge and peace that he had secured through his adoption of Gautama's truths. After inquiry, Sariputra came to accept the new faith also and in turn brought his friend Maudgalyayana into the fold. Sariputra was noted for his keen intelligence. When Gautama had difficulties arising from questions brought by others, especially those within the *sangha* or congregation, he would turn to Sariputra for help. It is said that Maudgalyayana helped Gautama by being able to travel by will to the various heavens and hells in order to secure secret information on which additional conversions were made. Both were among the most eminent of the early disciples. But neither outlived Gautama. It is said that they did not wish to, but returned to their villages in old age in preparation for dying.

Later the time came when Gautama and his followers, upon the request of his father, returned to Kapilavastu. As Gautama approached the city, his father, Suddhodhana, and others went out to meet him. The father had known a Gautama who was young, well-dressed, of princely bearing, and with jet-black hair. Now he found that his son was dressed in a tattered yellow robe, his hair had been shaven, his face was weatherbeaten and drawn. The father apparently thought of his son as a returning prodigal who was seeking the father's forgiveness. At their meeting, the father was disappointed, and without even engaging in the traditional courtesies he turned away and went back to the palace.

On the following day, Suddhodhana was further embarrassed when he learned that his son was begging in the city. The father went out to the son and indicated how troubled he was about the begging for food. He invited Gautama into the palace, where a royal assemblage greeted the former prince and food was provided for all. A dialogue followed in which the king pointed out that his son should be pitied for not having perfumed baths, shoes on his feet, a soft bed, the comforts of family life. Gautama took up each item and sought to show that a person can be happy without luxuries. He pointed out that the religious life as he had come to know it offered advantages that far outweigh the benefits of the life he had left.

The dialogue over, the household further offered its hospitality to Gautama and his disciples. They were invited to take their one daily meal at the palace. This they did and in time succeeded in attracting many of the household to the new faith. Many converts also were made in the city.

But Yasodhara and her son, Rahula, were not in the initial reception in Suddhodhana's palace. They were in their own palace, according to the tradition. The wife indicated that if she meant anything to her husband, he would want to come to see her. Gautama with two of his yellow-robed followers did visit her. When she saw him, however, she was so struck with his changed appearance that she fell at his feet with copious tears. Later she sent Rahula, dressed in bright attractive garments, to ask that he be given his inheritance. The son indicated that he was pleased to meet his father, for he had been a mere infant when Gautama left. Rahula asked for his inheritance. Gautama instructed Sariputra to receive Rahula into the *sangha*, which he did. Suddhodhana, however, was angry, saying that no minor should be converted without the permission of his parents. Gautama agreed that this should be a rule of his new order, although Rahula remained a disciple.

According to tradition, Yasodhara was resistant at first to the new faith. But in time she too came to accept it, and when the order for women nuns was created, she is said to have been one of its first members. Suddhodhana was highly resistive to Gautama's claims. Even after Suddhodhana's three brothers and his second son, Nanda, who was Gautama's half brother, were converted, along with many other relatives and friends, the father still held out. Yet in time he is said to have been persuaded. It is said that he underwent the experience of going through the four degrees of saintliness before he too achieved buddhahood. Out of his sympathy for the movement, he gave the park in which his son and his followers were living and decreed that all noble families within the region with two sons give one of them to the movement.

Among the relatives of Gautama who joined the new faith were two cousins: Ananda and Devadatta. Ananda was especially beloved. He became the personal attendant of Gautama, waiting on his every request. He was most faithful and loyal. But Devadatta was another matter. Having joined the movement early, he became increasingly jealous of Gautama. Devadatta sought to displace Gautama as the head of the *sangha*. He won the support of Ajatasattu, the son of Bimbisara. He wished Ajatasattu to kill the king, his father, but he was foiled in the attempt by those around the king. He plotted to do away with Gautama on several occasions, but when killers were sent to assassinate him they were regularly converted on their way or in his presence. Once, it is said, Devadatta arranged for a mad elephant to run Gautama down, but as it approached, it became docile, attesting to the power of the Buddha to overcome all evil designs. Devadatta did form a rival *sangha*, but it did not succeed. The fact that Devadatta and his various activities are given such prominence within the Buddhist tradition is perhaps some indication that he was a powerful enemy.

At the age of eighty and after decades of successful preaching of the Middle Path, Gautama was ready to face death. In his later years he had lost some of his vigor and at times was ill. Near the end he was in Pava, where he stayed in the mango grove of Cunda, a smith. Cunda prepared a meal with excellent food, although some part of it appeared to be indigestible. Gautama was ill from it, passed some blood, and suffered sharp pains. But he asked that Cunda not be blamed. Along with Ananda he set out for the village of Kusinara. He indicated that he would die soon. Ananda implored him not to die in such a little village; he should die in a large city. That would be appropriate to his stature. But Gautama objected, pointing out that the past of Kusinara had been noteworthy. Arriving in Kusinara, he asked Ananda to prepare him a bed with the head to the north. Despite the imminent end, Gautama continued to converse. Ananda asked him what should be done when the followers no longer could visit with him. Gautama indicated that there are four places where they might visit and be reminded of him. These are: the place where he was born, the place where he attained enlightenment, the place where he had expounded the Buddhist *dharma,* and the place where he attained complete *nirvana.*

Again, Ananda asked the dying master how the believers should act toward women. Gautama answered: by not seeing them. Ananda asked, then, what they should do if they were to see them. Gautama responded: by not speaking to them. Finally, Ananda asked what should be done if they were spoken to. Gautama replied that mindfulness should be exercised.

Other matters such as the development of further rules for the order were discussed. An ascetic of the place, Subhadda, came to ask Gautama to try to resolve certain doubts that he had. Ananda wanted the man to go away, but Gautama allowed him to enter and to speak with him. Subhadda was converted.

Gautama, the Buddha, then spoke his dying words. He said that decay is inherent in all component things. He urged his followers to work out their salvation with diligence. The end had come.

The cremation of the body probably took place that very day, as was the custom. Usually those who survived gathered about the corpse to lament the death. Then the body was washed and reclothed with the simple monastic garment, put on a stretcher, and taken to the public crematory. Following the rituals, the pyre was lighted and the mortal remains were turned into ashes.

Gautama's followers, however, did not let the death of their master end the religion's course of development. They and others after them took the message to countless others. What had begun as an individual's strenuous search for personal salvation became in time one of the most influential forces in human history. And the Buddha who was Gautama became not merely the one who had shown no dependency upon the divine in his own lifetime but an avowed divinity to his followers. They venerate him as the true savior of mankind.

4
NANAK
AND
SIKHISM

The fourth religion to have originated in India (the others being Hinduism, Jainism, and Buddhism) is Sikhism. The word *sikh* connotes a disciple, a person who is a follower of Nanak, the religion's founder.

Sikhism is the latest of the various religions that are considered in this volume. If one dates it from the time of Nanak's birth, it is somewhat more than five hundred years old. Nanak was born in A.D. 1469 and died in 1539. Although it is true that some religions which have personal founders are more recent, sometimes they cannot claim to be truly original in that they are avowedly offshoots of traditional religions. Mormonism, for example, is a later religious form, but it must be considered as a variant within the Christian tradition. So with others. Yet there are other religions, such as the Baha'i faith, which claim to be genuinely new even though, to a greater or lesser degree, they may acknowledge and even draw upon the more traditional religions for their basic ideas. They too may have personal founders. But the assumption underlying the present classification is that only a religion which endures through a long historical period has clear claim to lasting significance and is thus well worthy of study. The ability of a religion to last for a period of at least five hundred years entitles it to consideration as a formative influence in history. Sikhism on such a basis is entitled to that consideration. On the other hand, it must be admitted that all such decisions are highly subjective.

Sikhism is one of the smaller religions in the number of its adherents. Probably only Jainism and Zoroastrianism have a smaller following today. Sikhism currently claims from four to six million believers. The size of a religion, however, is not to be taken as a test of its validity. Religion cannot be quantitatively evaluated, especially not in terms of such a factor as their adherents. It cannot be justified to assert that a religion which appeals to many is more valid than a religion that appeals to only a few. The value of a religion does not respond to that kind of reasoning. So, although Sikhism is a relatively small religion, it must be approached with the same seriousness as that given to those religions which have gathered large followings.

Also, Sikhism is not a religion of universal appeal as are Buddhism, Christianity, and Islam. Born in India, Sikhism has largely remained in India. Its founder, Nanak, however, did travel widely about India on his several missionary journeys and there is evidence, of doubtful reliability, that he also took his message to such places as Ceylon (now called Sri Lanka), Saudi Arabia (he presumably went to Mecca and Medina), and Iraq (there is reference that Nanak visited Baghdad). But historically Sikhism has been confined mainly to India and to one state within India—the Punjab.

Although Sikhism for the most part has become the religion of a particular people in a particular place—the Sikhs of the Punjab—it originally did contain within it impulses of a more universal character. Nanak did not proclaim a religion for a limited number of persons; his teachings were intended to embrace the ultimate truth about human existence for all peoples. His concept of divinity was preached as the most true of all that was known and was applicable to every one in every place. Similarly the other teachings of Sikhism were not restricted; they were made available to all who would believe. But the historic fact remains that it was predominantly Sikhism which formed the faith of the people of the Punjab. The people and the religion bear a very close identity.

The various living religions maintain that there is a desirable relation between religion and the surrounding society; each of these religions has a definable politics. In some cases, such as Jainism, the relationship is largely negative. That is, the relation is one in which the religion teaches withdrawal from active participation in society and particularly in governmental affairs. At the other extreme are those religions which bear a close and accepting relationship between faith and society. Shinto, for example, is the civic religion of the Japanese people. Confucianism is a religion of social responsibility to such an extent, in its original form, that matters of an otherworldly nature are minimized and even denied. One cannot think of Islam as a religious system without conceiving of its interpenetrating the whole gamut of social relationships, including government. Judaism is a very clear example of a religion that defines itself in terms of a particular people. In fact, Sikhism probably comes closest to Judaism as an example of the manner in which a religion and a people are inseparably interrelated. Thus it may be said that Sikhism is the religion of a particular political entity, the Punjab.

Some Sikhs, however, live beyond the Punjab. They are found throughout parts of Asia as stalwart guards and policemen. One sees them in the cities of India, Hong Kong, Singapore, and elsewhere. In the British colonies in Asia they gained favor as courageous civil servants who were valuable also because they were accepted by both Hindus and Muslims as well as by others.

Sikhism is perhaps most distinctive among the living religions by reason of its efforts to harmonize two preexisting religions: Hinduism and Islam. All the living religions are complex cultural developments in which can be traced the blending of preexisting religious forms. None of the living religions was fashioned from absolutely new and wholly unique beginnings. Each came into being within a cultural context that included prior faiths. Each developed from prior religious forms whose elements in combination became the new religion. This process of building on the past usually involved a minimum of highly conscious decisions about what would and what would not become a part of the new religion. The syncretic process may be termed latent in that it occurred without a declared and open effort of a clearly rational nature to combine variants in past religious experience.

The case of Sikhism is different. Nanak, the founder, sought to combine the most attractive features of two large and important religious traditions in India: Hinduism and Islam. Hinduism is the immemorial religion of the Indian people. Hindus refer to their religion as *sanatana*, which means "ancient" or "eternal." Hinduism as a designation for the traditional religion of the Indian people did not originate with the followers of that religion. Rather, it was a term employed sometime after Islam became a widely accepted religion in India. The term was introduced as a means whereby Muslims differentiated between themselves and those who held to the traditional faith.

Hinduism is a religion that is difficult to define. It has no single set of beliefs or practices. It is the expression of the traditional, the variant, the developing culture of India over a period of several thousand years. Not a single religion by any means, Hinduism is rather like a medley of religions. Yet, despite a large number of important exceptions, Hinduism may be said to have several features common to all, although the exact content of these varies greatly from time to time and from place to place. Hinduism involves a reverence for the Vedas, a set of sacred scriptures of early record. Hinduism also involves a belief in the divine. The gods of Hinduism vary from the earliest animistic and polytheistic to the later transcendental and pantheistic deities who at times are conceived in personalistic terms as well. The social system of caste also distinguishes Hinduism. This system differentiates nominally four groups of Indians on a hereditary basis, although in actuality there are several thousand castes and subcastes. Certain concepts are also representative of Hinduism. *Karma*, the belief that one's life is determined inevitably by one's past actions, is one such idea. The notion that one is reborn repeatedly through the transmigration of souls is another. Other features of Hinduism are: belief in the efficacy of the *guru,* or teacher, as a necessary spiritual guide; emphasis on the saving influence of ritualism; belief that the phenomenal world is *maya,* or illusionary; and belief that there are several ways to salvation, one of which is *bhakti,* or devotion. In brief, Hinduism is one of the two major religions that Nanak sought to incorporate into his new faith.

Islam (more will be said about it in the later chapter on Muhammad) is a religion that is far different from Hinduism. Hinduism was native to India, but Islam originated elsewhere. It was introduced by the armies of Arabic Islam which brought the religion, along with its correlative culture, into India about A.D. 650, only some twenty years after the death of Muhammad. The first incursion was into the north. From there they moved down the west coast and later down the east coast until the whole of India, through successive stages, came under Islamic influence. But it was the eleventh century that brought the invasions of one of the greatest military leaders and rulers of all time. Mahmud of Ghazni through seventeen campaigns thoroughly conquered the Indian subcontinent. He returned each time to Ghazni (present-day Afghanistan) with great treasures, including the notable riches from the temple at Somnath. Other Muslim invaders came in later centuries, thus extending Islamic influence throughout India. Today tens of millions of Muslims live in India, converts from Hinduism in the main. In Pakistan and Bangladesh there are almost a hundred million Muslims.

The principal feature of Islam is the conception of god. His name is Allah. In Islam, Allah is the core of life and of all reality. He is one and transcendent. He is god alone; he is eternal; he has no companion or son; he needs no helper in his rulership. This estimate of divinity, as will be seen, became the chief feature of Nanak's religion. Islam, however, contains other aspects worthy of note. It possesses an array of extraterrestrial beings, or angels, who mainly act as Allah's messengers. The cultic life of the Muslim is relatively simple. No pictures or music are used in worship. There is no extensive priesthood. Usually a knowledgeable person in the faith, sometimes called an *imam,* conducts the frequent worship. The faithful Muslim prays five times a day after washing himself, and he hopes to make a pilgrimage to Mecca, the most holy city of the faith, at least once during his lifetime. A number of proscriptions regarding the family, the law, and the nature of ethical requirements are also a part of the faith.

Hinduism and Islam, then, were the two dominant religions at the time of Nanak and in the place where he was born. They presented an essential choice of world views. Although cooperation between Hindus and Muslims was prevalent in the Punjab as well as throughout India, the presence of such a sharp conflict of basic attitudes and values permeated the outlook of the people.

As with the founders of the other religions, there are many unsure aspects of the life of Nanak. Scholars are far from agreement as to what information concerning his life is reliable. Nanak's life is shrouded with fancies that have been added to the original account of his life by those faithful who sought by such means to express their deepest respect for him. These stories provide insights into what his followers, both early and late, esteemed him to be. For faithful Sikhs, Nanak is not just another man, an ordinary person. He is the center of their faith and the pivot about which they are able to make sense of their lives. In this context the nonhistorical aspects of the tradition are of clear importance. But for the person not ultimately committed to the faith the requirement of historical accuracy is a troublesome one.

What are the sources for constructing a biography of Nanak? The chief scripture of Sikhism is the Adi Granth. Granth means "book" in Sanskrit. It was compiled by Guru Arjan in A.D. 1603 to 1604. Presumably the Adi Granth contains more than nine hundred compositions by Nanak. Yet within the whole of the sacred scripture there are very few bits of information about the founder's own life. It is possible to infer that Nanak lived and taught at the time of one of the invasions by Babur, a Muslim military leader, into northwest

India. Also there is some evidence that Nanak was aware of
the Nath *yogis,* a group of Hindus who practiced self-
discipline as a means of gaining salvation. Aside from such
items, there is little information available in the Adi Granth to
throw light on the actual life of Nanak.

The most useful sources come from a body of literature
called the *janam-sakhis. Janam-sakhis* means life stories or evidences of his life. They are hagiographic accounts of various
events in Nanak's life and they are supposed to be arranged to
some extent in chronological order. From this large body of literature there is ample information available to reconstruct a
complete life story of Nanak. Unfortunately, however, many
doubts must be raised regarding their reliability. For example,
the strict chronology of the stories must be doubted. There are
too many gaps and too many conflicts in the accounts themselves to make them genuinely reliable. Of greater importance,
there is no presently known way whereby what is historical
can be separated from that which is nonhistorical. Fact and
fancy seem inextricably blended in the *janam-sakhis.* The
present telling of the life of Nanak, therefore, cannot avoid
using stories that some scholars are unwilling to accept as au-
thentic. Obviously, too, many stories about Nanak's life will
not be included here because of the need to present his life
within acceptable limits.

It is said that Nanak was born in the early-morning hours of
April 15, 1469, in Talwandi, a small village about forty miles
southwest of the city of Lahore, the capital of the Punjab. Sit-
uated on the river Ravi, Talwandi was near one of the two
main routes of invasion into northwest India. As a consequence, it both suffered and benefited from its geographic
position. It is said to have been destroyed thirteen times and
rebuilt each time. It was obviously a center where the impact
of Islam was felt upon the preexistent Hindu culture. At the
beginning of the fifteenth century, Rai Bhoe, a convert to
Islam who held vast lands in the area, rehabilitated Talwandi
and made it a thriving center. Upon Bhoe's death his son, Rai
Bular, continued to enhance the town. Additional families

were attracted, among them was that of Shiv Ram. Shiv Ram
was a Hindu. He was a member of the Bedi clan of the *kshatriya* caste. The *kshatriya* caste was the second highest, next to
the priestly brahmins, whose members consisted mainly of
military and governmental administrators. Shiv Ram was the
accountant for the local ruler, Rai Bular. He kept track of the
revenues from the rental of lands, and in other ways managed
the financial aspects of the Muslim ruler's enterprises. In time
his place was taken by his son, Kalyan Chand (sometimes
given as Mehta Kalian Das Bedi). Perhaps in his own lifetime,
but probably later, Kalyan Chand's name was abridged and
became Kalu. Kalu, the town accountant, was the father of
Nanak, the founder of Sikhism. Kalu was married to Tripta,
the daughter of Rama of Chahalwala, a village south of Lahore. Kalu also had a brother, Lalu, and a daughter, Nanaki.
It was into this family that the hero of faith was born in 1469.

As with the other founders of religions, the birth of Nanak
was seen to have celestial implications. According to the
janam-sakhis, "unbeaten sounds" were heard at the doorway.
A strong light flashed through the mud room in which the
birth took place. By these and other signs the birth of a great
personage was heralded. The father, Kalu, rejoiced over the
birth of a son and called the *pandit* (teacher) Hardyal to
come to his house to interpret the meaning of Nanak's birth. It
was the custom of the times to chart a horoscope for the newborn's life and Hardyal proceeded to do this, sitting on a cush-
ion and sprinkling a long scroll with saffron water. Having
charted the heavens, he called upon the midwife, Daultan, a
Muslim, to tell him if there were any experiences connected
with Nanak's birth that should be noted. She declared that
never had she aided the birth of so extraordinary a child. She
said that Nanak's first cry was that of the laughter of a grown
person. She was amazed. Hardyal asked to see and hold the
child. Against the protests of Tripta, the mother, he was
handed the infant Nanak. Upon deliberation, Hardyal declared that Nanak was indeed an unusual child and that his
birth held great promise for all mankind. He said that both

Hindus and Muslims would come to revere him, that his name would resound in both the heavens and the earth, and that Nanak would come to worship the one, true god. He indicated that he would return to the household on the thirteenth day to give the child his name.

The accounts say that the family and the town rejoiced over Nanak's birth. Village minstrels came to the household to sing and recite poetry. Hindu and Muslim friends and relatives visited to share the family's joy. Kalu supplied all his visitors with great signs of hospitality and even had special sweets sent to their homes. In addition he gave food and clothing to the poor of Talwandi. As was the custom, on the sixth day after Nanak's birth the men of the Bedi clan or subcaste were invited to witness the ceremonial bath of the infant and to enjoy a sumptuous feast.

Legends have it that the young Nanak was precocious. It is said that when he was only one month old he could focus his gaze and respond to calls from his parents and his nurse. In his second month he could hold his neck stably. At six months he could begin to lisp; at seven months he could sit up. By the time he was ten months old he could creep about and even stand. He spoke freely when he was a year and a half old and at two years he played with children of his age. His family and relatives and the people of Talwandi all noted his striking progress and abilities. Much later, in keeping with the honor felt toward Talwandi's leading citizen, the name of Nanak's birthplace was changed to Nankana in his honor. It also is called Nankana Sahib (*sahib*, meaning great). As Nanak grew up he played with the children of the town and impressed many by his generosity. In fact, his father, Kalu, sometimes reprimanded Nanak for giving away his possessions too freely. Also, Nanak impressed his elders by his wisdom. Hindu and Muslim alike found knowledge in him that was very unusual in a child. Townspeople remarked that Nanak was indeed a handsome child, full of wisdom, and shaped in the image of the divine.

At seven years of age Nanak began his formal schooling.

Hardyal was consulted to determine the most auspicious day for Nanak to begin. The child went to a small school for the town's children carrying a betel nut, rice, sugar, and a silver rupee as presents for his teacher, Gopal. Gopal, knowing of the abilities of Nanak, gave the child a preferred seat at the front of the class. The teacher wrote down the first few letters of the alphabet on a slate and handed it to Nanak for his lesson. So began his schooling. In the evening of the first day at school, Nanak came home in a pensive mood. His parents respected his thoughtfulness and on the next day gave him a bath, dressed him in new clothes, and sent him back to school. One day the young student took a slate and listed upon it the letters of the alphabet. To each letter in Punjabi he attached a learned saying, thus composing a kind of poem or acrostic. Gopal had not expected such advanced work. He read the poem with astonishment. Each line held a profound truth. Nanak asked, for example, who is truly learned and answered this by saying that a learned one is one who gains understanding through the use of the alphabet. He declared that true learning consists of unraveling divine knowledge. He proclaimed the benefits of worshiping the one, true god, of loving and serving him.

This kind of achievement amazed Gopal and Nanak's fellow students. But Kalu had other ideas about education. Kalu wanted Nanak to learn arithmetic, the compilation of financial ledgers, and other matters that ultimately would lead Nanak to take over his father's responsibilities. Kalu was a practical man and he wanted a practical education for his son. Nanak was not inclined to this sort of learning. The father relented and arranged for Nanak to be tutored by a Hindu scholar, Brijnath Shastri, who was steeped in the ancient texts of Hinduism. From him Nanak learned Sanskrit, but failed to be attracted to a sustained education of this nature. Following this schooling, Nanak went to a local *maktab*, or Muslim school, which was led by Qutb-ud-Din. There he showed great proficiency in learning Persian and Arabic. In this new setting Nanak not only learned the two languages but also developed skill in poetry, although all he wrote was of a highly religious character.

The marriage of Nanaki, Nanak's sister, was an important event. Her husband-to-be was Jairam, a civil servant attached to the office of the governor of Sultanpur. Jairam was responsible for an annual visit to Talwandi to collect that portion of the town's revenues which were owed to the governor. He spoke one day to the local ruler, Rai Bular, about his interest in marrying into one of the families of the caste and subcaste that Kalu represented. In time an arranged marriage was held. Both Hindus and Muslims brought gifts to the wedding, and there was great rejoicing in the families and throughout the town. Nanak always held his sister in deep affection. She in turn believed in him implicitly. She is said to be the earliest to have recognized his religious genius, and the two apparently were very close. But Nanak also came to respect and love Jairam.

At age eleven Nanak had arrived at a significant ceremonial occasion. According to custom, at that age he was to be invested with the *janeu*, or sacrifical thread. This thread was woven into a cord-hoop of cotton and was religiously blessed. The thread is worn around the head and draped over the shoulders. This sacred thread is a sign of high birth and high caste. It would mark Nanak as a *kshatriya*, distinguishing him from the members of the lowest caste, the *sudras. Sudras* were not invested with a thread.

The occasion of investiture was a happy one. Relatives and friends of the family were invited. At the center of the ceremony the family's spiritual counselor and priest, Hardyal, sat on a special seat that was raised and purified with cow dung. He chanted ancient *mantras*, or sayings, over the thread while he also lighted lamps, burned incense, and drew meaningful designs on the floor. The preliminaries finished, Hardyal proceeded to place the thread upon Nanak, who sat facing the priest. But Nanak would not have the thread placed upon him. He rejected it. The ceremony was shattered, and his family and friends were mortified. Hardyal told him what the thread was supposed to mean: it marked him off from those of lower birth. But Nanak responded that persons could not be marked off by the use of badges; what should characterize a person is not any outward sign, but the person's actions. The thread, said Nanak, would get soiled in time and would rot and break. Upon the rejection of the thread, Nanak proceeded to recite spontaneously a hymn in which he again reaffirmed his rejection of the physical thread and spoke eloquently of the nature of the spiritual threads that bind the person to virtues and endure beyond the life of the physical thread. The ceremony was over. The people returned to their homes in astonishment. Nanak believed that he had done the right thing. His parents felt that they were disgraced.

Nanak continued to be a disappointment to his father. Kalu was used to thinking that a boy ought to prepare himself to take up his father's work. For many hundreds of years the Indian caste system had held to that plan. Youth, according to the design, is a period of vocational preparation for later work within the accustomed caste and subcaste. The hereditary designation for Nanak as for Kalu before him was supposed to be that of a revenue collector and accountant. The *janam-sakhis* reported that Kalu had several agonized discussions with Nanak about his need to prepare for the work of an accountant. But Nanak was not compliant. He turned his father's suggestions from worldly literalities to spiritual symbols. He declared himself on the side of the one, true god. He looked for deeper realities than those which made up the ordinary world. His father was sad.

At times Nanak combined the practical with the spiritual. Kalu owned a herd of cattle (sometimes called buffalo) and probably also owned land near the town. Nanak had the assignment to watch over the herd. On his way to and from this task he would come into contact with various Hindu holy men and would have the opportunity to learn from them the mysteries of the Hindu way of life. It is said that he also had opportunity to learn about Islam from a Muslim scholar, Sayyid Hasan.

A number of legends tell about Nanak's boyhood experiences, combining fact with fancy. One day the moody Nanak was meditating, neglecting to watch the cattle. The cattle wandered into a neighbor's wheat field, trampling and eating the wheat. When the neighbor was apprised of the happening, he was enraged. He shouted at Nanak, who tried to appease the neighbor, saying that god would bless the field. But the neighbor remained angry. He hauled Nanak to the local ruler, Rai Bular, and made his complaint. Rai Bular called for Kalu. After a discussion, sometimes heated, the ruler decided that he would not hold Nanak accountable if Kalu would compensate the neighbor for his losses. Agreement was reached. The ruler sent some footmen to the neighbor's field to assess the amount of the damage. When they arrived, however, they found there was no damage. Not even a blade of wheat seemed to be harmed. Of course, the neighbor was surprised, although his veracity was not questioned. According to the account, the neighbor simply did not know that a miracle had been performed. Today in Talwandi, now called Nankana Sahib, there is a shrine that has been built on the site of the miracle.

Nanak's moods deepened as the years went by. When he was about sixteen years of age, it is said that he became very introspective. He no longer wished to tend the cattle. He lay on his bed most of the time, eating little, and not even engaging his parents in conversation. One account indicates that his mood continued for three months. During this time his parents tried various strategies to bring about his return to normal life, but they did not succeed. A *mullah,* a Muslim who is learned in the law, was brought to Nanak. The *mullah* sought to cast out the demon within Nanak, but failed. Nanak then lectured the *mullah* on the inadequacy of amulets and incantations. But in time and without any help from others, Nanak returned to his more ordinary self. His parents were pleased to see him leave his bed and take care of the cattle.

Kalu all the while was seeking ways to interest Nanak in the family-designated vocation. He devised a plan. He gave

Nanak twenty silver rupees and suggested that he go to Chu-
harkana, a nearby commercial town. There, Kalu proposed,
Nanak should invest the money in some sort of goods that he
could later sell at a profit. Nanak was also given an escort and
helper, Bala. Kalu also accompanied the pair for a little way
and then turned back, thinking that he may have succeeded in
instigating some business interest in his sensitive, meditative
son.

On the way, however, Nanak and Bala came upon a group
of *sadhus*, or Hindu holy men, who were without clothes and
poised in various meditative positions. Nanak asked why they
wore no clothes. He was told that the absence of clothes was
part of the discipline of the group. He also was told that the
sadhus were extreme ascetics who ate only when they were
given food. Nanak knew what he must do. He went to Chu-
harkana, and over the continuing protests of Bala, purchased
wheat flour, sugar, and *ghee* (a kind of liquefied butter).
Upon returning, he gave it all to the holy men. Kalu was
wroth with his son. What had seemed to be a good plan had
turned into a fiasco. He was so angry with Nanak, it is said,
that he would have beaten him, but Nanaki intervened. Kalu
told his story to Rai Bular. Although Rai Bular commiserated
with the enraged father, he asked that the unique qualities of
Nanak be recognized. Rai Bular even offered to recompense
Kalu for his losses; he also proposed that Nanak live with him,
an offer that was refused.

One day Kalu and Nanak both received letters from Jairam,
who was employed in Sultanpur, a governmental center about
a hundred miles from Talwandi. Jairam was inviting Nanak to
come to visit with him and with his sister, Nanaki. Kalu
thought the invitation was a blessing in that it might enable
Nanak to broaden his experience. Tripta, the mother, was saddened by the loss of her son. Rai Bular gave his approval and
even prepared a feast for the departure. Nanak apparently
was willing to go to Sultanpur. According to tradition, Nanak
set out from his home in the company of his faithful aide,
Bala, and with Mardana. Mardana was a *dum*, one of those

Muslim musicians who beat a drum or play a stringed instrument to accompany the singing of others. Some interpreters of Sikhism say that Nanak met Mardana, who was to be his close companion in later missionary journeys, only in Sultanpur. Others suggest that the two were boyhood companions in Talwandi. At any rate, Nanak reached Sultanpur in five days of travel. There he was well received by Jairam and Nanaki.

Sultanpur was the governmental location for a *satrap*, a province of Muslim rule. The ruler was termed a *nawab* (sometimes referred to as a *nabob*), who was in effect a viceroy for the supreme leader who lived in Delhi. Nawab Daulat Khan Lodhi was the formal title of Sultanpur's ruler. Jairam held a respected position within the councils of the *nawab*. Through Jairam, Nanak secured an interview with the *nawab* and was offered a job as the manager of his granaries and stores. Nanak accepted. By accepting, Nanak was taking upon himself a serious administrative responsibility that entailed considerable trust and knowledge. He appears to have assumed this responsibility gladly. During the day he worked, but at night he would engage in religious discussions, prayers, and hymn singing. Mardana was his constant companion.

In various ways Nanak was noted for his generosity. He especially favored the poor. When his father came to visit him, he found that his son did not have any savings from his official position. Nanak had given away whatever he had gained. In time, moreover, there were rumors throughout Sultanpur that Nanak was giving away the property of the *nawab*. The rumors reached Jairam and Nanaki. Some said that the rumors were created because Nanak gave his charities without regard for caste or religion. When Nanaki finally told her brother about the rumors, he immediately went to the *nawab* and asked that there be an accounting of the stores. The *nawab* appointed his treasurer, Jadurai, to make an investigation. Jadurai found that the stores were intact and that all of Nanak's accounts were correct. He even found that there was some money owing to Nanak. This money Nanak then gave away to the poor.

Several accounts indicate that Nanak married at the age of nineteen. But other traditions say that he married at twelve, fifteen, or sixteen. Nanaki was especially anxious to have Nanak married and asked Jairam to help in the arrangements. Jairam located a suitable bride from an appropriate caste, a *kshatriya*, and Kalu gave his blessing to the match. The bride, Sulakhni, was said to be long-suffering, helpful, and very considerate. Surely she had ample opportunity to demonstrate her virtues, for, following the foundation of her family, she was left alone for long periods of time while Nanak and Mardana went about India and elsewhere bringing the new message of salvation to the people. Apparently, too, her parents, after Nanak started out on his journeys, were very critical of their son-in-law for his neglect of their daughter and her children.

Some evidence suggests that Nanak was not too attached to his family. One account openly declared that he took no interest in his family. Even his duties under the *nawab* seemed in time to lose their appeal. But to Nanak and Sulakhni were born two sons, Sri Chand in A.D. 1494 and Lakhmi Das three years later. Sri Chand was known for his disdain of worldly matters and for his interest in asceticism. Later he founded the Udasis, an ascetic order within Sikhism. Lakhmi Das apparently grew up, married, and raised a family, although he attained to no position of religious leadership.

Nanak, despite his various successes, was apparently not completely satisfied with his life. He had deep spiritual needs that went unmet even though he continued in the evenings to be engaged with his companions in spiritual exercises. He had perceived faintly the true realm of spiritual reality. Yet something was lacking. He still longed for salvation. Through a striking event he was to be illumined and given a full awareness of the true god and his requirements for salvation. According to his custom, after a long night's vigil Nanak would go to the river to bathe before returning to his daily work. One day he did not return from his bathing in the river Bein. His clothes were found on the bank. People flocked to the site, searching for him. He was nowhere to be found. Even the *nawab*, Daulat Khan, came to the place where Nanak had disappeared and ordered fishermen to throw their nets into the river to seek Nanak's body. But they had no success. Nanak's disciples were distraught. Jairam assumed that his brother-in-law had drowned. Only Nanaki was confident that somehow Nanak was still alive.

On the third day after his disappearance, Nanak reappeared. His friends and relatives were puzzled. They asked him where he had been, but he remained silent. The *janamsakhis*, however, record that during his time in the river he was caught up in a mystical experience in which he conversed directly with the "high" god. Nanak had praised the one god who is the supreme truth, the creator who is without fear and without hate, the omnipresent who pervades the universe yet has not been born, nor will he die; he is the truth and evermore will the truth prevail. In return god recognized the attributes that Nanak had offered in his praise. He declared that just as he was the supreme god, so would Nanak be the supreme *guru* of the supreme god. God declared that whomever Nanak blessed would be blessed by the supreme god. It is said that Nanak received a robe of honor from the hands of god himself. God asked Nanak to rejoice in his name and to go and teach others to do so.

Nanak's friends were distressed by his experience. The *nawab* came to see him, but getting no satisfaction from Nanak, he departed sadly. Nanak left the inquiring people to go off into the woods to meditate upon the overwhelming experience that he had with the one, true god. The next day he returned and announced, "There is no Hindu and there is no Muslim." This statement was regularly repeated on this occasion and everywhere Nanak went in his missionary journeys. It became the hallmark of the new faith. It signified that Nanak had found through his mystical experience a religion that transcended both Hinduism and Islam. He had founded a new faith for mankind.

When the people complained to the *nawab* about the new religion that Nanak was preaching, Daulat Khan asked that

Nanak be escorted into his presence. There he received him with homage and seated him in a place of honor at his side. Later when the *nawab* and others went into the mosque, Nanak went along. A service was being conducted and as the time came for all to kneel, Nanak did not kneel. The leader of the worship complained to the *nawab*. But the *nawab* rejected the complaint. The *nawab* said he believed that Nanak had come into the truth. The people, moreover, both Hindu and Muslim, acknowledged that god was speaking through the mouth of Nanak. Nanak in turn addressed the assembly, pointing again to the new truth that god had given to him.

Perhaps it was in the year 1496 that Nanak prepared to preach the new faith. According to some calculations he spent the next twenty-three years traveling about India and elsewhere, enduring hardships that were appropriate to the times, proclaiming the word to those of lowly circumstance as well as to those who were highborn and of great worldly status, speaking at times to individuals and at other times to large assemblages, taking his rest often under the open skies and at other times within luxurious settings. He was inspired. He deemed himself to be charged by god to maintain the course he had chosen. All men needed *gurus*. That is how one learns about the weightier matters of the spiritual life. God in this sense was the *guru* of Nanak, and in turn Nanak was god's appointed *guru* who directly and authentically would instruct all men in the true requirements of the true faith. With this motivation Nanak was sustained as he engaged in his missionary journeys.

The parting was impressive. Jairam and Nanaki were sad to see him leave. Nanaki had not been able to have children, so Nanak with his wife's agreement arranged to leave his older son, Sri Chand, with Nanaki. Sulakhni took the younger son and left Sultanpur for her own home in Batala. There she remained through the years faithful in the knowledge that Nanak was abroad in the land doing what he considered to be the will of god. Nanak left with a song on his lips. He declared that he was the bard of god who intended to serve him from morning to evening every day. As he started away he was clothed in an unusual garb. It represented various elements of Hindu and Muslim adornment. He wore a mango-colored jacket over which he threw a *safa*, or white sheet. He wore the *qualandar*, the hat of a Muslim, on his head, and a necklace of bones, and a saffron mark on his forehead as would a Hindu. In so doing he sought to show by his appearance that "there is no Hindu and there is no Muslim."

It is said that the first journey of Nanak, always accompanied by the minstrel Mardana, lasted about twelve years. In this time the pair traveled widely throughout northern India. They made it a practice to visit many places that had been made famous because they were the goal of pious Hindu pilgrims: Delhi, Hardwar, Allahabad, Benares, Hajipur Patna, Ayodhya, Jagannath Puri, Rameswaram, Ujjain, Mathura, and other places. In general this long journey took Nanak across the north of India, easterly, and then south to the very tip of India, and presumably even beyond.

The adventures of Nanak in those twelve years are more numerous than can be cited here. Several may be recounted to give the flavor of his experiences. Leaving Sultanpur, he went to Lahore, where he stayed for seventeen days. Then he went to Talwandi to see his parents and others. The aging Kalu was less than happy to see his son, especially in his strange garb, but this time he did not argue with Nanak about his choice of vocation. Tripta was very glad to see her son again and was delighted to cook his favorite foods. Rai Bular, the local ruler, had come to admire Nanak greatly and was pleased to have him return to the town. But Nanak stayed in Talwandi only a few days before starting again on his long journey.

On one occasion Nanak came to Panipat, where there was a center for the Sufi order established by the noted Abu 'Ali Qalandar. The Sufis are Muslims who tend toward asceticism and mysticism. A disciple of the order came upon Nanak and Mardana as they sat resting near a well. The disciple had come to fetch water for his master. Observing the unusual dress of Nanak, the disciple took him to be a foreign dervish (perhaps from Persia) or a Muslim devotee noted for ecstatic practices. The Muslim greeted Nanak with the salutation: "Peace be to thee!" Nanak responded with a greeting that was strange to the ears of the disciple: "Salutation to the Ineffable Lord!" The disciple, impressed with this irregularity, went to tell his master of the event. The master hastened to the place where Nanak was and began to question him about his dress, his mission, and his religious identity. Nanak responded with a lengthy hymn which concluded that neither the Vedas (the holy books of the Hindus) nor the Quran (the bible of the Muslims) can encompass the holiness of saintly men. He appealed to a new way, the path of utter obedience to the one, true god. The master and his disciples were thoroughly impressed and praised Nanak for his direct approach to god.

Sometimes the reception he received seemed to indicate that his fame had traveled before him. For example, when he came to Delhi, it is said, a loud applause arose among the people. They were happy that Nanak had come their way. Hindus and Muslims in great numbers came out to greet him and to listen to his message. Even the Sultan, the ruler of Delhi, left his palace to come to hear the impassioned preaching of the new religion. A legend says that the Sultan came upon a royal elephant that had died, but that Nanak had resurrected upon his entry into the city.

Another source tells of the visit of Nanak to the holy city of Allahabad, a place of pilgrimage for Hindus, where the rivers Ganges and Jumna are conjoined. The day of the visit was a special religious day that brought large numbers of the faithful who sought to wash away their sins by bathing in the river. Nanak sat on the riverbank, but did not seek to enter the river. He sang a hymn that gave praise to the one, true god, while Mardana accompanied him on the rebeck, a small stringed instrument. The crowd was astonished at this display and many listened attentively. A Hindu priest, however, reminded Nanak that he had a golden opportunity to wash his sins away in the river and that such an opportunity might not often come. Nanak, however, took the occasion to preach his doctrine. He asked his hearers how truly they expected their sins to be absolved. He told them that water could not wash away the impurities of the heart. Breaking out in another hymn, Nanak proclaimed that persons are made pure in heart by dwelling solely in god. The inner attitude was substituted for the outward observance.

While traveling in Assam, Nanak showed his powers to defeat witchcraft. One day as Mardana was walking down a street a woman standing at the door to her house called him inside. When he entered he was immediately turned into a ram and was held secure in his place by a thread. Nanak, missing Mardana, searched for him and came to the sorceress' house, where he demanded that she release Mardana. She, however, sought to work a spell upon Nanak. When she did not succeed she called for other conjurers to join her in applying their black knowledge. They tried to work their spells upon Nanak, especially by tying the threads of magic which they brought with them. But they also failed. Finally the queen of the sorceresses, Nur Shah, in the company of her assistants, arrived, but their skills did not avail. She had her women dance and sing. She brought great wealth of gold and jewels and placed them at Nanak's feet, imploring him to obey her charms. But Nanak was not to be won. By a mere glance at the place where Mardana was, Nanak broke the spell that held him. Nanak then sang a hymn in which he declared that the true bride is the one who seeks always the favor of her bridegroom who in spiritual terms is the one, true god. The life of purity in obedience to god is the only defensible and satisfying life for women and men. Nur Shah was penitent; she threw her scarf about her neck as a sign of her penitence. Bowing before Nanak, she announced her acceptance of the new life that Nanak had brought to her. She and her followers, according to the story, became loyal Sikhs.

The travels of Nanak, accompanied by Mardana, covered a great part of India. Sikh tradition also says that the pair visited Ceylon (now Sri Lanka). But scholars who have looked carefully into the matter have generally concluded that Nanak

probably did not get to Ceylon. One example of the evidence
may be provided. Sikh tradition says that Nanak visited the
raja of the land, whose name according to the *janam-sakhis*
was Shivanabh. But at the start of the sixteenth century Ceylon was divided into three kingdoms: Jaffna, Kotte, and
Kandy. Kotte and Kandy were Buddhist; Jaffna in the north
was inhabited by Hindu Tamils. There is no historical record
that any of the kingdoms had a ruler by the name of Shivanabh. But legend has it that Nanak went to Ceylon and was
well received by Shivanabh. It is said that the ruler had some
knowledge of Nanak and his teaching through a trader from
the mainland, Mansukh, a follower of Nanak. The *raja* called
the trader into his presence and asked him why he, a Hindu, no
longer practiced his faith. Mansukh responded that he had
come into the new knowledge of the divine through the
agency of Nanak and was freed from his past religion. The
ruler was impressed and asked that Nanak be invited to the
realm. When Nanak arrived, having sailed from Rameswaram
off the southern coast of India, he encamped in the ruler's garden. The *raja*, however, applied several tests of the supreme
guru before he went to visit him. In Nanak's presence, Shivanabh bowed and asked Nanak for some knowledge of the ultimate mystery of life. Nanak obliged by reciting a hymn. He
told of the way in which men are unsatisfied when they are
not obedient to the one, true god. He said that the ego is a
strong barrier against dependency upon god. But by giving up
self and being obedient to god, the person is able to find lasting happiness. Shivanabh was deeply impressed by the words
of the teacher, and he and his wife and son, along with many
of his subjects, became disciples, or *sikhs*.

Making his way north again, preaching as he went, Nanak
finally arrived at Talwandi. There he rejoined his aging parents, who were delighted to see him. Kalu by this time was resigned to his son's being a religious leader. In fact, he was
pleased that his son had become so famous. The whole town
turned out to greet and honor Nanak upon his return. He was
a religious celebrity. Rai Bular also welcomed Nanak but, ac-

cording to tradition, lived only a short time after Nanak's arrival. Nanak was present at his bedside when he died. Later Nanak traveled to Sultanpur. There he visited Jairam and Nanaki, who were pleased to see him. Here too he was received by his earliest disciples who, along with Daulat Khan, begged him to remain and make Sultanpur his permanent base. But after a time Nanak was moved to take up his missionary cause once more. This time he went to the north and then to the east. It is said that on this journey he visited Mount Sumeru, Multan, Hinglaj, Saidpur, and elsewhere. According to tradition he went far into the Himalayas and even into Tibet, Nepal, and Sikkim, bringing to all who would hear his message of the new faith that combined features of both Hinduism and Islam. As with his other journeys many notable events occurred. This journey took perhaps a year.

Nanak's travels are said by the faithful to have taken him to lands beyond India and Ceylon. Some accounts indicate that he visited Mecca and Medina in what is now Saudi Arabia, Baghdad in what now is known as Iraq, Egypt and some of the areas of Africa. Some even say that he brought his message into Europe. There is some evidence to support the claim, but in general scholars who have investigated these trips are prone to be skeptical. According to the legends, Nanak scored impressive victories wherever he went. In Mecca, a most holy center of Islam, his visit was marked by successes. One version tells in detail the route that he took to get to Mecca, and another says that he was transported instantaneously to the place. One account tells that he was guided in his journey by a cloud. Another story says that upon his visit to Mecca, fresh water issued from the city's wells. Nanak also prevailed in his religious teaching. He is said to have been tired by his long journey to Mecca. Entering the Great Mosque, he fell asleep, with his feet in the direction of the Kabah. The Kabah is a small cube-shaped building in the Great Mosque. It contains the sacred stone, said to have turned black by the tears of the penitent. It is the most sacred shrine of the Muslims. It would be considered an act of impiety for anyone to recline with his feet toward the Kabah. So, when the *quazi*, the man learned in Muslim law, came to conduct the evening prayer he was shocked to find Nanak in this position. He upbraided Nanak for his lack of respect. But Nanak said to the *quazi:* "Where the house of god is not, turn my feet in that direction." The *quazi* took Nanak's feet and turned him around full cricle. But in whatever direction Nanak's feet were turned, the Kabah also turned. The *quazi* was astounded and fell to kiss Nanak's feet. He declared that on that day he had seen a true believer. As a result of the miracle many of those worshiping in the mosque gathered about Nanak to question him. Nanak declared that in god's court there are no Hindus and no Muslims. God only requires obedient service from all. Then, uttering a hymn in Persian, he told the assembly more about the one, transcendent deity who bridged the gap between Hinduism and Islam and who was able to bring genuine satisfaction to those who believed in him. Similar great experiences are said to have taken place wherever Nanak went in his western journeys.

The stories indicate that a new faith had been founded. It attracted believers close to the area of its origin and through the efforts of Nanak it gained adherents far and wide. The new religion was not simply an exercise of a highly devout leader, Nanak, but a social reality. This social reality was obviously influenced by the time and place of its beginnings. And the religion also, interpenetrating its surrounding culture, became a social influence of marked proportion. Over the years, however, Sikhism retracted from its geographic spread. At the present time it is, for the most part, the religion of the people of the Punjab.

What, in essence, is the nature of Sikhism? What is the character of its doctrinal, cultic, and social expressions? In a sense Sikhism is deceptively simple. The key element, which supersedes all other features, is the belief in one, transcendent, kindly god who is possessed of all virtues. He is nameless; so it is not proper to think of Brahma, the chief deity within Hinduism, or of Allah, the god of Islam, as adequate names for god. God is nameless, yet he is also the true name. In this manner the deity of Sikhism is intended to supplant the gods of all the other religions. The gods of the other religions are particular; the god of Sikhism is absolute. It is clear that the idea of god in Sikhism owes most to the concept of god in Islam.

Yet, from Hinduism the new faith accepted the idea of *maya*, or illusion. God is real beyond all realities, according to Sikhism. But the world as it is known is basically unreal. God has drawn a veil between himself and his creation. The creation seems to be real, but it is not. Escape from the transitoriness of the world is achieved by the endless repetition of the name of god.

Again, from Hinduism two other important concepts were incorporated into Sikhism. The Hindu idea of *karma* was taught by Nanak. *Karma* signifies the inexorable moral law of human behavior. It proposes that every human thought and action leaves an indelible, permanent impress upon the soul, which prevails even beyond the present life of the person. *Karma*, an ancient Indian concept, became a part of the new religion of Sikhism. The notion of the transmigration of souls, also borrowed from Hinduism, became a feature of Sikhism. This idea suggests that the individual is not obliterated at his physical death but proceeds from one bodily form to another. Nanak accepted this doctrine, but he taught that the disciple should seek to overcome the fated succession of rebirths by concentrating on the name of god. Through such concentration and repetition of the name of god the believer is able to break through the bondage of *karma* and the transmigration of souls and attain a blissful existence beyond that encompassed by *maya*. This blissful existence is not like the worldly paradise of the Muslim; rather, it is like the *nirvana* of Hinduism by which the liberated soul is absorbed in god himself.

Nanak also held disdain for all ritual. He was critical of the rites of the Muslims, saying that they tended to direct the attention of believers away from god and toward the human form of action. He also spoke against the various rituals of

Hinduism. He claimed that going on pilgrimages, which were thought to be especially meritorious by the pious Hindu, were distractions that took the mind of the believer from his basic obligation, which is obedience to the one, true god. Like the Muslims, he strongly criticized the creation of and the belief in idols, a popular feature of Hinduism.

The religious service in Sikhism is relatively simple. Sikh temples are like those of Hinduism, but they contain no idols. The Adi Granth, the sacred scriptures, hold the principal place in the temple services. The recitation of the hymns of the book and the murmuring of the name of the one, true god are the main activities of worship. There is no extended priesthood, although there usually is a leader or priest (*pudjari*) who conducts the service and a *granthi* who reads from the Adi Granth. Marriage is favored for all Sikhs.

Nanak was opposed to the Indian caste system. He asserted that castes are foolishness, since all men are equal before god. Later, however, aspects of the caste system entered into the social relations of the Sikhs. Sikhism does call its adherents into the *khalsa*, a social-spiritual community. A consecration ceremony, called the *pahul*, may take place at seven years of age, although generally it is held at the time of adulthood. The consecrated member of the *khalsa* takes the second name of Singh, or lion, as a sign to others of his membership. Although the teachings of Nanak himself set forth a quietistic religion that laid stress upon the individual and his relationship to god, the religion which developed after Nanak became highly political, leading to a religious state in the Punjab. Also, the original emphasis on individual virtues and piety became in time a faith that emphasized strength, combativeness, and even militarism.

Nanak was the chief architect of Sikhism. But his genius lay in his ability to shape successfully a new religion out of religions of the past: Hinduism and Islam. He also was influenced by religious teachers who lived about his time. Kabir was one of the chief of these. Kabir (1440-1518) was born near Benares to a poor Muslim couple. He became a disciple of the

Hindu reformer Ramananda, who was active in seeking a basic harmony among the various religious expressions in the India of his time. Kabir seized upon *bhakti*, or devotion, as the chief clue to the worship of god. This element enabled him to appeal to the followers of both Hinduism and Islam. He too taught the one, true god who is wholly transcendent and he practiced an essentially nonritualistic religion. Obviously many of the features of Sikhism as taught by Nanak are to be found in the teachings of Kabir.

Nanak also was succeeded by nine other *gurus*. These in turn shaped the religion of Nanak even further, consolidating it, institutionalizing it, and contributing significantly to its doctrines, social life, and political emphasis.

Nanak continued to make journeys. One of the last, at the age of sixty-one, took him briefly to the southeast of India. But in the main he stayed in the city of Kartarpur, which became his official seat. In 1522 his parents died, Kalu having reached eighty-two years of age. Previously his sister and her husband had died. It was in Kartarpur that Mardana in his seventy-sixth year fell ill. Nanak had asked him how he would like to have his body treated after death. Nanak had told him that he would be willing to take the minstrel's body and encase it in a tomb that would make Mardana famous all over the world. But Mardana replied that he saw no reason to put his body in a tomb, since death would signify the release of his soul from his body. A tomb would be the wrong symbol to relate to his death. So upon Mardana's death Nanak placed his body in the river Ravi while the faithful gathered at the shore to sing hymns and to partake of the *karah prashad*, a communion type of meal that was partaken of by the Sikhs in their *khalsa*.

Sikhs officially date the death of Nanak as September 7, 1539. Before his death he came to the Ravi and there placed five copper coins before Angad, who was to become the second of the ten leading *gurus*. Bowing to Angad, Nanak established the succession to his leadership. Nanak continued to instruct his followers with fresh hymns that praised god. Ac-

cording to tradition, in his final hours his disciples fell into an
argument about what to do with his remains. Those who were
Muslims had previously said they would bury the body. Those
who were Hindu said they would cremate it. But Nanak said
they should put flowers at his sides, the Hindus on the right
and the Muslims on the left. He said that they whose flowers
remained fresh should have the choice. Then, after reciting
more hymns, he laid down and pulled a sheet over his body.
The followers waited. When finally they raised the sheet the
body was gone. The flowers of both the Hindus and the Muslims remained fresh. Each took its own flowers. They fell to
their knees and blessed god for giving them and the world the
guru of all *gurus*.

Sikhism, the latest of the living religions, founded by Nanak
in India, sought generously to harmonize the then existing religions of the land. Nanak succeeded to a degree, for the religion of Sikhism did attract many who followed the combined
way.

5
LAO-TZU
AND
TAOISM

Although India has given rise to four of the world's living religions, three with known founders, China has been the homeland of two. Each has a founder: Taoism, whose founder was Lao-tzu, and Confucianism, which developed from the teachings of Confucius. The founders of these two Chinese religions lived mainly in the sixth century B.C. That century, as has been seen, was a remarkable one in various parts of the ancient world. In India it was the era in which Vardhamana was founding Jainism and Gautama was founding Buddhism. At about the same time in Persia (modern Iran), Zoroaster was beginning the religion that generally is called Zoroastrianism. Although Judaism appeared before the sixth century B.C., that period was characterized by a great outpouring of religious spirit as exemplified by the Hebrew prophets Jeremiah, Ezekiel, and the Isaiah of the exile. In Greece also, important intellectual and religious innovations were being made. In China, Lao-tzu and Confucius lived and founded their new faiths in this unusual period.

Taoism and Confucianism are the two religions indigenous to China. There have been more than two religious expressions of the Chinese people through the centuries, but Taoism and Confucianism are probably the most significant.

Over the centuries the Chinese people have shown hospitality toward other religions that have not originated in China. Zoroastrianism had some acceptance there. In the province of Honan in A.D. 1912 the site of what once had been a Jewish synagogue was sold to a church group. The sale marked the end of an eight-hundred-year period in which the Jews of K'ai-feng-fu had worshiped in their synagogue. At that time only seven families remained of what was once a large and flourishing Jewish community. But the community had dwindled, they had no rabbi, the synagogue had fallen into disrepair, the sacred scroll of the law had been destroyed—they had no basis for continuing. They had survived through centuries of wars, rebellions, fires, floods, and other calamities, preserving their faith and customs. The Jews were noted by the Chinese because they would eat no pork, a special delicacy in China, and because they would not worship idols or burn incense to their ancestors. Jews have also been known to live elsewhere in China.

Christianity has had a varied history in that country. It was first known from the seventh to the ninth century through the missionary efforts of the Nestorian Christians. They were followers of Nestorius, patriarch of Constantinople in the fifth century A.D. From about the middle of the thirteenth to about the middle of the fourteenth century the Franciscans were active. From the later decades of the sixteenth century until the persecutions of 1724, the Jesuits, along with other Roman Catholic missionaries, spread Christianity far and wide within China. The nineteenth and twentieth centuries saw the influx of both Protestant and Roman Catholic missionaries in China. This period lasted until 1949, when all foreign missionaries were expelled by the dominant Communist group. In each period the missionary movements failed because of persecution. At no time did Christianity find acceptance by more than a tiny fraction of the total population of China, although the impact of its schools, colleges, hospitals, and to some extent its religious outlook, was influential beyond its size and even its popularity.

Islam also is woven into the context of Chinese history. Its start in China is usually said to have been in A.D. 651 when an embassy from Caliph Othman was well received by the emperor of the province of T'ang. The Muslims did not come to

China in the same way the Christians did. The Christians came openly to convert the Chinese to their religion. The Muslims, on the other hand, contrary to their practices elsewhere, came primarily as traders or immigrants. They married Chinese women and were largely integrated into Chinese society, with the exception that they maintained their Islamic faith and required that their children be raised in it. They founded no distinctive sect of Islam and in the main followed the Sunnite tradition. The cultic forms, such as prayer five times a day, circumcision, the facing to Mecca, the removal of shoes upon entering the mosque, were maintained. The number of Muslims in China, historically and presently, is hard to establish. An estimate provided by the government in 1924, for example, gave the total as between fifteen and twenty million.

Buddhism also has had a long and complicated history in China. Traditionally it is said that Buddhism came to China in A.D. 67, but a more probable date is A.D. 148, when Shih-Lao arrived in China and spent twenty years there as a monk-missionary. It was the Mahayana form of Buddhism that was brought to China. This was less severe than the Hinayana form and more adaptive to non-Indian cultures. It was marked by a quiet tolerance of other faiths and it appealed to those who lived under the hard conditions of political and economic oppression. It provided a way by which the masses could gain liberation from their world-weariness. Mahayana Buddhism, moreover, appealed to the masses through its acceptance and development of magic, superstition, and mythological accounts of the universe. Buddhism grew in China. In the Tartar states of northwest China, for example, Buddhism was so widely accepted by the fourth century A.D. that it is said that almost everyone there was a Buddhist. The Buddhists not only developed their doctrines in conformity to the reality of Chinese thought and life; they also founded various charitable institutions, such as rest houses, bathhouses, hospitals, and dispensaries. They also engaged in the planting of trees, in the building of roads, in the digging of wells, and in other forms of community service. They probably reached their zenith in the ninth century A.D.

The several religions that are not indigenous to China failed to make notable headway with the Chinese people. The reasons for this are numerous. Some of them reside within the "imported" religions themselves. Others are thoroughly secular or nonreligious. For example, Buddhism had great appeal to the Chinese masses, but its stress upon celibacy ran counter to the stress within the traditional culture of China upon the importance of the family and the sense of respect that is owed to one's elders generally. Similarly, the Buddhist emphasis upon asceticism clashed with the Chinese ideal of social responsibility as embodied in the gentleman-sage who was looked upon by the Chinese as being the embodiment of civic virtue. Buddhism tended to give up on the reformability of society, whereas Chinese culture in the main taught that the good life is attainable through the corporate agencies of society, and notably through government even though for many centuries government did not give evidence of its redeeming capacities.

The Chinese at the time of Lao-tzu and Confucius believed they were the inheritors of a vastly honorable and admirable culture from past ages. Sixth-century B.C. Chinese looked backward historically to their golden age or ages. Their myths and historical knowledge encouraged this outlook. They were proud of such a major figure from the past as the Emperor Shih Huang-ti who, it is said, invented vessels of wood and clay, discovered the way to make bricks, and invented the calendar and money. It is also said that his chief wife introduced the silkworm culture to China. In addition, other heroes of the past were claimed by name to have introduced the making of fire by rubbing one stick upon another, the domestication of animals, the use of iron for hunting and fishing, the making of nets for fishing, the beginnings of medicine, and other achievements. Chinese history was said to be composed of ten great eras, which totaled some two million years, and at least one account suggests that Chinese history was ninety-six million years old. Obviously by these few illustrations the Chinese historically have been proud of their heritage and not at all prone to accept foreign ideas in a major way.

The world view of the Chinese at the time of Lao-tzu and Confucius also reflected the Chinese past in other ways. It expressed a particular cosmic outlook. The Chinese who thought about such matters proposed that there is a basic harmony in the universe. All the movements of the cosmos were regular and constant. This view represented a kind of pantheism by maintaining the fundamental unity of all existence. The Chinese also believed that they inhabited the earthly center of the universe and that as one went out from the middle kingdom, especially from the emperor's palace and its altars, one met with increasingly inferior peoples. Demonic forces, however, were recognized as operative in the universe. They accounted for disruptions in nature, such as floods and fires. They also accounted for human aberrations. But the basic harmony of the universe and of man's life on earth had the capacity of righting the disequilibriums of natural and human reality.

The Chinese, moreover, recognized two cosmic principles, the *yang* and the *yin*. These two forms of energy are present in all reality. The *yang* is masculine by nature; it is positive, active, warm, dry, procreative, and bright. Evidence of this principle is seen in fire, in everything that is brilliant, such as the sun, and in all male properties. The *yin* is feminine by nature; it is negative, cold, wet, dark, secret, mysterious. Evidence of this principle is seen in quiescent things, shadows, the shadowed south bank of a river, and in all female properties. These principles are present in all things. In human events they account for the ups and downs of personal and social history. They account for the creation of and disintegration of material objects. Sometimes an object will seem to represent only one of these principles, but in reality both are present. A piece of wood, for example, may seem to be thoroughly *yin* in character. Yet when wood is burned it shows that its *yang* property was actually inherent within it.

The harmony of the universe was expressed by the Chinese

with another concept, the *tao*, or the way. The *yang* and the *yin* accounted for the evident ways in which reality possessed a dynamic nature. But hidden on an even deeper level of reality the *tao* operates. The *tao* is a cosmically impersonal principle that is the cause of the harmony of the universe. It represents the cosmic plan that existed before the universe was called into being. But it also represents "the way-to-go." In this sense the *tao* indicates that there is a necessary purpose or essential channel by which the universe properly reaches its fruition. The *tao* represents and works for everything that is valued: peace, prosperity, and health. The *tao* is hindered in its goals by the demonic forces and by the evil actions of persons. But it points to the ultimate way, the path by which all parts of the universe, including human beings, must follow in order to reach fulfillment.

This complicated cosmic outlook held consequences for the Chinese understanding of their history. As a result of these ideas they believed that their emperors held an especially important role in the making of the good life. They regularly referred to two very good emperors, Yao and Shun, who ruled well because they were in harmony with the *tao*. Their ages were known as golden ages, for they were times in which harmony reigned among all beings, both human and animal. Peace, happiness, and prosperity in their times resulted from the ability of the emperors to realize the essential requirements of the universe both for themselves and for their people. The Chinese emperors traditionally have been thought to have ruled as tyrants. Their arbitrary powers have been stressed in Chinese accounts of history. But, without denying their great power, it must also be said that they possessed a heavy and compelling responsibility for themselves and for their people. It was their duty so to live and so to rule that they would express the requirements of the *tao*. Some emperors did not do so. They became indulgent of themselves, self-seeking, prone to luxury, and careless of the well-being of their people. Such emperors were not living and ruling in accordance with the requirements of the *tao*. In such cases it was considered that the people had a right to overthrow the non-*tao*-abiding rulers, placing in their stead emperors who would actively and faithfully follow the divine *tao*. Sometimes an emperor who thought he was following the *tao* would see calamities befall his people. In such instances the emperor, as the literature of several periods attests, would put the blame upon himself. He would cry out to heaven that he might be given the knowledge of how he had violated the requirements of the *tao*. The self-abnegation of the emperor before the mandate of the *tao* indicated that even a most powerful ruler felt himself to be ruled by an even higher or cosmic force. Historiography, then, is a corollary of the principle of *tao*.

The religion of the ancient Chinese, however, expressed more features than those of a cosmic outlook. There were also a number of reverential aspects within it that bear noting. From the earliest times the Chinese showed the highest regard for the earth. This obviously reflected an ancient agricultural society's respect for the fertility of the earth. Commonly every village had a *she*, a mound of earth, which was the center of a cultic religion devoted to the growth of crops. Each spring there was a festival, including dancing and singing, which centered on the *she*. Local gods were honored. Each fall another festival was held expressing thanksgiving for the crops that had been harvested. In later times, as China became a feudal empire, earth worship became more complex. In addition to the local *shes* others were formed and used as places of worship. Each province had its own *she* and the worship was led by the lord of the area. For the whole of China a *she* existed, composed of five different colors of earth, over which the emperor presided. At appointed times the emperor conducted rites, such as plowing a furrow, which were intended to show reverence for the fertility of all the soil of China.

As time went on, earth worship lessened in importance. But the worship of heaven increased. The concept of heaven included all that surrounded the earth. In earlier times a god by the name of Shang Ti was worshiped. Shang means upper

and Ti means ruler: the deity Shang Ti was a representation
of that respect in which heaven was held by the Chinese.
Later, during the period of the Chous, the designation of
T'ien, or heaven, was used. At this time and later the emperors
were thought to be the sons of heaven and therefore in an
especially close relationship to heaven. Complicated and attractive ceremonies were held in which the emperor performed the chief role and in which the harmonious relations
engendered by the *tao* were maintained. Thus, reverence for
heaven is another part of the ancient Chinese religion which
formed the backdrop for both Taoism and Confucianism.

The Chinese also held that both earth and heaven are filled
with specific spirits which inhabit rivers (the Yellow River
was a special object of reverence), hills, clouds, rain, roads,
and other places. The spirits were deemed to be of two kinds,
good and bad. Good spirits were called *shen* and were
thought to inhabit the sun, earth, stars, moon, winds, clouds,
rain, rivers, seas, and mountains. The evil spirits were called
kwei and were thought to inhabit all negative objects and
processes in nature and human affairs. Thus, the darkness was
inhabited by the *kwei*. Traditionally the Chinese have been
unusually fearful of the dark. Roosters have held a special
place in Chinese life because they herald the coming of the
new day. The sun is the locus of a good spirit who comes to
dispel the evil spirit of night. Representations of the rooster, in
wood or ceramic, are kept by the Chinese because of the symbolism involved. Similarly the blossoms of fruit trees are held
in high regard, for the blossoming trees in the spring are a
sign that the *kwei* spirits of the dark winter have been chased
away by the *shen* spirits that are seen in the renewal of life.

Ancestor worship is another part of the ancient Chinese religion. The Chinese have been noteworthy for their devotion to
the family. The Chinese family is not the nuclear family of the
West, consisting of husband and wife and unmarried children,
but the extended family. The extended family consisted of all
the members who would be included in a family reunion,
though the family in ancient China was even more than that.

It also included the dead along with the living. The Chinese believed that ancestors became spirits who were alive and active in their participation in the larger family. Ancestors were considered to be powerful agents for good or ill. If they were displeased by some circumstance, they would have the power to inflict evil upon the living members of the family; if they were pleased, the living members of the family would be blessed. The living members were obligated to make their ancestors a part of their prayers. They also provided food for their ancestors. It was not believed that the ancestors actually ate the food; rather, they ate the essence of the food, and after an appropriate time priests and others were permitted to eat what remained.

Within the context of ancestor worship, death and burial were important. Death was taken to be an auspicious event, and the passage from life to death was regarded as of great significance. Funeral displays were elaborate and costly. Among the very wealthy, as in Egypt and elsewhere, the deceased were deemed to be in need of objects and persons appropriate to their status. Thus they would be buried with such objects as hunting weapons, bronze pots, and other prized possessions. Sometimes even the person's horses, dogs, and servants would be killed and buried with him. Certain inscriptions, for example, indicate that some of the Shang emperors were buried with from one hundred to three hundred servants to attend them in the afterlife. But for the lowly as well as for those of high position, becoming an ancestor was taken very seriously and the power of the deceased was regarded as an awesome reality.

Both Taoism and Confucianism, despite their divergent natures, were the inheritors of the ancient Chinese religion which has just been described. Neither Lao-tzu nor Confucius developed religions without regard for their past culture and the dominant religious and social ideas that surrounded them. Neither Taoism nor Confucianism can be understood adequately without some knowledge of the cultural context in which they arose.

But in addition to the ancient Chinese religion that has been outlined, the social setting of the times of Lao-tzu and Confucius comprises another influential and perhaps determining factor in the shaping of their religions. They lived in socially unsettled times. In large part the religions that they developed were intended to be responses to that unsettlement. For a period of five hundred years, starting about 722 B.C., the feudal order in China was in the process of breaking up. A number of factors brought about this vast change. For example, the Chou emperors were unable to protect their people from the invasions of the Tartars, who regularly came into China from the northwest to pillage and destroy. Because of this inability, local lords or strong men arose who sought to defend their more localized jurisdictions against the Tartars. These nobles not only waged war with the invaders; they also warred among themselves. The Warring States Period in Chinese history is named for that long and costly time in which the nobles were at one another's throats. In due course the weaker rulers were conquered, and only seven larger and more powerful states prevailed. These also continued their warfare. In order to maintain himself, the emperor from time to time made arrangements of accommodation with one or more of the strongest lords. This method, however, did not succeed, and in this the emperor became a mere figurehead with little or no influence politically or militarily. At the end of the period of social unsettlement, in 221 B.C., Duke Cheng of the state of Ch'in was able to subdue all his rivals and bring the whole of China under his rule. As had Emperor Shih Huang-ti, he not only consolidated and centralized the disparate provinces of China but also succeeded in practically obliterating the feudal order of past times. Those who previously held localized power were deprived of all their power and in effect became merely common people.

Other factors contributed to this period of social unrest. New classes, among them farmers and merchants, came to hold significant social status and influence. By means of their rising wealth, they were able to challenge the positions of those wealthy aristocrats who had held their benefits on a hereditary basis. Even the serfs gained in importance. They succeeded in securing ownership of the land; previously they had worked only the land of wealthy owners. The serfs also banded together and shared their lands with each other. This added to agricultural effectiveness. A merchant class also arose to meet the needs of a more complex economy and they also were new centers of social and political power in the five-hundred-year period of unsettlement.

Thus the times in which Lao-tzu and Confucius lived and taught were highly unstable. The past had given way to a present that was unfamiliar. New modes of understanding the present were needed. Generalized solutions to the changes were invited. The new religions of Taoism and Confucianism constituted two formulations that proposed solutions to the dilemmas of their times. In the main, Confucianism expressed the point of view that the former feudal order ought to be reestablished. It represents those Chinese noblemen who advocated a social salvation that looked essentially to the past. The Confucianists, however, advocated no mere return to the past. They called for a return to a feudal order in which the best of former times would be conserved and the more blatant defects eliminated. They worshiped at the shrine of an idealized past.

The Taoists, on the other hand, saw things differently. Essentially, from a social perspective, the Taoists represented those groups within Chinese society, notably the intellectuals, who had become disillusioned with the course of events. They were not enamored with the past. They knew its injustices and they felt that the past simply could never be recalled. Yet they also did not like the present. They had lost faith in the ability of rulers of any sort to bring about the welfare of the people. They opted out of the political processes of their times, believing that human satisfaction could be and should be achieved primarily by means of withdrawing from society.

Drawing upon the resources of the ancient Chinese religion and responding to the unstable social order of the time, Taoism and Confucianism proposed divergent social and world views that formed the bases for the resulting religions. But there were other responses as well. Two may be mentioned. The Legalists thoroughly accepted the decay of the feudal order. They tended to look upon the changes as beneficent. They advocated the final dissolution of the feudal arrangements and the development of a more egalitarian society. Those who favored this position were mainly those who had prospered as a result of the changes, such as the new class of landlords. Another school of thought were called Mohists, after their chief exponent, Mo-tzu, a philosopher who may have lived a generation after Confucius. The Mohists proposed a return to the ancient religion of China as the likeliest possibility for providing a high degree of unity to the Chinese people. They believed that as a result of the recultivation of the ancient religion a new period of benevolence would arise in which persons would be more mindful of the need to respect each other. By this means the basis for a new social order would be laid.

Having said all this about the historical and cultural context in which both Taoism and Confucianism got their start, it is necessary to turn to the lives of the founders. Confucius is the subject of the next chapter. For a genuine life of Lao-tzu, unfortunately, there is very little reliable evidence. The evidence that seems to be available has led a number of scholars to doubt that Lao-tzu ever lived at all. It may well be that Lao-tzu was simply a legendary person, and the final truth of the matter may never be known. Yet there are other scholars who, despite the scant evidence and conflicts within it, do assert that there was a historical Lao-tzu. It is on the assumption that there was that this chapter is written. Without looking at some of the problems presented in forming a life of the founder at this moment, we may simply outline the main features of what has traditionally been said about the founder's life.

It is said that Lao-tzu was born on September 14, 604 B.C., that he was born in the village of Chu Jen which is in the county of K'u and in the kingdom of Ch'u. This would place his birth in what is now known as the Honan province of China. Presumably this date places Lao-tzu's birth at about fifty years prior to that of Confucius. As with the other founders, the birth of Lao-tzu is said to have had celestial implications. His mother conceived him some sixty-two years before his birth when she admired a falling star. Lao-tzu was able, after so many years in the womb, to speak as soon as he was born. Immediately after his birth he pointed to a plum tree and announced that he would take his surname from this tree: Li. Since his ears were unusually large, he announced that his second name would be ear or Erh. Thus the name he gave himself was Li Erh. But at birth, perhaps because of his age, Li Erh's hair was snow-white. Most people, therefore, called him Lao-tzu, meaning Old Master. It is this name which has commonly been employed as a designation for the founder of Taoism. After Lao-tzu died, however, he was given yet another name, Lao Tan, *tan* meaning long-lobed.

Aside from the suggestions that Lao-tzu's mother gave birth while leaning against a plum tree, little else is known about her or the family of the founder. Not even her name is available. Whether the family was high- or low-born, what their occupation was, whether they had other children, and so forth, is not known.

Again, little or nothing is known about the life of the child and his growth into manhood. There is a natural curiosity about how a great man grows up; in this case it must remain unsatisfied. It is assumed that he married, and it is said that he had a son by the name of Tsung. Apparently Tsung was a soldier of note under the Wei, for there is an effort on the part of later generations to trace their ancestorship to Tsung, including the line of T'ang emperors.

The one fixed reference to Lao-tzu's employment indicates that in maturity he became first the palace secretary and later the keeper of the archives for the court of Chou in the capital city of Loyang. Evidently, in addition to his work, he became a philosopher who attracted disciples. His outlook constituted a response to the unsettled conditions of his times. People were looking for satisfying answers to their dilemmas. It is not known whether the group that followed Lao-tzu was small or large, nor under what circumstances he taught them.

One of those who visited Lao-tzu, it is said, was Confucius himself. Confucius, who was perhaps some fifty-three years younger than Lao-tzu, held a lengthy discussion with the founder of Taoism in the year 517 B.C. Lao-tzu heard from Confucius how he had been searching within China's past to find the principles by which the present instability in society might be remedied. Lao-tzu reminded the sage that looking into the past brought no solutions for the present. He chided Confucius that the men about whom he spoke were all dead and that their bones had all turned to dust. He told Confucius to put away his proud airs and his desires. Lao-tzu in turn besought the younger man to look within himself in order, through quiet and mystical experiences, to find the great *tao,* that underlying force which is the ultimate basis for a proper understanding of life's meaning.

Confucius was perplexed. He told the old master that he had been searching for the truth by studying books for twenty years. He was indeed a devoted scholar. To this Lao-tzu replied that the *tao* was not something that could be handed on from one person to another. If it were, he said, the child would want to give it to his parents, parents would wish to give it to their children, the citizen would wish to give it to his ruler, every person would wish to give it to his neighbors. The *tao* is not of the nature of an object that once being possessed can then be given to others. The *tao,* continued Lao-tzu, can only be found by each person as an individual who, setting aside external matters, concentrates within his heart. The *tao* must be given asylum in one's heart.

With great scorn for Confucius and his ways of searching for the truth, Lao-tzu continued to chastise the youth. He said that a clever merchant whose coffers are filled with wealth will go about as though they are empty, that the princely man who is known for his moral excellence will go about as though he were a simpleton. He did not perceive these traits in Confucius. Thundering on, Lao-tzu called upon Confucius to abandon his arrogant ways and his countless desires, his suave demeanor and his unbridled ambition, for they do not promote the inquirer's welfare. The lecture was ended.

Confucius was astonished at the manner in which he was treated. He declared that he knew how birds can fly, how fish can swim, and how four-footed beasts can run. He declared that those which run can be snared, those which swim can be caught with hook and line, and those which fly may be shot with arrows. Then he spoke of the dragon, saying that he was unable to conceive how the dragon can soar into the sky, riding upon the wind and clouds. To this he added that on that day he had seen Lao-tzu and could only liken him to a dragon.

Confucius, the philosopher of social responsibility, must have appeared as an ineffectual busybody who really thought that he would be able to remake Chinese society. Lao-tzu, the philosopher of social withdrawal and inner realization, must have appeared as an otherworldly mystic who really thought that life's ultimate meaning could only be apprehended through fragile intuition. Thus the two founders of religions met and parted, each dissatisfied with the other. The meeting, if it did actually take place, was a most unusual event in the history of religions, for at no time among the other living religions is there evidence that two founders ever personally met.

Given his particular outlook on human affairs, Lao-tzu is said to have become increasingly disillusioned with the trends in his society. In his view the Chou dynasty was in a state of decay. So believing, Lao-tzu decided to give up his post as keeper of the archives, and apparently also his disciples. He wished to find a place far removed from worldly concerns where he could concentrate more fully on self-realization through attachment to the *tao*. He left the Middle Kingdom, riding through the Han-ku pass in a chariot drawn by a black ox, going westward from Loyang. The keeper of the pass was Yin Hsi, who by means of the signs of the weather had anticipated that a very wise man would be arriving. Yin Hsi, therefore, spoke to Lao-tzu, saying that as he was about to withdraw from sight he should consider writing a book for the pass keeper. The Tao-Te-Ching, the sacred scriptures of Taoism, it is said, was written by Lao-tzu at this time. It is a relatively brief book, containing some five thousand Chinese characters.

Little evidence is available to tell what then happened to Lao-tzu. In a very late source it is said that during his first three nights after going through the pass he meditated in the mountains. There he was sorely tempted by demons and by beautiful women. But he succeeded in resisting all the temptations. It is said that he considered the beautiful women to be merely bags of skin filled with blood. It is not known how much longer he lived. It is said that he was one hundred and sixty years of age when he left Loyang. The date of his death is traditionally given as 517 B.C., although its accuracy cannot be ascertained. Nothing more is known about the man responsible for the first personally founded religion in Chinese history which is still existing today.

It is fair to say that almost every aspect of the life of Lao-tzu as provided has been placed in doubt. Some scholars say, for example, that he was not born in 604 B.C., but may have been born in 571, 480, 390, or 300 B.C. One account says that he spent not sixty-two years in his mother's womb, but eighty-one. Another account indicates that he may have left for his final journey from Loyang at the age of two hundred, rather than one hundred and sixty. Some scholars doubt that the encounter of Lao-tzu and Confucius is historical, noting that there seems to be no good reason to assume that the two would have to be so bitter in their personal relations as the accepted account assumes. Again, it is suggested that Lao-tzu may have been the treasurer to the Chou emperor rather than the keeper of the archives. Much of the information available about Lao-tzu was compiled by the great Chinese historian (some call him the Herodotus of Chinese history) Ssu-ma Ch'ien, who probably wrote his account about 100 B.C. Even he despaired of uncovering the real facts about Lao-tzu's life.

In time the historical or legendary Lao-tzu and his teachings attracted many. His disciples increased until there were millions. The philosophic teachings of Lao-tzu were made the basis of a flourishing religion in which Lao-tzu also was considered a divinity. In the first century A.D. the government ordered that sacrifices be offered to Lao-tzu. An emperor in the seventh century A.D. proclaimed him as a former emperor. So it went. The humble, mystical Lao-tzu, who was well aware of his personal defects, became in time not merely a human hero but a god. In addition, although Lao-tzu apparently did not teach the existence of a single, personal deity, Taoism in its later development taught the existence of an almost limitless number of deities. The later development of the religion saw the original teachings transformed into a cultic religion in which superstition, magic, and extended mythology prevailed. What later emerged would probably not have been recognized by the founder, Lao-tzu. Most probably, Lao-tzu would have been strongly opposed to it.

The Tao-Te-Ching is the depository of the early expressions of Taoism. As with the life of Lao-tzu, there are varying opinions among scholars regarding the book. Some think it was written much later than the time that Lao-tzu presumably lived. It is well known that authors in China did attribute their works to earlier, known writers so that their words would have greater acceptance. Other scholars believe that the book was not written by one person, but that it is a collection of sayings from various people who lived at various times. But there is some basis for thinking that the Tao-Te-Ching was written by one person and even that it may have been composed at about the time of Lao-tzu. It is not probable that a work of such balance and insight could have been dashed off by a Lao-tzu hurrying through a mountain pass on his way to retirement. It is too thoughtful and skilled for that.

The Tao-Te-Ching has been an immensely popular book in China over the centuries, and its popularity in the West is also great. One scholar notes that by 1955 there had been some thirty-four translations of the Tao-Te-Ching into English alone. One basis for the book's acceptance in the West may be that it teaches an ethic which at many points closely parallels the teachings of the New Testament. The same scholar who counted the number of English translations of the Tao-Te-Ching has arranged in parallel columns fourteen passages from the Tao-Te-Ching and the Gospels that are impressive for their literal similarity.

The two main thrusts of the early Taoist movement, as exemplified in the Tao-Te-Ching, were the emphasis upon the concept of the *tao,* and the quietistic, long-suffering ethics. The Tao-Te-Ching teaches that the *tao* is one, eternal, impersonal being known through intuitive or mystical experiences. The *tao* is described as having a number of attributes: all-pervading, unpretentious, sustaining all things, original, formless, primeval, before heaven and earth, the ultimate, formless, unchanging, nameless, unstriving, and inactive. Yet the *tao* is also conceived to be, even by reason of some of the enumerated characteristics, beyond any human description.

Taoist ethics also comprise an important emphasis in the Tao-Te-Ching. The person is urged to be calm, at rest, serene, even as the heavenly *tao* possesses these attributes. Taoist ethics does not enjoin persons to enter into social responsibility. It has no vision of a reordered society in which its structures will bring about the happiness and the welfare of the people as individuals. It calls upon the individual to withdraw from society and to seek individual perfection through control of the inner life. Heaven is long-enduring, so the individual should be patient and long-suffering. Striving to get ahead or to dominate others is an evil to be shunned. In a remarkable passage in the Tao-Te-Ching it is said that the Taoist should be good to those who are good to him, but he also should be good to those who are not good to him. The teaching is: recompense injury with kindness. Yet the perfect person is the inactive, contented, indifferent person.

The idea of doing nothing, non-striving, or inactivity is the core of Taoist ethics. Only quiet non-striving is successful in human relations. It is the basis for universal good order. This doctrine of *wu-wei,* or inactivity, is subtle in its meaning. It suggests that one should do nothing about even tyranny, pillage, and murder; not because those things are not worthy of human response, but because evil begets evil. To respond to force with force will only compound the first evil. Thus the very things that one wishes to overcome are increased and there is no end to the cycle. The idea of *wu-wei*, then, is a calculated inactivity, an inactivity by design. It grows out of the conviction that evil cannot conquer evil. It should be remembered, however, that Taoist ethics is for individuals. It is not to be considered a basis for the maintenance of societies. The Tao-Te-Ching is relatively silent on how non-individualistic human relations should be conducted. For example, it has no ethical wisdom to impart to governments. This is so because Lao-tzu, despite his participation in government as the keeper of the archives, saw no hope for the social order. He was thoroughly disillusioned with the decay in social institutions that he perceived in his own time. Essentially his message was to withdraw from institutional responsibilities and to concentrate upon being a calm, quiet, inactive, restful, simple, and humble person.

It is easy to perceive that Taoism provides insights by which human beings may make responses to the cultural crises of their times, whether in China or elsewhere in the world. Its message, although not acceptable to everyone, retains its appeal to many.

6
CONFUCIUS
AND
CONFUCIANISM

Confucianism is the most impor-
tant religion to have originated in China, and it had a personal
founder. Taoism, founded by Lao-tzu, is the other Chinese religion that has gained international recognition and also has
played a significant role in the cultural history of the Chinese
people. After the Han dynasty broke up, Taoism and Buddhism challenged the preeminence of Confucianism in China.
In these times various rulers found that Taoism and Buddhism
provided more otherworldly dimensions than did Confucianism. These religions tended to seek answers to questions that
are naturally reflective of truly religious concerns, such as:
how to deal with pain and suffering, what follows death, what
makes the human being distinctive, in what manner is human
life a part of a divine plan in which an ultimately personal
deity is in control. Buddhism was found to be especially attentive to such questions and found acceptance by some rulers
even beyond Taoism.

But aside from those periods when Taoism and Buddhism
made significant headway, especially among the rulers, Confucianism has been the most universally accepted religion
among the Chinese rulers and their people. It has been the
chief religion of China. It became, after the time of Confucius,
the official religion, acknowledged and practiced by successive
governments. It was the religion that bolstered the authority
of the emperors. The intellectuals with aristocratic tendencies
also found that Confucianism supported them in their admin-

istrative responsibilities within government. Its teachings encouraged social peace for the masses, exhorting them to practice respect toward one another and toward their superiors (especially those in governmental control). Civil service examinations, preparatory to governmental service, were thoroughly based upon the teachings of Confucianism. In these and other ways Confucianism has been the most significant single force that has nurtured and guided the long historical development of the Chinese people. Confucianism has been one with the Chinese way of life.

The descriptions of Confucianism in this chapter and of Taoism in the previous chapter are largely relevant only until 1949, at which time the Chinese Communists came into control of the land. However, a marked decline in the official acceptance of Confucianism came much earlier. In 1905, for example, the examination system for civil service, based on Confucianism, was abolished. More importantly, when the historic rule of the emperors was abolished and the republic established in 1911, the state character of Confucianism was eliminated. There were efforts to maintain the religion as the official religion of the republic, but they failed. The president of the newly founded republic, Yuan Shih-k'ai, asked that the annual spring and fall sacrifices to Confucius be continued. Confucius had been recognized as worthy of one of the three great sacrifices that were maintained by the government, the other two being to heaven and to earth. The president also declared that Confucianism was a most appropriate expression of the revolution. For long centuries it had been a firm support of absolute rulers in China, but it also had democratic elements within its teachings. It was to these that the republican leaders pointed. These leaders were comfortable with the thought that Confucius was truly a great Chinese sage and that in his teachings much of the national heritage could be found.

But the more youthful followers of the republican leadership were not of a mind to agree. They had been educated abroad and had come under many foreign influences, including non-Chinese religions. They tended to be skeptical of all religions. In their enthusiasm they looked upon religion as a conservative social force, opposed to the essential meaning of the revolution. They looked to so-called modern (meaning largely Western) theories of education, economic organization, and political governance. To many of these, Confucianism was the enemy of the people.

The ascendancy of the Communists in 1949 brought about even greater changes. Mao Tse-tung, for example, declared that he had hated Confucianism since the age of eight. Marxism was an avowedly atheistic system in which belief in the *tao* appeared to be superstitious in the face of the doctrine of dialectical materialism. Under Communism it was further said that Confucianism had been the chief support of the feudalism of past centuries. It had maintained a social system in which two main classes existed. The one class was the aristocrats who possessed great wealth, enjoyed leisure and the available education, benefited from hereditary status, and practiced the Confucian virtues. The other class consisted of the masses who lived in poverty and ignorance. To Communists the Confucian heritage had enforced the subjugation of women, made the family more important than the individual, and lessened the growth of nationalism. On these counts and others, Confucianism was found wanting and has been opposed in the main by the more recent Chinese leadership.

It is not possible at present to know precisely how Confucianism (and Taoism, too) is faring in the new China. The future of the Chinese religions is even more problematic. Several elements in the current situation, however, are rather clear. Although the present leadership has been in control of China for only about twenty-five years, it seems to have broken the hold that traditional Confucianism had over Chinese life for many centuries. No turning back seems possible. Also, since the present leadership is so strong and secure, there has arisen recently some recognition of the cultural heritage prior to 1949. Some of the Confucian temples that had fallen into disrepair are being restored, and some of the Chinese classics, including the Analects, the sacred scriptures of Confucianism, are being translated into modern form. If in the future the doctrine of the "hundred flowers," or cultural pluralism, were to prevail, a resurgence of Confucianism well might take place, although in a highly modified form. Confucianism is still the religion of many millions of Chinese who do not live within modern China, and for these Confucianism has yet another constellation of meanings.

There is a sense, however, in which Confucianism is now a part of the universal inheritance of mankind. It remains a cultural force to a greater or lesser degree among the Chinese in China and outside China. Historically, Confucianism has been a strong force in the shaping of the societies of Korea, Japan, Indochina, and elsewhere. It also has been admired in the West, especially from the eighteenth century when Jesuit missionary scholars returned to Europe with knowledge of the religion. Leibniz and Voltaire, German and French philosophers, for example, were greatly interested in this religion and were undoubtedly influenced by it. All those persons who seek solutions to modern personal and social problems will find its study rewarding.

Confucianism offers a number of strengths. It is primarily an ethical religion that makes morality the obligation of all people. This morality is envisaged as being in harmony with the nature of the universe. Thus it provides more than human sanction for its ethical principles. Confucianism is relatively optimistic about human nature. It has confidence that persons are able through the expression of their wills to shape social relations so as to promote universal human welfare. It is not a religion that preaches social withdrawal. It has a strong sense of social obligation for every person. It emphasizes the importance of the family as the basic social unit and the center of moral influence. But it also recognizes the significance of government as another primal means for advancing human welfare. Its teaching of "nothing to excess," or the idea of the golden mean, appeals to reasonable persons, and its tenet of the golden rule relates positively to such Western religions as

Judaism and Christianity. In these and other ways Confucianism is not a relic, but a live option for modern man.

Lao-tzu and Confucius both offered their religious reflections as responses to the historical and cultural situation of their times. Neither founder claimed to be introducing uniquely new teachings. Both found support for their teachings in the accumulated wisdom of the past. Both tried to locate within that past those fundamental principles by which the unsettled Chinese society of their times could be made secure.

Yet, despite the fact that both Lao-tzu and Confucius accepted the same body of evidence and had the same goals for their teachings, their religions are quite different. Some scholars say that in part these differences reflect factors in the lives of the two men. Confucius, for example, was more widely traveled than Lao-tzu. Confucius went from state to state preaching his ideas of social reform. Lao-tzu, on the other hand, was restricted to the state of Chou; thus he had a more limited outlook. Others say that Lao-tzu grew up in a state that valued naturalistic simplicity, whereas Confucius grew up in a state that had a more highly developed socioreligious awareness.

The teachings of the two founders are divergent in several ways. Lao-tzu stressed the unity between persons and things in the universe to a greater degree than did Confucius. Confucius stressed clearly the great importance of human beings and society. The first arena of his thought was that of people; nature was important, but secondary. They also seem to have held different conceptions of heaven. Lao-tzu recognized the *tao* as a prior and creative force in the universe, whereas Confucius was more ambiguous about the relation between the *tao* and heaven. Confucius did believe, however, that heaven is an active principle that even intervened in human affairs. But the chief difference between the two founders lies in their estimate of the value of social activity. Lao-tzu believed that social activity is ineffectual. He urged that his followers withdraw from social participation. He held that social institutions are not constructive forces in promoting human welfare and that a person could find satisfaction only by retreating from them and through mystical experiences become attached to the *tao*. Confucius, on the other hand, held that social responsibility is the core of religious reality. Social relations are the nexus in which the basic requirements of religion are expressed. One rejected society; the other embraced it.

Before reviewing the life of Confucius, the question should be faced as to whether Taoism and Confucianism are really religions. This question has engaged the attention of many learned sinologues, but the conclusions are varied. Some say that these two religions are primarily ethicopolitical systems of thought, and that they do not qualify as full-blown religions. Others say that historically and culturally they have always been regarded as religions by those who practice them. The answer to this dilemma lies in what is meant by a religion. If a religion must feature a belief in a transcendent and personal deity who has created the world and who bears a fatherly relationship with human beings, then Taoism and Confucianism are not religions. But this would seem to be an arbitrary claim, based in large part on theological features found in other religions. Both Taoism and Confucianism, however, do have concepts of the *tao*, heaven, earth, various spirits, and other features that for them provide a cosmic orientation for their followers. Both religions do have a sense of the holy in the universe and teach the requirement of reverence toward it. A number of other features of the two religions, such as the nature of life after death, are not so clearly and well defined as those in some of the other living religions. Yet these themes are not always neglected in these religions, as, for example, in the doctrine of ancestor worship.

It is necessary to say that Taoism and Confucianism are basically culture religions. They are part and parcel of the Chinese civilization. They are largely earthly, shunning the otherworldly. Both may be said to be humanistic, by which is meant that they are fundamentally concerned with human affairs. Taoism affirms the importance of human life even though it is pessimistic about the efficacy of social relations. Confucianism is much more positive in its assertion that persons are able to manage their own lives successfully through the social institutions in which they find themselves. The primary focus of both faiths is on the human condition.

Although it is difficult to establish whether Lao-tzu was actually a historical person, no such doubt arises regarding Confucius. Almost common agreement exists that Confucius did live, and considerable detail regarding his life is available. This does not mean, however, that all the details of his life are known or that they fall into a neat package of acceptable facts. Many gaps exist in the record, and the record itself is not entirely harmonious.

The sources for knowing about the life of Confucius include the historical literature that has grown up in the early life of the movement. This literature is usually classified in two parts. The first part consists of five works, which are considered to be the oldest in the Confucian tradition. They are assumed to have been written, in whole or in part, by Confucius himself; however, it is now believed that more ancient sources are embodied in them. The five are taken to be canonical scriptures, by which is meant that they are authoritative. The first is the I-Ching, or Book of Changes, a work of prophecy that deals with supernatural powers and their relation to one another. It is said that the book actually was written by the emperor Fu-hsi, perhaps in 2950 B.C. The second, the Shu-Ching or Book of the Records, is a compilation of governmental decrees and other statements of a political character. This document is said to date from the times of the semimythical emperors and great heroes in ancient China, although those who have looked into the book think that it may have been composed in the ninth to the seventh centuries B.C. The third, the Shih-Ching or Book of Poetry, is a collection of poems, which because of its simple grammar and archaic language is dated in the centuries during which the Chou dynasty reigned supreme (1000–600 B.C.). The fourth, the Ch'un Ch'iu, or Annals of Spring and Autumn, is a history of Confucius' native state of

Lu. Presumably this book was written entirely by Confucius and covers the period 722–481 B.C. The fifth, the Li-Chi or Book of Rites, is a collection of various statements on religious and social customs. It may well have been compiled in the first century A.D. These five works, then, are the most authoritative within the Confucian tradition. They are said in that tradition to have been written by Confucius or his disciples, although historical scholars now believe that they came from a variety of authors, both early and late, and that whatever Confucius may have contributed was built upon sources that existed before his time.

In addition to the five canonical works of Confucianism there are four classical works from various writers and different periods. The first, the Lun-Yu or the Analects, constitutes a collection of conversations between Confucius and his disciples. The Analects has been widely translated and read in the West. It is indeed a great Chinese classic as well as a basic document which throws light on the life of Confucius. Commonly it is taken to be the sum and substance of the whole religion, especially by those who know it from some distance. The second is the Ta-Hsueh or the Great Learning. Originally this treatise was Ch. 39 of the Li-Chi, but it was removed because of its usefulness in education. Usually it was the first text studied by young students. The third is the Chung Yung or the Golden Mean. This work on the equanimity of Confucius is said to have been written by his grandson. The fourth is the Meng-tse or the Book of Mencius. This document was probably written in the third century B.C. It represents the originative and systematic thought of Mencius, one of the leading Confucian interpreters of that time. Thus, with the five canonical and the four classical works in the Confucian tradition the nature of the religion may be understood, although it must be stressed that the nine works themselves do not provide a simple, unified, consistent, or reliable account of the life of Confucius.

The name Confucius, the Latinized form for the name of the founder of Confucianism, was brought to the West by Jes-

uit missionaries. The Chinese name is composed of three characters that represent K'ung Fu Tzu. K'ung was the family
name of Confucius and Fu Tzu means a master, a distinguished person, a sage, a great teacher. Thus Fu Tzu is an
honorific designation that was granted to Confucius by those
who revered him. Actually the personal name of Confucius
was Ch'iu, making his name K'ung Ch'iu. Sometimes, also, he
was known as Chung Ni, although the exact meaning of this
name is not known.

It is not possible to ascertain the historical facts about Confucius' forebears. Legend has it that he was descended from
the royal house of Shang. According to Ssu-ma Ch'ien, the
great historian of early China, Confucius' grandfather, Fang
Shu, migrated from the state of Sung and settled in the state
of Lu, the place where Confucius was born. According to the
various sources, the family was noted for its royal connections
and its abilities in warfare. These accounts appear to be exag-
gerations.

The Analects mentions that the father of Confucius lived in
Tsou in the province of Shantung, which is in northeast China.
Presumably Confucius was born there in the year 551 B.C.
There is reasonable agreement among scholars that this date is
probably correct, although some give the date as 552 B.C. By
some accounts the father's name was Shu-liang Ho and the
mother's name was Cheng Tsai. It is said that the father was
an officer who served the Meng family, one of three noted
families that ruled the state of Lu. The mother, Cheng Tsai, is
thought to have come from a relatively undistinguished family
called Yen. It may be that the mother was a secondary wife or
concubine of Shu-liang Ho. Her common background and the
prestigious status of the husband suggest that. The historian
Ssu-ma Ch'ien, although he is not always sure of his facts, indicates that Confucius' father was a warrior retained by the
powerful Meng family and took part in many heroic military
exploits. If this is so, Shu-liang Ho held a status far above that
of his wife. Ssu-ma Ch'ien suggests that a proper marriage
may not have existed between Confucius' father and mother.

It may be, then, that the father was a member of a growing group called *shih*, who did not have full noble status but who could trace their lineage to the nobility.

After Confucius' death a large number of legends grew up about the celestial implications of his birth. One says that, prior to the birth, Cheng Tsai had a wonderful dream in which five old men, who represented the five planets, approached her, leading a sacred unicorn covered with dragon scales. Paying her homage, they knelt before her. The unicorn spewed out before her a tablet of precious jade on which was written that her child would be the essence of the waters and that he would succeed as an unsceptered king to the decaying dynasties of Shang and Chou.

In another story, Cheng Tsai ascended the hill Ni to pray that she might have a son. As she went up the hill, the leaves of the plants and trees stood up straight as a sign of the importance of the mission; they drooped as she came down the hill. On that very night she dreamed that a black emperor came to her and promised that she would bear a son. The son would be born in a hollow mulberry tree. The mulberry tree turned out to be the name of a dry cave on the south side of the hill Ni. It was to that cave that she went on the night of her labor. In the morning, when the child was born, she bathed him in the waters of the spring that flowed from the cave.

When Confucius was an infant (some say when he was three years old), his father died. No information is available as to the cause of Shu-liang Ho's death. It is said that he was buried in the original location of the K'ung family, Fang, rather than in Tsou, where his family lived. It is said also that Cheng Tsai never told Confucius where his father was buried. Perhaps the husband and wife were estranged.

The death of his father was a decisive event in the life of Confucius. He obviously came under the full influence of his mother, who apparently did not cherish the life of the military. Confucius' education was devoted to nonmilitary matters, and his teachings show no reverence for warfare. Also, his early life was one of poverty. Later he declared that this early poverty gave him insights into the nature of human existence that were denied to the aristocracy.

Despite the poverty of the K'ung family, Confucius did have opportunity to devote himself to learning. Probably at an early age he showed ability in intellectual affairs and was helped by the Meng ruler to enter a private school for high-born children. Confucius himself declared that at the age of fifteen his mind was bent on learning. No reliable records exist to tell the events of his life prior to that time, although he may have begun his education as early as seven. Later he may have combined his studies with administrative responsibilities in the state of Lu, being encouraged by his superiors to develop his many intellectual interests. The first thirty years of his life apparently were largely devoted to learning. The subjects that Confucius studied were varied and many. According to the Analects, he took an interest in history, poetry, archery, music, science, government, literature, and the proprieties. The proprieties were contained in the ritual codes available at the time. These he deemed to be very important in instructing the citizen in the proper ways of maintaining positive social relations. It is said that he also avoided certain subjects: feats of strength, prodigies, and the supernatural. At one point in his early life he became a teacher, although under what precise circumstances is not known. He founded a school that was especially receptive to impoverished students and is said to have grown at one time to about three thousand students. At any rate, the youthful Confucius was a very bright student who eagerly sought knowledge and who impressed all who knew him with his wide and deep learning. His students may be said to be the first disciples of the new religion of Confucianism.

Two special events of a personal nature occurred in his youth. At the age of nineteen he married. It is said that his bride was a daughter of the Chien-kuan clan of the state of Sung. No reliable sources tell of the family life of the two, although it is said that a year after their marriage (532 B.C.) a son was born to them. The K'ung family rejoiced along with their friends, and the ruler of Ku made a ceremonial presentation of a carp. The son was named Li (carp), although later he was called Po-yu (fish) the elder. Another source indicates that Confucius also had a daughter. Nothing is known about her, but the son apparently preceded the father in death. The father was disappointed that the son did not follow a life of learning.

Confucius also had other family responsibilities. It is said that he was the youngest of eleven children and that he was the only able-bodied child among them. This meant that early he had to take heavy responsibility for his family's welfare. According to tradition he had a lame elder half brother for whom he took responsibility even to the point of finding a suitable husband for his niece.

The second event was the death of his mother in 528 B.C. In the Chinese tradition such a death would be mourned for a period of three years in which severe restrictions would be placed upon the mourners. They would be required to refrain from hunting, fishing, music, drinking, and even visiting friends. It is not clear what Confucius did, although the Analects say that he reprimanded his son for mourning the death of his mother. Cheng Tsai was buried in the capital of Lu. Much later when Confucius learned from an old woman that his father had been buried at Fang, Confucius had his mother's remains transferred to the family plot in Fang. Traditional Chinese culture requires children to show respect to their parents, both in life and in death. But undoubtedly the teachings of Confucius that emphasized filial piety were reinforced by his own attitude toward his mother.

Confucius was basically interested in learning and teaching, and to these he devoted much of his time throughout his life. For him any impulse for action rested upon the storehouse of knowledge which had been provided by the past but which he had carefully reviewed and edited to fit the present circumstances. But Confucius had another overriding interest: politics. He believed that the central source for human welfare was government. No other social unit, with the possible excep-

tion of the family, held such promise for the achievement
of true human welfare. The well-managed state had the
possibility of improving the lot of all its citizens. Yet Confucius did not hold a positive estimate of governmental administrators. He was firmly convinced that his teachings and his
teachings alone held the prospect of creating good government. Those who governed were politicians, not grounded in
his teachings. They had little respect for the principles that he
espoused. It was appropriate, therefore, for Confucius increasingly to seek high public office for himself so that he might
fearlessly apply his moral teachings to the conduct of government.

Confucian tradition describes how in many instances
Confucius sought for and held various public offices. Mencius
records that Confucius was at one time simply a clerk who had
minor responsibilities in connection with the state granaries.
Later he was connected with the administration of the pasture-
lands of the state of Lu. In these duties Confucius was an
able, conscientious servant of the government. It is said that
he later became chief magistrate of his town, a post that enabled him to show his wisdom and his ability to make ethical
decisions regarding human problems. Then he became an assistant superintendent of works within the state and finally the
chief justice. Stories abound of the excellent way in which he
carried out these responsibilities. It is said that he increased
the mutual respect that people had for one another and for the
state. He was able to bring about peace within the state and
between the state and other jurisdictions, as well as having a
role to play in the start of disarmament. In all his public posts
he maintained his teachings. He declared, for example, that
the primary aim of good government was not to increase revenues so that the state treasury would be full. Rather, it was to
develop reciprocal relations of a high quality in which all persons would perform their social functions properly. In the Analects he advised that the person should behave when away
from home as though he were in the presence of a most important guest. He urged government officials to deal with the

common people as though they were officiating at an important sacrifice. Declared Confucius: Do not do to others what you would not like yourself. Then, whether one is governing the affairs of the state or of a family, there will be no feelings of opposition. The result will be genuine peace based upon proper respect and goodwill.

Certainly the state of Lu had its problems. At the time of Confucius it had a population of about one million and included a territory of twenty thousand square miles. The Duke of Lu was able to trace his ancestry to the famous Duke of Chou, but his kingdom had fallen upon hard times. Compared with other states, Lu was in the backwaters of the time. Confucius found that the state of Lu was not actually ruled by the Duke, but by three rival baronial families. These had in reality seized the power and had made the Duke a mere figurehead. Running the government was considered to be their proper role. They were the great officers of the court. They held the real power. The day-by-day administration of the state, however, was left in the hands of a secondary group who might be called gentlemen knights. It is to this group Confucius undoubtedly belonged. Thus it was not possible that Confucius could attain to the very top position within the state of Lu. To a degree members of every ruling group prided themselves on their patronage of intellectuals who not only gave prestige to the rulers but also provided them with the expertise necessary for the practical administration of the government. The highest ambition of Confucius, then, was thwarted.

An example may indicate the nature of political conditions in Lu at the time of Confucius' youth. The prime minister at one point was Chao-tzu, who belonged to one of the three ruling families. But he was prime minister in name only. Chi Ping-tzu, who was a member of a rival family, actually wielded the power of the office. The Duke of Lu remained powerless. At the age of thirty-six (or in 515 B.C.) Confucius was aware of these facts. He knew that the Duke was so poor that he was not able to pay the dancers and musicians who ordinarily took part in the ceremonies of respect for ancestors.

But Chi Ping-tzu was so rich and demonstrative of his power that he held elaborate ceremonies, including eight rows of eight dancers, sixty-four in all. The practice humiliated the Duke and irritated Confucius greatly. The powers of Chi Ping-tzu, however, did not go unchallenged. Various factions in Lu developed a plan whereby he would be curtailed in his blatant displays. However, they did not succeed, for the three main families, perhaps sensing what was at stake for them as well, came to his defense. Probably because the plot implicated the Duke, it became necessary for him to flee into exile in nearby Ch'i, where he remained for seven years until his death.

These and other incidents were not accepted with equanimity by Confucius. His passion for applying moral principles to government was offended. From all accounts Confucius was always capable of expressing moral outrage. He seldom remained silent when he perceived politicians resorting to questionable practices. On the occasion when Ching Ping-tzu held his elaborate ceremonies to the derogation of the Duke of Lu, Confucius was outspoken. He declared that if Ching Ping-tzu could be endured, then there was no man who could not be endured. Such public declarations certainly did not endear him to those who held the ultimate power in Lu.

As a consequence, it became necessary for Confucius to leave Lu. It is said that he went to Ch'i, where the Duke was in exile. Apparently he was well received by the Duke of Ch'i, who, like the other rulers, enjoyed having persons of learning about him. Confucius became his adviser. The Duke is said to have offered the revenues of the town of Lin-chu to Confucius, but Confucius was unwilling to accept. He said he had not earned the privilege of such income through acceptable services to the Duke. He also said the advice that he had so freely given to the Duke had not been heeded. Confucius was not only highly principled but also capable of recalcitrant emotions as well. Later the Duke wanted to assign some local fields to Confucius but was persuaded against this decision by his prime minister, who reported that Confucius was an im-

practical person, conceited, placing too high a value on ceremonies, and who had his "peculiarities." Confucius apparently
was a hard man to get along with.

Confucius lost the confidence of the Duke of Ch'i and left
the state to return to Lu. Some fifteen years passed before he
was able to receive an official position in Lu. During these
years, however, he reestablished himself as a teacher, bringing
to his side a band of loyal disciples. His students came mainly
from the group of secondary governmental administrators.
These young people were primarily interested in the workings
of government so that they could take positions later with one
of the three leading families or within the central administration of the state of Lu. Confucius taught them much more
than the science of statecraft. He brought to his students the
full range of his learning. It was his view that the processes of
government could not be divorced from such matters as the
long history of China, the importance of ceremonial codes, the
ways of expressing proper respect to others, especially to one's
superiors, and the basic principles of the moral life. His students may have included sons of the royal families.

In a sense it was fortunate that during this time Confucius
was somewhat removed from politics, for unsettling events
were taking place. After Ching Ping-tzu died in 505 B.C., several factions within the Ching family vied for power. A re-
tainer of the family, however, Yang Huo by name, seized
power and ruled for three years as a despot. During this time
Confucius was invited to serve in the government, but he declined. He did not approve of the rule of the Ching family,
and he found his successor, Yang Huo, to be morally no better. The brutal Yang Huo, however, overreached himself, even
to the point of plotting to murder the head of the Ching family. Kung-shan Fu-jao, the warden of Pi, within the province
of the Ching family, arose. He did battle with Yang Huo and
defeated him, sending him into exile. Yang Huo managed in
his fleeing to take with him the hereditary state treasures.
Confucius was emotionally torn by the social uprising. His
quick sympathies were on the side of the warden of Pi, but he

did not act upon his sympathies. He did not because he believed, as did many in his time, that so-called inferior persons should remain loyal to so-called superior persons. In this instance Confucius apparently neglected to take into account another operating principle of Chinese society. It held that rebellion was proper when an overlord failed in his responsibilities to the people. Confucius was torn between the two alternatives but was dissuaded by his loyal disciple, Tzu-lu, from entering into the revolt. For this decision Confucius was later criticized.

With the defeat and flight of Yang Huo, Confucius was offered the post of chief magistrate of the town of Chung-tu. Possibly he was fifty years of age at the time. At this age Confucius entered into a group that was known as the Ai, or the elders. The elders were those by reason of age and experience who were considered especially suitable for governmental positions of some note. It was in this period, as indicated previously, that he rose in governmental responsibility. He was promoted to be the assistant superintendent of works within Lu. The position of the chief superintendent was not open to him because it was assigned on a hereditary basis to those of the highest class. It is said that later he was appointed to the ministry of crime, although this can be doubted on the grounds that this position also was reserved for the aristocrats. On this point the testimony of Mencius, the later sage who amplified the teachings of Confucius, must be doubted.

Aside from his public posts, Confucius was held in high regard by many. By this stage of his life he had developed his philosophy of social responsibility to a point where his wisdom was widely acknowledged. His disciples also were doing him honor. Some of them had been given worthwhile appointments within the administration of Chi K'ang-tzu, who had come to head the Chi family. Although his wisdom was widely praised, especially among the rulers of Lu, his counsel was not always heeded. He became an ornament of the court, and he felt that his teachings were not put into practice. He grew disillusioned with this state of affairs. His positions were regarded as sinecures by which he could maintain himself and continue teaching his disciples. Sometimes his advice, openly sought for, was not respected. It is said that his resignation from all public posts came about because the Duke of Lu appointed a group of courtesans to office. Probably Confucius had deeper reasons for his decision. He was fast approaching old age. He firmly believed that his teachings were important to the recovery of China. He thought they would restore the broken harmony of the Chinese people by overcoming their social and political divisions, and that by his teachings the welfare of all would be made secure.

Given the attitude of Confucius and his inability to achieve a position from which he could have free rein in applying his teachings, it is perhaps easy to understand why he resigned from all official duties in Lu. He may have been fifty-six years old at the time, but he did not retire from life. He still sought an opportunity in public life in which he could bring to bear his principles of social responsibility. He began a period of at least ten, perhaps as many as thirteen, years of travel, in which he went from state to state in an effort to attract the attention of the rulers. He had said that if a ruler would employ him for twelve months, he would have sufficient time to show the value of his teachings. If a ruler would employ him for three years, he would be able by then to accomplish his total program of governmental reform.

Almost everywhere he went he was well received, for it was customary in his time that leading sages were well respected by most of the rulers. In the visit he made to the neighboring state of Wei, he was taken into the home of a leading official, Yen Ch'ou-yu. When he arrived in Ch'en he was lodged with Ching-tzu, the minister of work. There as elsewhere he interviewed the leading government officials, offering them advice on their several functions. He visited other states, although it appears at this time that he made the state of Wei his temporary home, leaving it perhaps on five occasions to visit elsewhere. In Wei he experienced events that encouraged him to look farther for a state that would acknowledge his teachings.

One day in Wei, the ruler, Duke Ling, was riding in his carriage, along with his hated adviser, Nan-tzu, followed by Confucius in a second carriage. As the crowds viewed the procession, they cried out that there was lust in front and virtue behind. The outburst angered the Duke and cast Confucius in an embarrassing situation. Again, as Confucius was on his way to the state of Ch'en, he traveled through the states of Ts'ai, Sung, and Cheng. While in the capital of Sung, he had an audience with the ruler. He carefully expounded his teachings on the nature of good government to the eager interest of the ruler. The speech finished, the ruler said that he was able to accept the teachings, but he thought that he was too stupid to put the ideas into practice. At this, enraged and disappointed, Confucius left and went farther on his journeys.

Confucius, however, was not always haughty. One time, while speaking with the minister of crime in the state of Ch'en, he was asked whether Duke Chao of Lu knew the rules of propriety. The Duke was an especial favorite of Confucius'. Confucius sprang to the defense of the revered ruler by saying that he certainly did know the rules. But the Duke had violated the rules of propriety by marrying a daughter of the house of Wu, who had the same surname. This was a clear violation of the rules of marriage at that time in China. The minister, then, after Confucius left, called one of his disciples and pointed out the misjudgment of the sage. The minister said that he had always heard that Confucius claimed to be absolutely impartial, but his response was partisan. Later, when the disciple told Confucius of the minister's remark, Confucius acknowledged his mistake, saying that he was indeed a lucky man, for whenever he made a mistake, people were sure to notice it. Confucius was strongly convinced of the rightness of his views, but he combined his conviction with a corresponding sense of his frailty. Humility was known and advocated by the founder of the major Chinese religion.

Wherever Confucius went as an itinerant teacher and adviser, he took with him three of his most perceptive and loyal disciples: Yen Hui, Tzu-lu, and Tzu-kung. Together they planned their trips, arranged for interviews, and evaluated the results of their visits. The disciples, moreover, supported the master when he was discouraged. Once, Confucius was greatly discouraged and asked his disciples whether they thought his teachings were false. He pointed out that they were at the time without provisions and sick to the point of not being able to stand on their feet. The most understanding of the disciples, Yen Hui, responded that the teachings of Confucius are so profound that the world can hardly comprehend them. He suggested that Confucius should continue to expound his doctrines even though no ruler accepted and applied them. Said Yen Hui, the responsibility for promulgating the teachings belonged to Confucius, whereas the task of implementing them fell to the rulers. If the teachings were not accepted and applied, that would be the shame of the rulers, not of the great teacher. Confucius was encouraged. At other times, however, it was Confucius who had to encourage his disappointed disciples. When he was asked by Tzu-lu whether as gentlemen they should have to endure such deprivation as they were suffering, the sage responded that a gentleman stands firm in his misery and that it is the small man who gives up in times of trouble.

After years of travel through a number of states, enduring the extremes of luxury and deprivation, always failing to receive the kind of acceptance that he considered appropriate to the fulfillment of his life's aim, Confucius returned finally in the year 484 B.C. to the state of Wei. By this time the situation there had changed. Duke Ling, who had been the ruler, had died and his grandson, Duke Chu, reigned. The grandson, however, held only nominal power. A minister, K'ung Yu, possessed the real power. But K'ung Yu received Confucius well and even arranged a government stipend for him, relieving him of any worldly anxieties.

At this time, when Confucius was sixty-nine years old, Chi K'ang-tzu, head of the Chi family in the state of Lu, sent messengers to invite the old man back to Lu. Confucius returned. He found that he was received royally and noted that some of his earlier disciples had come into positions of high trust. One of them, Tzu-kung, had been the ambassador to the state of Wu and had performed well. This gave credit to Confucius as well. Another disciple, Jan Ch'iu, had been the steward of the family of Chi and the commander of a part of its army. Another disciple, Fan Ch'ih, was the right-hand helper of Jan Ch'iu. Jan Ch'iu became even more prominent when in 484 B.C. he repelled an invading army of Ch'i. Near the end of that year, one of the officers of Ch'i killed the duke of the state. It seemed to Confucius that Duke Ai of Lu should respond by attacking the murderer. He so advised the Duke, but the Duke rejected the advice. Naturally Confucius was disappointed. His disillusionment increased when the head of the Chi family increased taxes greatly. Confucius thought the increase was oppressive and called upon his disciple, Jan Ch'iu, to resist his lord, but Jan Ch'iu did not. On the only occasion when Confucius publicly denounced a disciple, according to the Analects, Confucius declared that Jan Ch'iu was no disciple of his. He said that he gave permission for the common people to "beat the drum" and to set upon him.

But in his old age in the state of Lu, Confucius was still held in very high regard. It appears that he was a respected adviser who ranked only below those who held the top positions by reason of their heredity. In his final years Confucius became more of a private person. Aside from age, the deaths of a number of persons may have influenced him. It was at this time that his son died. This event was followed by the death of his foremost disciple, Yen Hui. In 481 B.C. another disciple of note, Ssu-ma Niu, died. In the following year his oldest disciple, Tzu-lu, also died.

In his last years Confucius wished to write about his experiences and his teachings. He is one of the few founders of the living religions who is known to have written in regard to his ideas. It is said that Lao-tzu wrote the Tao-Te-Ching, the sacred scriptures of Taoism. The only other founder who may have contributed directly to the formation of a religion's basic literature was Zoroaster, who may have written a part of the Avesta, the sacred scriptures of Zoroastrianism.

The extent to which Confucius wrote the several works of Confucianism that have been previously described in this chapter is debated by scholars. The most generous view is that he compiled the whole of the Confucian classics. But it well may be that only the Ch'un Ch'iu, or Annals of Spring and Autumn, were written by him. The Ch'un Ch'iu consists of a history of the state of Lu covering the period 722–481 B.C. It is clear, however, that Confucius was not a composer of original ideas. All that he expressed came to him from the past. He did not claim to be innovative. He believed that no new ideas were needed to meet the requirements of good government and good citizenship. All such ideas as were needed were to be found in the teachings of the past. Confucius may be said to have been a compiler and an editor. Yet such a designation should not be viewed as demeaning. Confucius did not merely repeat the ideas of the past. He selected from among them, dropping out those which were unworthy and attractively arranging those which were enduring and constructive. The result was the formulation of a revised, evaluated, and rearranged compendium of the wisdom of past Chinese history and culture. The work, moreover, was satisfying to future ages and not simply to the times in which he lived.

The circumstances of Confucius' death are not reliably known. The account given by the historian Ssu-ma Ch'ien seems not to be in accord with the great man's character. In the Ch'un Ch'iu, presumably written by Confucius himself, there is the mere statement that he died in summer on a day in the fourth month. It is said also that he died after a week of serious illness on the eleventh day of the fourth moon in the sixteenth year of the reign of Duke Ai of Lu, or 479 B.C.

Tradition says that at death the eyes of Confucius were sealed and three pinches of rice were placed in his mouth. He was then dressed in ceremonial garments, a valuable jade ring, and a fancy headpiece. The body was placed in a double coffin, the inner one made of one kind of wood and the outer of another. The coffin externally was embellished with various signs and about it were placed symbols of the three earliest dynasties in China. His body was taken to a spot on the river Ssu north of the Lu capital and buried.

Confucius' disciples mourned him, as was the custom, for three years. Even on the day of their departure they cried so much and chanted so loudly that they lost their voices. One of the disciples, Tzu-kung, it is said, after seeing the others depart, returned to construct a mud hut at the graveside, where he remained to mourn his master for yet another three years.

In life Confucius was noted for a number of characteristics. Surely he was a learned man. He gave his whole lifetime to constant study. He never believed that he knew enough. The main content of his study was the past cultural inheritance of China. But he also was interested in archery, music, and other activities. He was not an ascetic. There is evidence that he enjoyed life and even the luxuries that were given him in his various state connections. Yet he did not live ostentatiously. He apparently believed that the life of social responsibility did not call for a denying of creature comforts. He clearly placed the life of learning and ethical purity above that of material and sensual pleasures.

Confucius was well aware of his early background. He knew that poverty was part of his own life. In his teachings he showed interest in and respect for those who were poor. Oppressive taxes were criticized by him, illustrating his concern for the masses of his time. But for much of his life, Confucius was not poor and did not immediately identify with the poor. He was a gentleman first and foremost. It may even be said that he was an aristocrat, for in his court positions he ranked just below the very top class that held power on a hereditary basis. Clearly, too, he was quite sympathetic with those in power. Not only did he spend a large part of his life in advising them, he also wished, perhaps above all else, to become one of them. His ambition, however, was not for his own advancement, but as a way to apply his teachings, which he believed would certainly make for the welfare of all.

Some persons in Confucius' time thought him to be difficult in human relations, contentious, easily hurt, overly concerned with the details of the ceremonial codes, insensitive to the requirements of political reality, and haughty. But such characterizations in the main came from his detractors. On the other hand, he always seemed to place the welfare of persons first in his scale of values. He had a charm that drew to him the leading political figures of his time and, in addition, a sizable band of disciples who carried on his work after his death, making sure that Confucianism would survive. He was a person whom many not only respected but loved. Also, he always thought that he was capable of further improvement. In the Analects he confessed certain moral defects, including the overdrinking of wine, and he wished that he might have fifty more years to live, that he might study more and improve himself.

His disciples held a somewhat enlarged view of their master. Little is known regarding them. It is said that there were more than seventy in Confucius' lifetime. These may be considered in two categories. First, there were those he taught very early in his career, who had been attracted before he set out on his journeys. Second, there were those who were the disciples of his maturity.

After his final resignation from official life, Confucius gathered about him those who were to carry on his teachings and were instrumental in forming the basis for the later religion of Confucianism. These were not all of the same mind. There were eight Confucian schools that were established after the sage's death; three of them are said to have been founded by disciples of his later years.

Although Confucius had a rather humble view of himself personally, his disciples tended to see perfection in him. They declared that he had no foregone conclusions, no arbitrary predeterminations, no obstinacy, and no egoism. They declared that he was not like ordinary persons; in fact, they held him to be above comparison with anyone else.

As the centuries went by, Confucius was further elevated. Some of the later Confucian classics say that he was the equal of heaven, that all things on earth honor him, that he was unequaled in the history of the whole of humankind. Later his stature was even further increased. Before the Christian era the emperor of China offered animal sacrifices at his tomb. He was given various royal titles, such as duke, earl, and finally emperor, and his statue was placed in line with those of the other emperors of China. He was canonized, and temples were constructed throughout China for his worship. Finally, through an official rescript of an emperor, Confucius was raised to the rank of co-assessor with the deities of heaven and earth. The Chinese sage who shunned prayer, advocating the importance of human responsibility, became himself a god who was worshiped.

The teachings of Confucius were primarily ethical and social, yet they did not ignore cosmic beliefs. The Confucian scriptures make many references to the divine order in the universe. In the main these references are to an impersonal heaven, or *t'ien*, which not only orders the physical aspects of the universe but also constitutes the moral basis for the conduct of human affairs. The designation *ming* signifies a notion of impersonal destiny, another name for the supreme order in the universe. Whatever is decreed or fated cannot be resisted. It is the fundamental requirement or harmony in all things. The concept of *shang ti*, meaning supreme ruler, indicates also the controlling nature of the divine way. Confucianism also taught that the divine rule is expressed as *tao*, or way. For Confucius the *tao* has an ethical character as it pertains to human beings. It is that fated requirement of the good life whose aims must be met. It constitutes that divine path which persons ought to follow and neglect at their peril. Thus, the ethical principles of Confucianism are rooted in universal realities that are beyond human initiative and control. It is not proper, therefore, to think of Confucianism as lacking transcendent features on which human relations are grounded. In this sense, Confucianism may well be considered a religion rather than only an ethical code.

The ethical teaching of Confucius, although a working totality, may be viewed in some of its parts. Central to the ethics is the notion of *jen,* or the true gentleman. The true gentleman is that person whose actions are consonant with the *tao.* Practically speaking, the *jen* is a supreme moral perfection that human beings seek to emulate, although few if any actually achieve it. It is characterized, as many passages in the Analects make clear, as requiring benevolence, love, good human relations, kindness, and mutual respect. According to Confucian teaching, human nature in its original form is not synonymous with *jen.* The ideal life is achieved ethically. Living calls for constantly maturing action whereby through discipline the *jen* is attained. Confucianism, therefore, calls for rigorous self-discipline.

Brotherly love is a part of the requirements of *jen* and as such is a major component in the teachings. This love is usually portrayed as filial piety or respect for one's elders within the family. The idea of filial piety did not originate with Confucius; it was a characteristic of Chinese life for long centuries before him, but he incorporated it into his teachings in a prominent way. Filial piety required that the person respect his parents in life and in death. He should defer to them. He not only should be attentive to their material welfare but also should humbly be instructed by them, following their teachings in his own life. This did not mean that children always thought their parents were morally or otherwise accurate. Parents could be reproved. But in the end, children were to show respect toward their parents.

The teaching of brotherly love, moreover, was not restricted to the relationships of children to their parents. Family relationships of all kinds were to be guided by brotherly love. It was a principle by which all human relationships should be guided. Beyond the family the principle of brotherly love was basic to all social relationships and particularly to the maintenance of government. For right or wrong, Confucius was committed to the assumption that the family and government are coterminous. A set of requirements proper for the family was proper also for government. The teachings of filial piety, therefore, although relating primarily to the family, became a basic social duty.

The practice of brotherly love, however, was not limited to generalized attitudes. Confucianism teaches the importance of *li,* which is a composite of the various inherited practices and customary rules by which the true gentleman should be guided. Originally *li* signified a set of ceremonial observances relating the influence from heaven to life on earth. But it also came to mean specific elements of deportment, the ways by which brotherly love is expressed through courtesy, politeness, formality, decorum, good form, and good manners. This code of conduct regulated the five great relationships that constituted the field of action for the moral life: ruler and subject, father and son, husband and wife, elder brother and younger, and friend and friend. Reciprocal propriety was the rule of Confucian ethics.

The ethics of Confucianism encouraged the development of the superior person. The concept of the superior person occurs 105 times in the Analects. There it is contrasted with the idea of the mean man. The superior man is that one who is the true gentleman, a *jen,* who is guided by the attitudes engendered by brotherly love and concretely expressed in *li,* or the practical code of reciprocal propriety.

Confucius, as much as any of the founders of the living religions, placed heavy emphasis upon education as the fundamental means for achieving his religious goals. There is little emphasis in Confucianism upon the role of ecstatic experiences in attaining the good life. Confucius shunned mysticism. He did not teach that the intervention of god was needed. In contrast, his teachings assumed that human beings are malleable and that human reason is the basis for growth in the ethical life. For Confucius, education did not consist of factual information; it was primarily aimed at the improvement of character. True education led to the achievement of the moral life. He urged his followers to set their minds on the *tao*, to lay hold on every right attachment, to trust in goodness, and to find relaxation in the arts. Not only did Confucius found a religion in the sense that his teachings later led to an official state cult, he also laid the foundation on which the general system of education in China was built for many succeeding generations.

Confucius was the single, most influential force in the shaping of one of the richest, most renowned, and highly workable civilizations known to history.

7

ZOROASTER
AND
ZOROASTRIANISM

In considering Zoroastrianism, the geographic scene turns westward. The religions that have been portrayed in the past chapters through the lives of their founders have all been founded in Asia, particularly in two countries, India and China.

Zoroastrianism is a religion of the Middle or Near East. It is the first of three religions from this area whose founders' lives will be delineated in the next three chapters.

The religions of the Middle East may well seem more familiar to Western readers. For one thing, their deities are transcendent, personal gods who bear a close relationship to individual and social life. They are more like what the Western person conceives gods to be. It is difficult for many to understand how Jainism and Buddhism can be classified as religions, since they appear to deny, in their earliest forms, any sense of a personal god. Sikhism does offer a supreme deity who is more familiar to Westerners, but in this case the concept of god was taken directly from Islam. It is difficult also for Western man to understand how Taoism and Confucianism can be classified as religions, since their concepts of divinity are so impersonal. The concept of god, moreover, is only one attribute of the Asian religions that makes them seem somewhat strange to those who share the Western cultural inheritance. The nature of religious organization, the role of sacred scriptures, the freedom of the person, attitudes toward asceticism, beliefs regarding the nature of the afterlife, and their ethics are also alien to Western thought.

In the main the religions that originated in the Middle East are distinctive in that they give a prominent place to the relationships that individuals are able to have with a highly personal deity. This relationship may account for the high value that in general is placed upon human life. These religions also regard ethical decision-making as central. Human beings are not one with an all-encompassing nature; through their freedom they stand on a higher plane in the cosmic order of things. God, man, and nature are three separable and distinct spheres of creation. Nature, as god's creation, is the area in which man operates. But the primary realm of meaning lies in the personal encounters that take place between god and man. Ethical relations, moreover, constitute the core of the relationship between god and man. Zoroastrianism, with its own special content, is representative of the Middle Eastern religions.

In comparison with the number of adherents of the other living religions, Zoroastrianism is today rather small. With a membership of about 180,000 it is probably the smallest. The next larger religion is Jainism, with a membership of about 2,600,000. Historically Zoroastrianism appealed to many millions and influenced several of the basic tenets of Islam. But it was brought low by the latter religion in A.D. 651, when in its surge through the Middle East, Islam conquered the people of Iran, converting, sometimes by force, as it went. Zoroastrianism almost became extinct in the land of its birth. But, as has been true of some other persecuted religions in history—for example, Judaism—a small number of Zoroastrians survived and kept their faith in secret. The Muslims called them the Gabars, "infidels." The Gabars maintained the rituals, dress, beliefs, and other aspects of their ancient religion. Today there are only about 12,000 of them in modern Iran, where they are completely tolerated by the government.

Following the Arab conquest, however, tens of thousands of Zoroastrians in Iran migrated to India. They moved first to the mouth of the Persian Gulf and then to an island off the Indian coast. Later they entered India, settling chiefly in what is now the city of Bombay within the province of Gujarat. The Hindus of the region received them well and characteristically permitted them to worship as they wished. About 100,000 Zoroastrians live today in and about Bombay, although there are Zoroastrians in isolated communities elsewhere in India and beyond. Zoroastrians today are commonly called Parsis or Parsees. This name, given them by the Hindus, refers to the city of Pars in Iran from which they originally came.

The Parsis of today are few, but they are influential far beyond their numbers. As a group they are among the wealthiest people in India. They know how to make money. They are the leaders of India's industries, stores, hotels, and other business enterprises. They are noted for their philanthropies providing help for social services, medical facilities, and other forms of aid to persons in distress. But the Parsis in general remain aloof in their religious practices. They are characteristically confident and dignified in their respect for their religious heritage. They do not permit persons of other religions or of no religion to worship with them. Like their cousins, the Gabars of Iran, they remain protective and even secretive about their most sacred rites. The religion of the Parsis today is regulated by two orders of hereditary priests. They claim to be able to trace their ancestry back to the Iranian tribe of the Magi. The Magi are known to Christians and others as that group from which the wise men traveled by the guidance of a bright star to the place where Jesus was born. Their interest in celestial guidance and similar features of their religion also has given birth to the term "magic." The high priests of the Parsis are called *dasturs* and they are often highly learned persons. The ordinary priests are called *mobeds*. They undergo strict procedures of initiation and are known for their memorization of large parts of the Avesta, the sacred scriptures, even though they do not understand what they have memorized, since the Avesta is written in what for the *mobeds* is an archaic language. The lay Parsis also memorize portions of the sacred text which they use in their temple worship.

Like the founders of the other religions, Zoroaster did not originate a wholly new religion. He was dependent upon the culture, including the religion, that preceded him. It was a culture formed by the Aryans, who originally were a large group of Indo-European-speaking wanderers who moved essentially in three directions, perhaps as early as 2000 B.C. One part of them left southeastern Europe to settle further west in Europe. Another part went into India and there conquered the native Dravidians and established their own special blend of religion, which became known in early times as Vedism and later as Hinduism. Another part, however, settled in parts of the Middle East, in the Soviet Union, and in Iran. It was the Aryans, having settled in Iran, who gave shape to the religion that preceded Zoroastrianism.

The religion of the Aryans who settled in India and Iran was similar. In both early Iranian religion and in Vedism two classes of deities were acknowledged: the *daevas* and the *asuras*. They were spirits that personified the forces of nature: the sun, moon, stars, fire, water, wind, and so forth. In the Rig Veda, the earliest account of Vedism, the *asuras* were more remote from man and the *daevas* were closer. In the Rig Veda, for example, Varuna, the great protector of truth, is an *asura*. He also is the great protector of the moral law. On the other hand, Indra is viewed as the greatest of the *daevas*, a war deity not fundamentally concerned with the moral law. These two classes of deities are found also in early Iranian religion. But over a period of time and especially due to the attack of Zoroaster upon the *daevas*, the ranking order of the deities developed differently. In India the *daevas* became more exalted, while the *asuras* were held in less regard. In Iran the *daevas* were defined as evil; thus the *daevas* became demons, while the *asuras* became essentially good forces in the universe.

Another common conception, held both in India and in Iran, has to do with the moral nature of the universe, including its effect upon human action. In Vedism this idea was expressed by *rita* as it applied to the natural order. The principle of causation was perceived in the whole of nature. The idea of *karma* in Vedism applied the causative principle in nature to human affairs. What a man sowed, that he also would reap. In Iranian religion there was also a recognition of the causal principle. The deity that personified it was called Asha. Asha was the principle of truth, and truth is that which cannot be resisted. Asha is associated with light; error is associated with darkness. Followers of the Iranian religion were required to be followers of the light, for it is only the light that is necessary. Asha is therefore supreme in nature and in human relations.

Again, the kinds of sacrifices that were practiced in the two religions appear to be similar. Fire held a central place. In Vedism the god Agni was the personification of fire and was held to have a major role in Vedic sacrifices. Fire worship has been a chief characteristic of the ancient Iranian religion and has been a feature of Zoroastrianism throughout its history. Sacrifices were of both a cereal and an animal variety, but the consummation of the sacrifice by fire was the key feature. Also in sacrifices in India a fermented juice called *soma* (also the name of the god) was enjoyed. In Iranian religion the fermented juice of the *haoma* plant was employed in various ways, including its use for inducing intoxication. The practice must have been very widespread at the time of Zoroaster, since he upbraided those who drank the juice. He called upon the good god to strike down the practice of drunkenness, which, he said, the priests and the rulers encouraged. In these and in other ways the religions of the Aryans in India and in Iran were similar, having a common source within a historic people.

Yet the religions that ultimately developed in India and Iran were not similar. In fact, they are highly divergent. Hinduism, for example, in one of its major strands, emphasized asceticism. The world was viewed as *maya,* or illusion. The religious person was encouraged to withdraw from the world in order to concentrate on saving his soul. Zoroastrianism, however, stresses engagement in and with the world. The world is the battleground in which the issues of good and evil are fought out and the believer is encouraged to take the side of the good and to seek actively to overcome the evil.

Hinduism, in the main, never considered itself a religion for all men. In part this was due to the restricting idea of caste, the hereditary social arrangement by which the Hindus lived. Zoroaster, however, believed that his religion was superior to all others. He held it to be universally applicable. For a time, especially through early missionary efforts, Zoroastrianism did succeed in winning many thousands of converts. Not having a caste system as a part of its doctrine, it could appeal to a large audience. In time, however, its universalism was lost and its missionary efforts dried up. The onslaught of the Arabs in the seventh century A.D., along with other factors, brought about its decline. A further review of later Hinduism and Zoroastrianism will show their dissimilarities.

Living religions commonly have an influence beyond their memberships. This is true of Zoroastrianism. It influenced the thought of cultured Greeks and Romans. Knowledge of the thought of Zoroaster is said to have come into Europe, perhaps in the sixth century B.C., through Hostanes, the Archimagus, who went with Xerxes in his expedition against Greece. Probably such Greek thinkers as Plato, Aristotle, and Theopompus were acquainted with some aspects of Iranian religion. Hermippus in the third century B.C. indicates that the writings of the founder of Zoroastrianism contained not less than 120,000 verses. At the time of the Christian era, various references were made to purported works of Zoroaster by such notables as Pliny, Pausanias, Dio Chrysostom, Strabo, and Nicolaus of Damascus. Clement of Alexandria, a leading Christian theologian of the third century A.D., shows an awareness of its scriptures. The Gnostics, who claimed to have superior knowledge of spiritual matters, also were attracted to the rich cosmological references contained in Zoroastrianism. Eusebius, the Christian bishop of Palestine and a noted church historian, indicated that in the third century there had been collected a set of the sacred scriptures of Zoroastrianism. These and other references show that the religion was known beyond the borders of Iran.

It is especially interesting to Jews, Christians, and Muslims to note also that Zoroastrianism is referred to in the Old Testament, although the religion is not mentioned by name. The kings of ancient Iran were Zoroastrians and they are mentioned in eight books of the Old Testament, usually in a commendatory way. Cyrus, for example, is mentioned in Isa. 45:1 as Yahweh's own messiah, a term that later came to be identified with Jesus. Again, Cyrus, the Zoroastrian king, is said by Yahweh to be his shepherd.

Earlier it was said that the wise men who came to see the infant Jesus may well have been priests of Zoroastrianism (Matt. 2:1).

Scholars are not of one mind when it comes to understanding the manner in which Zoroastrian ideas influenced the religious thought of Judaism and Christianity. Any influence that would have been made upon Islam would have been through Judaism and Christianity, since Islam in certain aspects is a direct outgrowth of these religions. It is suggested, for instance, that the concept of Satan in Judaism was introduced after the Babylonian exile in 586 B.C. Prior to that time everything in creation, including both good and evil, was attributed to Yahweh. This view is also found in the perspective of the Isaiah of the exile. But following that time the concept of Satan is introduced as a means of separating responsibility for good and evil. Yahweh is the creator of good; Satan is the creator of evil. The shift in assigning responsibility is made very clear in two passages of the Old Testament which attempt to account for the same events. In II Sam., ch. 24, it is stated that Yahweh moved David to number the people and then killed seventy thousand of them by a pestilence. This was a punishment for David's sin. But in I Chron., ch. 24, the story is changed. This later account, written after the exile, is largely the same as the earlier one. The chief difference is that the census of the people is suggested not by Yahweh, but by Satan. This theme of the duality of the ultimate creative forces in the universe, a principal Zoroastrian contribution, is found in many instances and forms throughout Western civilization during many centuries of poetry, religion, and philosophy.

Zoroastrianism also contributed other ideas to Judaism and Christianity. The notion that the dead will be physically resurrected was not found in early Judaism, although after the exile it became a standard view. Obviously this idea formed a foundation for the doctrine of the physical resurrection of Jesus and for all later acceptance of the fate of the person. The idea that there will be a final, great judgment in which persons will be evaluated for their earthly conduct is a teaching of Zoroastrianism. The peopling of the atmosphere with evil spirits and their countermanding guardian angels originated with the Iranian religion. The idea that a divine savior, a messiah, would come at a future time in human history to redeem the righteous is a key teaching of Zoroastrianism. The notion of the afterlife as a highly personal existence of ideal qualities was a further contribution. It is interesting to note that Jesus, in speaking to the thief on the cross, said that they would be together in paradise. The very word "paradise" (Luke 23:43), although it is Greek, probably was derived etymologically from *pairidaeza* in Avestan, the language of ancient Persia.

Modern anthropologists have warned that the nature of cross-cultural influences is not always easy to determine. Influences may be in only one direction, as in this case from Zoroastrianism to Judaism and Christianity (and later into Islam). Most of those who have looked into the matter have come to that conclusion. But there are at least two other possibilities. The influence may have been in the opposite direction, that is, from Judaism and Christianity to Zoroastrianism. That is a theoretical possibility, though hardly a probability. The other alternative is that the several religions developed similar doctrines independently. Perhaps more can be said for this alternative, but not enough to make it practical.

Like the founders of the other living religions, Zoroaster has been much misunderstood by those who lived after him. Perhaps the one reference familiar to most Western intellectuals regarding the founder of Zoroastrianism comes from the philosopher Friedrich Wilhelm Nietzsche (1844-1900), who often prefaced his views with the statement: "Thus spake Zarathushtra." The German philosopher's notions of the superman hardly have Zoroaster as a credible source. Similarly the original emphasis by Zoroaster upon a monotheistic vision of the universe was modified by his followers into a cosmic dualism of such rigidity that the Iranian master would probably not have understood. The idea, too, that Zoroaster primarily taught a kind of religious astrology, as became associated with the Magi, is surely not an adequate representation of the man and his teachings. These and other misinterpretations call for as objective a portrayal of his life as is possible from the earliest sources.

The basic source of information regarding the life of Zoroaster is the Avesta, the sacred scriptures of the religion. The language in which the Avesta is written is Avestan, a cognate language of Sanskrit. The Vedas of Hinduism were written in Sanskrit; Veda means knowledge. Avesta also means knowledge. The Avesta is essentially a miscellany and appears in its present form to be the remains of what must have been a much more extensive commentary. The scriptures are arranged into five main groups, each of varying value. The Yasna, meaning worship or sacrifice, undoubtedly is the earliest part. Within the Yasna are seventeen Gathas, or psalms (written in the Gathic dialect). These provide what is probably the most reliable information concerning Zoroaster's life. The Gathas are generally attributed to Zoroaster himself. The Visperad, meaning invocations to all the lords, is a liturgical book which is used in worship. The Vendidad, meaning the law against the demons, is basically a set of ceremonial instructions for the priests, although it also contains materials of historical, eschatological, and cosmological nature. Of lesser importance are the Yashts and the Khorda-Avesta. The Yashts, meaning worship hymns, contain poetry and invocations to angels. The Khorda-Avesta, meaning little Avesta, is a devotional work used by all Zoroastrians in their daily religious life. So it is mainly to the Gathas within the Yasna to which the biographer of Zoroaster must look.

The dates of Zoroaster's birth and death are usually given by scholars as 660 and 583 B.C. But other dates also have been suggested. Such classical writers as Xanthus, Pliny, Plato, and Plutarch say that he lived much earlier, from 6000 to 1000 B.C. Today there is little critical support for such views. Modern scholars, however, have placed him in various periods from 1200 to 800 B.C. Zoroastrians traditionally date their founder 258 years before Alexander. This probably refers to 330 B.C., the time of the death of Darius III, the sacking of Persepolis, and the fall of the Achaemenian empire to Alexander's armies. This would place Zoroaster at 588 B.C., referring not to his birth, but to the time when Zoroaster converted King Vishtaspa. At the time of the king's conversion, Zoroaster, it is said, was forty years of age. Such reasoning would date Zoroaster from 628 to 551 B.C.

The place of his birth is not clearly known. It is generally agreed that the locus of his preaching was Chorasmia, which today comprises the area of Iranian Khorasan, Western Afghanistan, and the Turkmen Republic of the Soviet Union. But Zoroaster probably was not born in that area, since he complains that he was persecuted in his homeland and apparently went elsewhere to find success. The Avesta contains only one geographic reference and that is to a suburb of present-day Teheran. It is possible that he was born in Amui, or Amvi, in the district of Urumiah in Media.

Like the birth of the founders of the other living religions, Zoroaster's birth was said to have been preceded by various supernatural events. It is said, for example, that his birth was foretold some three thousand years previously, and another account says it was only three hundred years. It is said, moreover, that Ahura Mazda, the source of goodness, transmitted his glory to the mother of Zoroaster and that the glory came down from the endless light and mingled with her. She was fifteen years old at the time. The tradition suggests a virgin birth for Zoroaster, with Ahura Mazda as the putative father. At any rate, the mother's family was hard put to explain the event and saw in it signs of witchcraft.

Tradition says that Zoroaster's father was Pourushaspa, a learned and pious man who was a member of the warrior clan of Spitama, related to a royal family. His mother was Dughdhova, also a learned and pious person of royal lineage. This couple had five sons; Zoroaster was the third. Zoroaster's birth was special. Even while the child was in his mother's womb he glowed with a spiritual light and the mother also was encompassed with a glow that was recognized by others. Instead of crying at his birth as newborn infants do, Zoroaster, even according to the Roman writer Pliny Secondus (A.D. 23-79), laughed outright.

Zoroaster's real name was probably Zarathushtra. Zoroaster is chiefly the name by which he is known in the West. But the exact meaning of Zarathushtra is not clear. The last part of the name, *ushtra,* means camel and the suggestion is made that the full name means the possessor of old or yellow-colored camels. Other suggestions are that the name means one whose camels are old and one who plows with camels. Probably the name was derived from a landowner who had camels as beasts of burden. His teachings reflect an essentially rural setting. But another tradition says that the name Zarathushtra connotes a high priest; and yet another proposal says that the title means "he of the golden light." The various founders of religions often are given honorific titles by their followers which in some instances have become the titles of the religions themselves. Probably the best that can be said is that the name has something to do with camels.

Very little is known about Zoroaster's early life. Probably, according to custom, he was given a tutor. From his earliest years Zoroaster showed remarkable intellectual ability. The scriptures say that at a time when other children were terrified by the silliness of their speech, Zoroaster was noted for his powerful intellect, his cautiousness in expressing himself, and the sagacity of his responses to questions.

At the age of fifteen, the youthful Zoroaster was given the *kusti*, or sacred thread. This was a part of the ceremony that leads the initiate into manhood, similar to the rite in Hinduism previously mentioned. It also had implications regarding the religious commitment of the initiate. But in Iran there was no caste aspect to the initiation. By taking the thread, Zoroaster was symbolizing his introduction into adult responsibility and also expressing his desire to devote himself to religious questions. At this time in his life he showed deep compassion toward all living things. The aged were a special concern to him, but he also sought to feed distressed cattle in time of famine. He continued to be concerned about the meaning of the inherited Iranian religion and the problems of the society of his times.

Some interpreters of Zoroastrianism say that the founder took leave of his family and at fifteen retired to the thick of the wilderness to contemplate. But the scriptures say clearly that when he became twenty years of age he left his parents in order to devote himself to religion. Apparently his parents resisted this decision.

Practically nothing is known about the private life of Zoroaster prior to his leaving home. Seemingly he was married. As was the custom, his father chose the bride, although Zoroaster wanted first to see her and approve of her. But the name of his bride is not known and no references are made in the Avesta to her. It seems clear, however, that when Zoroaster left his parents he also left his wife so that he might pursue what to him was a higher calling.

The next ten years were spent by Zoroaster in preparation for his first confrontation with Ahura Mazda. Where he went in the ten years is not known. It is said that for seven of these years he remained silent. Greek sources indicate that he lived in a cave. Other accounts say that he lived in the wilderness or perhaps in desert places. Assumedly he was solitarily concentrating on questions of an ethical and religious nature. One source says that he retired from ordinary life because he could not find even one just man, let alone two, or three. It also is said that in the ten years of his retirement from the world that he eagerly sought out others in order to ask of them what their views were on life's deepest questions. He even addressed throngs of people in an inquiring spirit. On one of these occasions, for example, he asked what the people considered to be the most favorable actions that would redound to the good of the soul. He was told that he should nourish the poor, give fodder to cattle, bring firewood to the fire, pour *haoma* juice into water, and worship many *daevas*. Zoroaster was open-minded. He agreed that the first four of these proposals were commendable. He balked, however, at the last, believing that it was improper to worship demons.

At the age of thirty, Zoroaster received his life-shaking and life-directing call from Ahura Mazda. As is usual, the period of deprivation, foreboding, and withdrawal led to an event of illumination, joy, and a sense of holy purpose. Realizing that by himself he was unable to secure the ultimate meaning of life, Zoroaster prayed that he might be able to come into the very presence of god. There he expected to have his life's longings satisfied. He believed that in one moment the mystery of life would be revealed. So he prayed, indicating the kinds of questions that he would ask of Ahura Mazda. Who was the first generator and father of Asha, the god of truth? Who determined the path of the sun and the stars? Who has ordained that the moon shall wax and wane? Who upheld the earth beneath and kept the heavens above from falling? Who created water and plants? Who yoked the two horses to the wind and clouds? Who is the creator of Vohu Manah, the embodiment of the good mind? Who created light and darkness? Who made sleeping and waking? Who created morning, noon, and night, that remind a man of his duty? These were the questions to which Zoroaster sought answers from Ahura Mazda.

According to tradition, Zoroaster was taken into the presence of Ahura Mazda in a striking manner. When the appropriate time had come, Vohu Manah, an archangel who personified the good mind, appeared to Zoroaster as he was on the bank of the river Daitya, near his home. Vohu Manah appeared as a figure nine times as large as a man. Vohu Manah asked Zoroaster a number of questions that tested his desire to be taken into the presence of Ahura Mazda. When the archangel was satisfied, he asked Zoroaster to lay aside the form of his material body and to proceed as a spirit-being to the heights where Ahura Mazda could be found. Ahura Mazda was described as being the supreme being of the universe who at the time was holding court along with his angels. Zoroaster, then, found himself in the presence of Ahura Mazda. He noted, as an aside, that in the heavenly abode he no longer saw his own shadow and accounted for this phenomenon on the grounds that the brilliant light cast everywhere about him by the angels eliminated all shadows.

What actually transpired between Zoroaster and Ahura Mazda is left largely to the imagination. Tradition does not record precisely what answers Zoroaster got to his questions. It is clear that the god did commend Zoroaster as the only one who had hearkened to his enunciations. Ahura Mazda had selected Zoroaster to be his holy prophet, and Zoroaster recognized Ahura Mazda as a beneficent and wise lord. He also declared that he knew that the deity was responsible for the moral law; he recompenses words and deeds. Ahura Mazda is ultimately responsible for returning evil for evil and good for good.

Although the exact details of the confrontation between Zoroaster and Ahura Mazda are not known, the effects of the experience are. Zoroaster concluded then, and held to the belief through his whole life, that he had been chosen by god to be his prophet. As a prophet, Zoroaster felt that he was charged with the duty to bring to all people the new faith that he had received. In this regard his prophetic message was not restricted to a particular people, such as the Iranians. It was universal in scope. The religion that originated out of Zoroaster's direct experience with Ahura Mazda, moreover, was not merely one religion among others. It was the one, true faith. Its claims were to be pressed upon all persons. By the message received from the deity he would convert all men, turning even the robber horde into the greatest people of righteousness. He prayed that he might bring about a great spiritual renovation, making the world progressive.

The first conference was followed by others. One account says that during the next ten years he had seven further meetings with Ahura Mazda. Another version says that in the next eight years he met with each of the six principal archangels. In each of these visionary meetings the teachings were further elucidated. Zoroaster was reconfirmed as the one, true prophet of Ahura Mazda. Zoroaster further dedicated himself as god's anointed spokesman. He declared that he brought the life of his own body and the choiceness of good thought, action, and speech as an offering to Ahura Mazda.

Amazingly, as Zoroaster went about the countryside of his own region for a period of about ten years, he was unable to make a single convert. It is hard to know why. Apparently he was opposed by all. His family was unresponsive. His friends shunned his message. As he wandered about he was rejected by those to whom he preached. In part his rejection may be understood on the grounds that he strongly condemned the religion that was popular in his time. Earlier he had opposed the worship of demons. This ran counter to the practices of large numbers of people. Again, he spoke against the use of *haoma,* the intoxicant employed in sacrificial ceremonies. *Haoma* was not only well accepted but also widely used. The intoxicated person, so the reasoning went, found himself in an extraordinary state. Such states are often interpreted to be a sign of divine possession. But Zoroaster rejected this conception and the resulting practices. He taught that it hindered one's relation with the divine. Also, with the typical forcefulness of a severe prophet, Zoroaster did not always present himself and his ideas in a winsome manner. He was primarily a man of deep and abiding convictions. He allowed no compromise with the teachings that he held to be divinely inspired. He called upon his hearers for complete acceptance and total obedience to the truths that had been revealed by Ahura Mazda.

So in this spirit he readily denounced those who opposed him. He declared that there would be woe to the end of their lives for any who would not practice his message as he conceived it and uttered it.

On the other hand, Zoroaster's religion was an advance over what was currently popular. For one thing, he taught the existence of a single, all-powerful, all-seeing, and benevolent deity. The popular religion of his time taught polytheism—the belief that there are many gods. His monotheism brought a more rational, comprehensive, and appealing view of the universe and man's place in it. Also, to mention only one other attractive feature of his religion, he magnified the significance of the individual in the important sphere of ethics. To Zoroaster the person possesses so-called free will. He is responsible for his actions. His actions truly count for good *or* evil. Zoroaster appealed to those who heard him to take a highly personal responsibility for the rejection of evil in their lives and for the encouragement of good. Such a view increased the worth of the person. It placed the individual in an ethical context in which he assuredly had a key role to play.

Yet the prophet who preached a universal message of the transcendent Ahura Mazda, which was intended to convert the wicked and purify the whole of life, was rejected by relatives, friends, and foes for ten years. Once, in wintertime, he lamented that he was unable to find shelter for himself and his two horses shivering in the cold. He grew despondent. Tradition says that he was also tempted in this period by the evil divinity, Angra Mainyu, who came to the prophet with promises of worldly success, calling on him to renounce the religion given him by Ahura Mazda. But Zoroaster did not relent. By prayer he dispelled the evil god and called to Ahura Mazda for aid. In his prayer he asked to what land he should flee, indicating that he was far from a success in his home country. He asked how he might please Ahura Mazda. He declared that he had few cattle and few kinfolk. Thus he called to Ahura Mazda for such support as a friend gives to a friend. On another occasion he asked that the god tell him whether he was on the right track and whether he would really receive the promise of reward, this reward being the acquisition of ten mares, a stallion and a camel, along with the future gift of welfare and immortality. But through it all Zoroaster maintained his ultimate faith in Ahura Mazda. He did not turn away from the course that he had chosen.

At the end of the ten-year period, however, he did make a convert. It happened to be his cousin Maidhynimaonha. Nothing is known about his cousin, although he must have been well received by his mentor.

Having no success in Media, his home country, Zoroaster decided to travel westward to Bactria. It is said that he developed a plan whereby he would aim to convert a ruler rather than continue trying to make converts of the common people. He reasoned that a converted ruler would immediately bring acceptance of his religion by the multitudes. It took time, but Zoroaster finally succeeded in gaining access to the court of an Aryan prince in Bactria. The prince's name is usually given as Vishtaspa, although sometimes it is given as Hystaspes. Some think that Vishtaspa was the father of Darius, but this is not sure.

Vishtaspa's conversion was not easy. It took two years. It also ran into fierce opposition from a group of dominating priests, the Karpans. They held the king in strict control, requiring his acquiescence to complicated animal sacrifices. They held him dependent upon their magic rites which were said to control demonic spirits, make the crops grow, and even thwart the invasions of the Turanians, a band of nomads in the north. Vishtaspa had much to give up, if he were to become a Zoroastrian. At one point, tradition says, the Karpans succeeded in having Zoroaster committed to prison. But ultimately Zoroaster prevailed. Aside from the appeal of his message, two other elements are said to have figured in the king's conversion. One was the loyal support of the king's wife, Hutaosa, who early saw the value in the new religion and urged her husband to adopt it. The other element was the miracle that Zoroaster performed when he healed the king's favorite black horse.

Vishtaspa became a Zoroastrian. As might have been expected, the king's decision profoundly affected the members of his family and court. The king's brother, Zain, was converted. The king's courageous son, Isfendir, also became a follower. Also in the court were two brothers: Frashaoshtra and Jamnaspa. They were nobles who were greatly trusted by Vishtaspa. Frashaoshtra gave his daughter, Huovi, to Zoroaster as a bride. Jamnaspa himself married Pourucista, Zoroaster's daughter by his first marriage. Obviously these two marriages greatly increased Zoroaster's prestige and power in the kingdom.

As was said earlier, little is known of the family life of Zoroaster. The Avesta declares that he had three wives, all three of whom survived him. Again it is stated that he had three sons and three daughters. Two of the sons were named Auvartad-Nar and Khursed-Chihar. The latter was a warrior who was a commander in the army of one of the sons of Vishtaspa. At the marriage of his daughter Pourucista, Zoroaster composed a bridal hymn which forms a chapter of the Yasna, a part of the sacred scriptures of Zoroastrianism.

Vishtaspa, with Zoroaster at his side, made the new religion current in his realm. It is said that the royal sons accepted the religion as a yoke and propagated the new faith in their travels about Asia Minor and even into India.

Not much is known about the last twenty years of Zoroaster's life. Under the influence of Vishtaspa the faith was more widely accepted. Zoroaster continued to be spiritual adviser to the king, leading him in the strengthening of his faith. But Zoroaster also was a key adviser in mundane matters. The requirements of statecraft at that time involved the use of violence. The Turanians, for example, were not content to leave Vishtaspa's kingdom alone. They made regular raids and during Zoroaster's last twenty years they engaged in two major wars with Vishtaspa. The king's son, Isfendir, showed unusual bravery and skill in military leadership in the first of these wars. In this and other military activities Zoroaster gave his consent and even justified the use of violence in the name of Ahura Mazda. The acceptance of violence was further developed in the later writings of the religion.

The exact circumstances of the death of Zoroaster are not known. In a document written at least a thousand years later, a part of the noncanonical literature of the religion, it is said that he was slain in the second great war against the Turanians. According to this account, Zoroaster was officiating at the fire-altar in the city of Balkh when one of the Turanians surprised him and slew him. He was seventy-seven years old at his death.

In life Zoroaster was a complex personality. He could be dominatingly certain of his convictions. Yet before the conversion of Vishtaspa, he was subject to doubts. He became a person who held significant power, politically and religiously, though in his lifetime he often expressed the virtues of humility and openness. He founded a religion based on ethical considerations beyond what was known prior to his time. Yet he could justify the use of violence and called for divine support in the waging of war.

After Zoroaster died, however, he was venerated. His disciples thought that his life was a clear testimony to his having been chosen by Ahura Mazda as a prophet who had received divine revelation. In his personal life he was said to have been morally superior, even perfect. They said that he was the head of the two-footed race, the wisest of all beings in the perfection of his holiness, and the only one who could daunt evil. He was said to have excelled in three ways: by being incomparable among mankind in his love of righteousness, his understanding of the means of defeating evil, and in his ability to teach his fellowman. In fact, he later was declared a divinity who was entitled to be worshiped along with Ahura Mazda. His preexistence became a feature of the faith. By this time, of course, the religion had found a firm footing, having spread as the nation of Iran spread.

For a period of about one hundred years (583-480 B.C.), Iran was stimulated in part by the new religion. Nationalism as an emotional cause was revived. The Iranians in this period conquered their powerful neighbor on the west, Babylonia, in 539 B.C. Iran, or Persia as it was known then, became a great power. Darius, the king, sought to press on into Europe, but was defeated by Greek forces at Salamis in one of the most decisive battles in history. By the middle of the fourth century B.C., however, Greek forces under the leadership of Alexander roundly defeated the Iranians. Later the Parthians also conquered the Iranians. Zoroastrianism now reverted to polytheism and fire worship as these were found in the religion of Mithraism. Mithra in Iranian mythology is the god of light and truth, later of the sun. In A.D. 226, however, Ardeshiri, a devout Zoroastrian, managed to reestablish the country's independence. He conquered neighboring Armenia and established the Sassanian dynasty. Zoroastrianism was secure in its native land from that time to the conquest by the Arabs, who were inspired by Islam.

The religion that Zoroaster taught had a number of features. Fundamental to the whole religion is the teaching regarding Ahura Mazda. Ahura means god and is similar to the Vedic designation of *asura,* which also means lord or god. Mazda means either the wise or the full of light. In some instances the deity is referred to as Mazda Ahura, meaning wise lord. Scholars say that there are ties between Ahura Mazda and Varuna within early Hinduism. Both were the gods of the physical and moral order of things. Certainly Ahura Mazda was not an invention of Zoroaster. The deity was a part of the long cultural tradition of Iran. But Zoroaster did reconceptualize the belief in Ahura Mazda, making the god the single, supreme deity of the universe. Zoroastrianism, then, teaches monotheism, the idea of a single and in this case a personal god. Not only did Zoroaster purify and exalt Ahura Mazda, he also ethicized the god. This means that Ahura Mazda became the ultimately supreme moral ground for the universe. A composite list of attributes of Ahura Mazda can be gleaned from the

Gathas, the part of the Avesta that probably was written by Zoroaster himself: greatest, most mighty, creator, all-seeing, friendly, most bountiful spirit, beneficent, father of justice and right, all-knowing, and father of the good mind (Vohu Manah). In later Zoroastrianism, Ahura Mazda was abbreviated to Auharmazd or Ormazd.

Zoroastrianism is perhaps distinctive among the living religions in that it openly acknowledges the existence of an evil deity who is ever competitive with Ahura Mazda. This god is Angra Mainyu. He is said to have existed from the beginning of time, is operative in human affairs and in the universe, and will finally be defeated by Ahura Mazda only at the end of time. Ahriman is the name for Angra Mainyu used in later Zoroastrian writings. Thus Zoroastrianism teaches a kind of ultimate dualism that is personified by Ahura Mazda and Angra Mainyu. But it is a qualified dualism. Angra Mainyu is a real power and a force for persons to resist. He is the enemy. But he is not supreme. The universe always and ultimately is in the control of Ahura Mazda. The final victory in human history will be that of Ahura Mazda. Zoroastrianism, therefore, may be claimed to be a monotheistic religion, for it asserts a belief in one, supreme, personal god.

Ahura Mazda and Angra Mainyu each have the support of spiritual beings who are aligned with them, doing their wishes. Those associated with Ahura Mazda are called *spenta mainyus*, or bountiful spirits. At least as often in the Gathas they are called *spenishta mainyus*, or most bountiful spirits. Some of these spirits are: Asha—truth, righteousness, order, justice; Armaiti—piety, love; Vohu Manah—good mind, disposition, thought; Kshathra—kingdom, power, dominion; Ameretat—immortality, eternal life; and Haurvatat—welfare, health, wholeness. The exact nature of the *spenta mainyus* is difficult to fathom. They have been treated in various ways in the history of the religion. They are said to be archangels who serve Ahura Mazda as his messengers and instruments of his will. Usually they are distinguished from Ahura Mazda and enjoy their own existence as personal beings. At other times, however, they are conceived as attributes of Ahura Mazda and not having separate existences. Another way of thinking about them makes them into the personification of common virtues that are a part of the religion and were inherited by Zoroaster from times that preceded him.

Angra Mainyu also has his supporting spirits. They are generally called *daevas*, or demons. It is said that there are countless demons acting as messengers and instruments of Angra Mainyu. They represent such evils as: false speech, winter, harlotry, arrogance, wrath, hunger, thirst, drought, and greed. *Daeva* through a long and varied history became the English word "devil."

The ethical teachings of Zoroastrianism rest upon the idea that all life is a constant battlefield between good and evil. The ultimate basis for the ethics lies in the cosmic battles between Ahura Mazda and Angra Mainyu, along with their supporting spirits of good and evil. But for the individual the conflict of good and evil is expressed within the soul. The believer is one who truly adheres to the good and who resists evil. A doctrine of human freedom is assumed, for without some form of genuine freedom the person could not actually decide for the good. The believer also is assumed to be in a genuine battle against evil to the extent that what he does actually counts toward the ultimate defeat of Angra Mainyu. He is called upon to be a deliverer of himself and others from the grip of demonic forces. Just what is the content of the good and the evil is not specified. The ethics of Zoroastrianism is not codified. In the main, the good person is he who accepts the supremacy of Ahura Mazda. Such acceptance is a recognition of the true religion. Those who are not good are those who do not follow the true religion, who fail to worship Ahura Mazda, and who are influenced by the evil forces or demons who are ultimately personified by Angra Mainyu. But practically speaking, Zoroaster did provide a number of specific injunctions. He taught that he who relieves the plight of the

poor makes Ahura Mazda king. The good man is not an ascetic; he participates in constructive work. Zoroaster identified
the good man as the farmer who sows the seed for his grain,
roots out weeds, cares for his cattle (especially cows), and in
general develops his natural resources. The ideal Zoroastrian
is a thrifty husbandman. Declared Zoroaster: he who sows the
most corn, grass and fruit, sows righteousness.

Zoroaster also taught that there is an absolute difference between the truth and the lie. He avoided moral ambiguities.
That which is true is clearly true. It is grounded in the nature
of things and is self-evident. A highly developed, rational system of ethics is not found in the religion. The virtues are inherently evident to the good man.

Attitudes and practices toward good people and evil ones
are firmly fixed in the religion. The believer is to do good to
those who are good. Zoroaster taught that whether one has a
little or a lot he should show love toward the righteous. When
in conflict with a good person, he said, one should proceed
with the approval of friends. But the believer is under no obligation to deal with his enemies with kindness. The believer
should give ill treatment to the evil. He should resist them,
even with a weapon, although enemies should fight fairly.

Zoroastrianism is not characterized by a highly complicated
ritualism. In its early stages it purified the preceding religion
of the worship of demons, as was seen earlier. It also abolished many superstitious practices, as interpreted by Zoroaster,
although later Zoroastrianism was associated with magical activities. At times Zoroastrians are said to be fire worshipers.
The worship of fire was a key element in the religion inherited
by Zoroaster; but it is clear that Zoroaster did not worship fire.
For him and for later followers, even those of the present, fire
represented a religious symbol. Ahura Mazda is spoken of as
light, fire, and other attributes of illumination. Thus Zoroastrians in making fire a central part of their worship are engaged in a symbolic acknowledgment of the lordship of
Ahura Mazda. The scriptures say that it is necessary to keep

the fireplace properly and to keep watch that the fire never goes out, also to see that nothing impure or polluted shall touch the fire.

Zoroastrians believe that at death, after the soul has escaped, the body should not contaminate fire, air, water, or earth. They refrain, therefore, from burying their dead in the earth or in water, neither do they practice cremation. The ceremonies surrounding the death of a person are complex, but when they are finished the body is taken to a Tower of Silence. Such a tower is placed on a hill and is uncovered. There the body is left, after prayers and a period of meditation, exposed and uncovered. Flesh-eating birds proceed to devour the corpse. The deceased's clothes and remaining bones are left to the eroding elements. In Bombay, however, the bodies are put into a well near the main tower where they disintegrate in an acid solution.

Zoroastrianism also teaches a distinctive view of the afterlife. Clearly the good ultimately will triumph over the evil. At the end of time a general resurrection will take place. This will be followed by a great day of judgment in which good persons and evil ones will be separated. All will go through an ordeal of fire and molten lead. The good will find that the ordeal is harmless to them, but the evil ones will truly suffer. In another version of what takes place at death, Zoroastrianism says that each individual comes to the Bridge of the Separator, the Chinvat Bridge, which spans the abyss of hell. Beyond the bridge lies paradise. At the bridge a list of the good and the evil deeds is recalled. If the good ones predominate, the person is waved by a hand to the farther shore. If evil deeds predominate, the hand points to the abyss of hell. Paradise, or heaven, is described in the most positive terms. It is the abode where the sun shines forever and people are eternally happy. Hell consists of agelong misery and punishment. It is characterized by darkness, foul food, and woeful words. Although the eschatology, or doctrine of last things, in Zoroastrianism is complex and not always consistent, it comprises a significant part of the religion. A certain feature of the thought has survived to this day in some of the other living religions, notably in Judaism, in Christianity, and in Islam.

Zoroastrianism, a Middle Eastern religion, founded by Zoroaster many centuries ago, remains, despite its relatively small membership, a significant shaper of the course of human culture.

8
JESUS
AND
CHRISTIANITY

To Western eyes, the statement that Jesus was the founder of Christianity comes as no surprise. For some, a review of the life of the founder of this religion may seem to be a thankless, trite, and familiar task. But for others, such a review may provide fresh insights regarding a person well known to them in name only.

With less knowledge of the lives of the founders of other living religions, the Western reader may be able to bring a certain detachment to his reading. The stories of the lives of Vardhamana, Gautama, Nanak, Confucius, and Lao-tzu may have a distant ring about them. Considerable objectivity may be brought to them. They stand outside the realm of our personal commitment. But Jesus is another matter. For many readers Jesus is a name they revere. So, whatever is said about him is taken as a matter of deep personal concern. For committed persons, he is not merely a man who lived and died in an ancient time and in a distant place. He is for them the central fact of human existence. This attitude leads to various complications in telling his life's story. Assumptions do color facts. No one ever is completely objective. Emotional stances that are derived from past experience and that have formed judgments regarding what is real and valuable influence all present evaluations and actions.

Past experience is always partial experience. The Christian, like the believers in the other religions, is necessarily born in a particular time and place; thus, his culture is only a slice of historical culture. Usually he is born into a tradition, whatever it may be. In this regard Christianity is an astonishingly rich and diverse religion. It is not one tradition, but many. The various churches and sects that constitute it naturally influence the perceptions regarding Jesus of those who are their members.

Those who stand outside the Christian tradition, especially in the West, have their own special problems in evaluating the life of Jesus. Jews, for example, have a commitment to Judaism, a religion that bears its own heritage of diverse interpretations. For those who claim no allegiance to Christianity or to any other formal religion, the problem is different, but a problem, nevertheless. Such a person's attitudes are formed by what he is against, just as the committed Christian's attitudes are formed by what he is for. Then, too, everyone in the West in subtle and pervasive ways is the inheritor of a cultural tradition in which Christianity has been one of the chief contributors. Seemingly, one cannot avoid being partial and even biased.

Yet it must be said that the situation which confronts the Western evaluator of the life of Jesus is not dissimilar to that which confronts persons everywhere in connection with any religion. The believer in one of the non-Christian religions will find that his commitment colors what he deems to be the facts of his religion. His commitment will also free him for certain kinds of evaluations regarding other religions.

The traditions and organizations of other world religions show a richness and variety similar to that of Christianity. All religions are historically complex, some more than others. No believer in any religion faces a religious homogeneity. Every religion has its churches and sects. One can only be an inheritor of some part of a total religion. Therefore, the problems of all believers in connection with their own religions and those of others remain rather much the same.

Within the living religions there are two sequences of interdependency that are worthy of note. In India, Hinduism was the mothering religion, and Jainism, Buddhism, and possibly

Sikhism can be considered its offspring. Sikhism may be a doubtful case in that it arose as an effort to synthesize two existing religions: Hinduism and Islam. In a sense it may be claimed as a half brother to Jainism and Buddhism. Yet it does have many features that were derived from Hinduism as a parent religion. In China, both Confucianism and Taoism drew upon the same cultural inheritance. Yet it is not possible to claim that one built upon the other or that they bear a close relationship to each other.

A closer sequence in the interdependency of religions occurs in the Middle East. It consists of the mothering religion of Judaism and its related religions of Christianity and Islam. Neither Christianity nor Islam can be adequately understood, historically, theologically, organizationally, or in any other way, except by reference to Judaism.

Both Christianity and Islam, moreover, recognize the sacredness of the scriptures of Judaism, those writings which Christians call the Old Testament and which they claim for their own traditions. While Christianity and Islam broke away from Judaism and at times in their histories were sharply opposed to Judaism, they have never repudiated its sacred writings. In this regard the second sequence differs from the first. While Jainism and Buddhism, and possibly Sikhism, are inextricably bound historically and otherwise to Hinduism, they early repudiated any dependency upon the Vedas, the sacred writings of Hinduism. These religions rejected the authority of the Vedas, believing that the teachings of their religions were in opposition to the teachings of the Vedas.

Christianity originated in the Middle East, as did Zoroastrianism, Judaism, and Islam. For a variety of reasons the Middle East has been termed a fertile crescent. The four religions that originated there and that have survived to become important determiners of human history represent a part of that fertility.

Christianity is one of the few religions that has become universal in scope. Several of the living religions have had universal intent. Zoroaster believed that the religion which he founded was for all men, and that it was superior to all other religions. Similarly there is a strain within Confucianism which claims universal validity. In fact, all religions are regarded by at least some of their members to be the final or most authoritative of all religious forms. Religion seemingly involves that kind of emotional commitment.

Christianity, along with Buddhism and Islam, has become international in its history. It is not evident that Gautama, the founder of Buddhism, initially was possessed of a worldwide vision for his faith. At one point he was concerned with the question as to whether the salvation he found was simply for himself or whether it was for others. He decided that it was for others as well. He did conduct what might be called missionary activities in large parts of India. But, due to a variety of circumstances, Buddhism was taken to other lands. In India, the land of its birth, the religion in time became virtually extinct. But Buddhism succeeded in becoming an international religion, being the faith of many millions throughout Asia and elsewhere. Islam, the subject of the next chapter, has also become an international religion.

It is probably more nearly correct to say that these religions are historically international than that they are universal. To say that they are universal seems to connote that they are found everywhere in the world. Such is hardly the case. But they are in fact international, that is, they are found within a relatively large number of nations, both historically and presently.

Christianity is an avowedly universal religion. It seeks to be the religion of all people. It does not restrict itself to a particular people or class or race. The factor of universalism is one of the key elements that marks Christianity as distinct from its parent religion, Judaism. Judaism in several senses also is an international religion. Through the various historical dispersals of the Jewish people, dating from Biblical times, Jews have been found in large numbers outside the land of the birth of the religion. They may be found today, in fact, in a large number of nations and in various parts of the world. In 1948, with the establishment of the independent state of

Israel, a new identification of Jews with their holy land was achieved, although several millions of Jews continue to live beyond Israel's boundaries. But Judaism largely remains the religion of a particular people, the Jews.

Christianity, however, succeeded in its universalizing tendencies shortly after the death of its founder. Many of the earliest Christians, and quite possibly Jesus himself, considered the new religion to be a reformation of the then existing Judaism. But others, notably Paul, adapted the new faith to other peoples. Two tendencies are apparent in the earliest Christianity. One was the Judaizing tendency which wished to see Christianity remain as a faithful expression of a revitalized Judaism. The other tendency is usually called the Hellenization of Christianity, by which is meant the effort to adapt the new religion to the non-Jewish world of the times.

In its historical development Christianity became the religion of large numbers of people in Africa, Asia, and elsewhere. It has remained present also in the Middle East, although it is clearly in a minority status in that region. But Christianity mainly developed in the West, in the various parts of Europe, including the Soviet Union, and in the Americas, both North and South. It is closely identified with Western civilization, participating in both its virtues and its defects. Western civilization in itself is enormously complex and its relationship with Christianity is rich and varied. Also, Christianity is not the only shaper of Western civilization. Influences of the cultures of Greece and Rome, along with other forces, provide significantly visible threads in the fabric of that civilization.

Christianity's missionary movement has been the chief means of its international expansion. The religion early assumed responsibility for bringing its message of salvation to all peoples. But the intent took the form of an organized effort that is unparalleled among the other religions. The missionary movement accounts in large measure for the success of the religion in Western history. The organized missionary work of the European and American churches in the recent centuries accounts for its extension to other parts of the world. The organization, financing, and motivation of this movement is probably distinctive in the history of world religions.

As a consequence, Christianity is certainly one of the larger religions in terms of membership. It is not possible to ascertain with a high degree of accuracy the memberships of the several religions, and the situation holds for Christianity as well. Yet at the present time various estimates indicate that there are several hundreds of millions of Christians, members of various churches and sects. It is claimed that Christianity is the most populous religion. Perhaps its membership totals half a billion. If so, this would place it well ahead of all the other living religions. Perhaps the sheer size of the religion also accounts in part for its tremendous diversity in beliefs, practical forms, and social organization.

Christianity is a relatively late religion. Only Islam and Sikhism followed it. No other religion came into being in that period that has lasted to become a currently prevalent faith. One might suppose that the later the religion, the more accurate and available the information would be regarding the life of the founder. But this is not necessarily the case.

The life of Jesus, the founder of Christianity, may be viewed appropriately against the backdrop of his time. He was first and foremost a Jew in his cultural inheritance and in his religious outlook. But he lived in a time and place where two powerful cultures influenced his world: the Greek and the Roman. The information about these two forces has filled many books; therefore, it is proper here only to provide sketches that are appropriate to an understanding of the life of Jesus.

In terms of government, Palestine was ruled by the Romans. In New Testament (the term for the sacred scriptures of Christianity) times, the Romans had extended their rule beyond the Mediterranean world, which was theirs, to the north as far as Great Britain, to Morocco to the south, and to Arabia to the east. Palestine had only recently come under their sway. The empire was held together by a Pax Romana which Augustus began. This was enforced by forts throughout the empire, and by over twenty-five military legions which were composed of about six thousand soldiers each. The empire, however, contributed more than occupation forces: there was a fine system of roads, an enforced public order, free sea travel, and the strengths of the Roman way of doing things. The empire was divided into regions or provinces. The imperial provinces were administered by procurators (called prefects until the time of Claudius), who were directly responsible to the emperor. A procurator held responsibility for all matters within his realm, including administration, political activities, and criminal trials. The responsibility for gathering taxes was given to companies of so-called publicans, although there were frequent abuses of the tax-gathering duties. The uniform system of coinage within the empire provided a common basis for commerce. Originally, Roman citizenship was closely restricted, but in time it was extended. Several references in the book of The Acts illustrate the advantages of limiting it. But the four basic accounts of the life of Jesus, the Gospels, are singularly silent about Roman administration, except for a few references in the account of the trial of Jesus before Pilate. This is not hard to understand when one realizes that the world of the Gospels is almost exclusively Jewish.

Herod the Great ruled Palestine at the time of Jesus' birth. At his death and according to his will, the land was divided among his three remaining sons. The three hurried to Rome, where the bequest was confirmed by Augustus Caesar. Archelaus was given Judea, Samaria, and Idumea. Herod Antipas was assigned Galilee and Perea (part of modern Jordan). Philip was given the region northeast of the Lake of Galilee (a part of modern Syria). Augustus, however, was not enthusiastic about Archelaus and placed some restraints upon his rule. His suspicions were borne out after nine years of Archelaus' rule, which was characterized by brutality and incompetence. As a result of serious charges brought to the emperor, Archelaus was banished to Gaul and his province was placed under another procurator.

Roman religion seems not to have been a significant force in the New Testament world. That religion had been influenced by Greek and other forms of thought and practice. The public cult of the Romans was well organized and extended throughout the empire. The Romans, however, did not look with favor on astrology, occult practices, and the mystery cults that had sprung up in various places. Some scholars have interpreted the Christianity of this period as being essentially a mystery cult that had to operate with great secrecy in order not to be crushed by the Romans. This view, however, seems hard to maintain. Paul, for example, does speak about mystery on a number of occasions, but his references seem to be to the profundity of some Christian doctrine concerning which reason is inadequate as a final determiner. In addition, the Gospels portray Jesus acting in the open; he preached to the multitudes, he healed the blind and infirm in the company of others, and so forth. The public charges that brought about his death were not that he practiced a secret religion. It would seem, then, that Roman religion had very little influence upon the religion of nascent Christianity.

Strangely enough, the most dominating foreign influence in Palestine at the time of Jesus was not Roman but Greek. Even the Romans in that part of the empire had been thoroughly Hellenized. The Greek influence originated with Alexander's conquest of the Middle East, dating from 334 to 323 B.C. Inspired by the Greece of the Golden Age, influenced by the teachings of Aristotle and others, imbued with the concepts of a rich literature, and possessed of an open-mindedness toward all subjects, Alexander the Great brought with his conquest a high civilization. At the time of Jesus, the Jews had to make some accommodation to the government imposed by the Romans. But their greatest challenge was the culture of the Greeks. Much of the history of earliest Christianity reveals the struggles within the church between those who viewed the new religion as primarily an extension of ancient Judaism and those who stood outside that tradition, such as Stephen and Paul, whose most deeply felt task was that of accommodating the new religion to the prevailing Hellenism. The book of The Acts (Acts 6:1-6) tells the story of the conflict in the church at Jerusalem between the Hebrews and the Hellenists. The Hebrew Christians represented a conservative kind of Judaism; they sought to maintain the importance of the Jewish law. The Hellenists, some of whom were Jews, were more progressive in their outlook, having been impressed with the appeal of Greek thought and life. Although the conflict can be found in various parts of the New Testament, notably in the writings of Paul to the early churches, the gradual ascendancy of the Hellenistic outlook and its final victory shaped Christianity as a new religion of universal intent rather than another variant within the historical context of a developing Judaism.

While early Christianity adapted itself to the thought forms of Hellenism to a great extent, it was not uncritical. Paul, for example, speaks against the prevailing philosophy of the times (I Cor. 2:6). This "wisdom" he refers to was probably Stoicism. This philosophy was founded by the Cypriot Zeno and was named from the fact that it was advocated from the *stoa*, or painted porch, of the *agora*, or marketplace, in Athens in the third century B.C. Stoicism taught that the individual should live the life of reason, with nothing to excess. The follower sought through self-discipline and ascetic practices to bring himself to a state of general apathy in which he would not be deeply concerned about good fortune or ill, sickness or health. Paul opposed this philosophy. To him the final meaning of life is secured not through reason, but by revelation. Jesus as the Christ was the central fact of human existence. The person should lead a wholesome life, devoted to god and to his fellowman. A pantheistic religion was rejected. The world ultimately would be redeemed through the agency of god, rather than destroyed through a final conflagration. On these and other points Paul, like the other Hellenists within early Christianity, was not ready to adapt the new-found faith to the features of Greek life and thought.

It is striking to note that the sacred scriptures of Christianity were written in a vernacular form of Greek. Many of the writers of the New Testament, if not all of them, were Jews and one might have supposed that they would have written in Hebrew, the language of the sacred scriptures of Judaism. But the entire collection of sacred writings was written in *koine,* or common Greek. This vernacular is characterized by simplified grammar, the widespread use of colloquial and idiomatic forms, and a coloring of Semitic features. Obviously the fact that the New Testament was written in *koine* Greek enabled it to be accepted and understood by many in the early church. It also enabled the writings of the new faith to be shared with very large numbers of people for generations to come.

The Jews of Jesus' time were troubled by two interrelated factors. First, they were anxious and divided regarding their own religion. Changing circumstances called for changing practices. How to be faithful to the traditions and yet maintain a vital faith constituted a dilemma for many. Second, they were mindful of the ever-present Roman rulers who irritated them, mostly by oppressive taxes. The Romans were a rather aloof people. Unlike the Greeks, they did not mingle with the people, seeking their views with sympathy and genuine interest. They were mostly content to let subject people, such as the Jews, maintain their own culture, institutions, and values. However, the Jews saw their taxes not only maintaining the Roman administration in Palestine but keeping the huge and costly empire elsewhere as well.

At this time the Romans began to rebuild several cities in Roman splendor. A few miles north of Nazareth, the home of Jesus, they began to rebuild Sepphoris, the largest city in Galilee. On the western bank of the Lake of Galilee they started a brand-new city, Tiberias, named by Herod after the ruling emperor in Rome. These two cities were grand in conception, but also costly. The Jews were required to bear the financial burden through tolls collected at bridges and harbors, custom duties on goods imported from abroad and even from city to city within the region, and by the salt tax. In A.D. 6, Quirinius, the governor of Syria, ordered that a census be taken of the people in Palestine so that an even more comprehensive sys-

tem of taxes might be imposed. The people were greatly dis-
turbed. Some of them started an insurrection. Jesus at the time
must have been quite young, perhaps ten or twelve years old,
but he may well have been aware and impressed with what
happened.

Those who took part in the insurrection were called Zealots.
They were a Jewish party founded by a certain Judas, a Gali-
lean, who was aided by Zaddok, a Pharisee. The contemporary
historian, Josephus, writes that the Zealots had an inviolate attachment to liberty, saying that only god is their lord and master. He states that they did not fear death for themselves or
for their relatives and friends in advocating their principles.
They opposed all taxes, except those levied by their temples.
In a sudden attack, the Zealots seized the city of Sepphoris
and took over its arsenal. The uprising must have been serious, for the Romans under Varus used two legions in
suppressing it. They sacked the city of Sepphoris and killed by
crucifixion several thousands of the Zealots. The movement,
however, would not die.

The Zealots were a Jewish group which presented Jesus
with a clear-cut choice to be made. Two of his disciples may
have been members of the group: Simon, called the Zealot,
and Judas Iscariot, who betrayed him. It was the crowd in the
courtyard of Pilate which, when given the choice, called for
the release of Barabbas, the Zealot, and thereby sent Jesus to
his death. Jesus was clearly not a Zealot. The Gospels give no
account of his having supported them. On several occasions,
such as when the Roman soldiers came to arrest him, he rejected the methods of violence.

The Essenes, another group of Jews at the time of Jesus,
were in sharp contrast to the Zealots. For one thing, they were
opposed to all violence. They met the challenges of their time
by withdrawing from the body politic and giving themselves
to the devotional life. They aimed to purify Judaism; thus, they
opposed animal sacrifices, which was unusual for the time.
They did not react to the Roman repression in any direct way,
for they believed that god would ultimately send them and all

Jews a savior, the lord's anointed one, the messiah, who would bring deliverance. Many lived in isolated communities and were celibate. They would till their fields by day, holding their possessions in common, maintain the Sabbath strictly, engage in prayer and fasting—in the pious hope that the messiah would save them finally.

One form of the Essenes' community life was revealed through the discovery of the Dead Sea Scrolls in 1947. These scrolls threw much fresh light on both Judaism and Christianity. The community is known as the Qumran community, after a nearby *wadi*, or riverbed. Probably the community was in existence from the last quarter of the second century B.C. until about A.D. 68. The membership consisted of about two hundred males, although they were probably local units of the order that existed beyond Qumran. Those within the community were celibate; those without were married. Once a year at Pentecost the whole membership would gather for a renewal of vows, the reception of newcomers, and the management of administrative matters. A strict hierarchy prevailed. The laity outnumbered the priests and together the laity and priests composed a council of the community. An overseer, who in effect was a pastor or chief administrator, cared for various matters, including the two-year program by which initiates came into the order.

The Qumran Essenes believed that they were the true Jews. They were the children of the light, while all others, Jews and non-Jews, were the children of the darkness. They revered a great teacher of their past who they said had received by divine revelation the truths that formed the basis for the community and its social organization. Although the community was called by various names (the new covenant, the congregation, the unity, sons of light, etc.), it was marked by a belief in the need for radical repentance and the acceptance of the great teacher of the past. Only the great teacher had understood the mysteries of the heritage of the prophets and he imparted this secret knowledge to his followers. The Qumran community, then, was something of a secret society. Actually this group of Essenes taught that ultimately two messiahs would come to deliver them. One would be a priestly messiah who would officiate at the temple in the last days and would show to all the purity and righteousness of the faith. The other messiah would dominate the political sphere. As a descendant of David he would wield a sword that would bring all nations into a righteous social order. Another figure, a prophet rather than a messiah, would also appear in the last days and he would be responsible for settling various questions regarding the law. The theology of the Qumran community is quite complex, but these elements show some of the features of its beliefs.

Some scholars have eagerly made Jesus an Essene and possibly a member even of the Qumran community. In this way they account for some of his attitudes and teachings and for the years of his early life concerning which there is no information. Jesus probably was well aware of the Essenes in general and perhaps of the Qumran community in particular. But whatever the influences, Jesus can scarcely be claimed as an Essene. There are a number of reasons for this. They were ascetics; he participated in ordinary social events freely, such as attending wedding feasts. They were legalists, maintaining a strict adherence to the Jewish law; he was the opposite, believing that it is the spirit that makes the law live, as is illustrated in his attitudes and practices regarding the Sabbath. They were participants in an essentially secret society; he maintained himself and his teachings in the open, eagerly seeking out others with his message. They believed that it was proper to hate one's enemies and that ultimately the kingdom of god would be brought about by the sword; he taught that men should love their enemies and he rejected the way of violence even in worthy causes. On these and other points, Jesus seems not to have been an Essene.

The Sadducees were religiously the most conservative of the Jewish groups at the time of Jesus. They considered themselves to be the only orthodox group. They wished to maintain the ancient Jewish tradition as they perceived it without making any changes in it. They believed that the religion of the first five books of their sacred scriptures, the Torah, was divinely inspired in every detail, and should not be modified. To them, being a loyal Jew meant keeping the traditions, despite all the activities of the Romans and those Jews who found other solutions to the problems of the times. Hardly anyone thinks that Jesus was a Sadducee.

The Pharisees, probably the largest of the groups, attracted many Jews in Jesus' time. In the main they were a learned lot. The scribes and the rabbis devoted themselves to a systematic study of the sources of their faith. They founded schools for this purpose; an especially large one was established in Jerusalem. Notable teachers, such as Shammai and Hillel, were members of this group. The Pharisees opposed the Zealots on the grounds of violence. They believed that there was no hope of an insurrection succeeding against the powerful Romans. They also were not as conservative as the Sadducees. On the other hand, the Sadducees in political matters were able to compromise with the Romans; thus they were far from being conservative in this sphere. But they did believe that the duty of Jews was to observe the Jewish traditions as strictly as possible. They advocated tithing, keeping the requirements of the Sabbath, honoring the Jewish festivals, being exact about ceremonial purity, having no legal dealings with the civil courts, and maintaining the dietary requirements. In these and other particulars, the Pharisees sought to apply their traditions to the whole of life. Jesus was no Pharisee. On a number of issues, such as the keeping of the Sabbath, he was openly critical of the Pharisees. In certain respects he believed that they were impeding the fulfillment of true Judaism.

There were also large numbers of Jews who did not fit neatly into any of the defined groups. Many of the common people were not rigid in their religion. They considered it a necessity to make various accommodations to the pressures of the real world in which they lived. This does not mean that in some sense they abandoned their heritage. Some of them were indeed pious and honored much of the tradition. But they were largely selective, pragmatic, and eclectic. The family into which Jesus was born may well have been representative of them.

The sources for constructing a life of Jesus call for review and evaluation. Few of the founders of the living religions wrote anything that has survived. This is understandable, for they regularly were men of action. They preached and taught, traveling about to bring their messages to others. In some instances, their disciples sought to preserve accounts of the lives and teachings of the founders. Jesus is not known to have written anything himself. All that is known about him comes from others and much of what is available dates from a period much later than his lifetime. Since this is so, what is known about his life and teachings is filtered through the memories of those who were engaged in churchly responsibilities. They were advocates rather than historians and biographers. This does not mean that what they wrote is inaccurate or unreliable. It means that they were not objective, and that the task of ferreting out the true account is both complex and difficult.

These difficulties are seen in the various letters of Paul, whose writings are probably the oldest of all the records regarding Jesus. I Thessalonians, for example, was probably written about twenty years before Mark, the earliest written Gospel. In the decade and a half that followed, Paul wrote many other letters to young churches, about ten of which have been accepted into the canonical scriptures of Christianity. But Paul provides very little information about the historical Jesus. Paul was concerned with such matters as the essentials of Christian moral action, the way in which churches should be organized, the relation of the new religion to the Jewish law, and other subjects. Nowhere with any exactness does he relate events in the life of Jesus, with the possible exception of his description of the Lord's Supper (I Cor. 11:23-26). And Paul was not one of the disciples of Jesus, and probably he never knew Jesus personally. Thus he had no personal basis for providing an account of Jesus' life.

The oldest extant recording of the life of Jesus has been provided by Mark. He is assumed to have written his Gospel in Rome after the death of Peter whose companion he was. If Peter died under the persecution by Nero in A.D. 64-65, Mark may have written his Gospel any time from A.D. 65 to 70.

Matthew and Luke provide accounts of the life of Jesus which in the main follow the Gospel of Mark in outline, style, and content. The three are called the Synoptic Gospels, for they share a common point of view. It seems that Matthew and Luke had Mark's writings at hand when they composed their own Gospels, although they added various elements with which they were familiar and which Mark did not include. Mark, for example, did not include some of the parables and the Sermon on the Mount. It is assumed, moreover, that Matthew and Luke may have had a document other than Mark's Gospel. Perhaps this document, commonly called Q after the German world *Quelle*, or source, was as old or older than Mark's writings. Both Matthew and Luke seem to use this document at times word for word as a basis for their stories. And Matthew and Luke each had other sources that were not known to the other. It appears that they worked independently and were not acquainted with each other's work.

The Gospel of John is another matter. It is basically unlike the Synoptic Gospels in both style and content. Contrary to the other Gospels, John includes no parables. According to the earlier Gospels, Jesus makes only one journey to Jerusalem for the celebration of the Passover, but John says that Jesus made three or four journeys to Jerusalem. The Synoptic Gospels say that the ministry of Jesus covered about a year in time. John indicates that it spanned at least three years. John, whoever he actually may have been, wrote out of a tradition different from the Synoptic writers and probably with a different purpose. He appears to have written his Gospel sometime between A.D. 100 and 110 for the purpose of interpreting the meaningfulness of Jesus as the Christ to a highly sophisticated audience already familiar with Greek thought, symbolism, and mysticism. For example, he adopts the idea of the *logos*, or the word, which was popular in Stoicism where it meant the rational order and energy of the cosmos. Modifying the idea somewhat, John seeks to show that this eternal *logos* was indeed that eternal wisdom of the Jewish tradition which became incarnate in the life of Jesus as the Christ. Again, John does not include most of the miracles of the Synoptic Gospels, although he contributes a few of his own, but these seem to be simply apt illustrations of the deeper Christian truths as seen from a Hellenistic perspective. John, then, is valuable for the way in which he adapted the essential Christian teachings to a foreign culture through the use of philosophic concepts. He provides little, if any, concrete and historical information regarding the life of Jesus.

The New Testament, then, is the chief source of information regarding the life of Jesus. There are no non-Biblical sources of any consequence for constructing the story of his life.

Probably more books have been written about Jesus than about any other person. Yet when one looks at the available information about his life, one finds that it is surprisingly scant. The four Gospels do not present a single or even a consistent set of facts about him. Like other founders of religions, the life of Jesus begins not with his earthly birth, but with certain celestial affirmations about him. The writer of the Gospel of John identified the human Jesus with the traditional idea of the messiah within Judaism and the notion of the *logos* in Greek thought, making him an eternally existing reality. From the very beginning of time the Word existed.

Two of the Gospels, Matthew and Luke, aver that Jesus was born of a virgin. These accounts are an effort to show that Jesus was not naturally born, but that god was his father. Matthew seeks to tie Jesus genealogically, through a long and complicated ancestry, to the ancient hero David, although his story of the virgin birth in effect denies such a paternal descent.

Angels also are connected with the birth. In one instance an angel visits Mary, the mother of Jesus, to announce that she is blessed among women, for she is to become pregnant and will bear a son who will be named Jesus. Again, at the time of the birth an angel appeared to shepherds in a field near Bethlehem. The angel, accompanied by the glory of the lord, announced that there had been born that day in the nearby city a savior who is god's anointed one. The angel tells them that they will know the child by his dress and place (swathed and lying in a crib). After the angel departed, the shepherds left their fields, went to Bethlehem, and found the child just as the angel had said. Another situation in which the holy spirit spoke involves a story that parallels that of the birth of Jesus, namely, the birth of John, whose parents were Zacharias and Elizabeth. This account in the first chapter of Luke's Gospel provides further support for the marvelous workings of god in the lives of contemporaries.

Another celestial sign related to the birth of Jesus is told in Matthew's account of the visit of the Magi. It is assumed that they were Zoroastrian priests from Iran who, following a guiding star, asked: Where is the king of the Jews who has been born? When they got to Jerusalem they told Herod the king of their purpose and he was strangely afraid, thinking that this newborn king would be a threat to his rule. Herod instructed them to continue in their search and to report back to him after they had found the child. The star guided the Magi to the very spot where Jesus was. There they presented him with gifts appropriate to the occasion: gold, frankincense, and myrrh. Tradition assumes that there were three wise men from the east, although the account in Matthew does not say how many made the trip. The wise men paid their homage and then returned to their own land without informing Herod of what they had found.

Little is known of the parents of Jesus. Probably they resided in Nazareth, where Joseph was a carpenter. At that time, however, a carpenter was something like a builder. Luke says that the parents went to Bethlehem because a census was being made and everyone had to return to his native place. It was there that Jesus was born. The story blends well with prophecy, for the messiah, it had been predicted (Micah 5:2), would be born in Bethlehem. The place of birth was possibly the house of a shepherd, not a cave, and he was placed in a crib that ordinarily was reserved for an animal. Quite probably Jesus was not born in the traditional year, but in 4 B.C. or a few years earlier. For one thing, Herod the Great would have been alive then, for he died in 4 B.C. Also, placing the death of Jesus in the fifteenth year of Tiberius Caesar, as the account reads, would place his birth at the close of the prior era.

The events that followed the birth are not too clear or detailed. Luke says that at the end of eight days Jesus was circumcised and given the name that the angel had previously announced. Then, after a period of about forty days, when Mary's purification was over (a woman at that time was "unclean" after parturition for seven days and had to stay at home for another thirty-three), the parents brought the child to Jerusalem to present it to god. Tradition (Ex. 13:2) required that the firstborn child be dedicated to god and redeemed by the payment of five coins, although the payment could be dismissed in the case of the poor. A sacrifice also was made at the temple: in the case of the well-to-do a lamb was slaughtered; in the case of the poor a pair of pigeons or turtle doves could be substituted. While Mary may have gone to the temple, she would not have entered the inner court, for that was reserved for men only.

The event was given special significance. In the temple was a pious old man named Simeon who was looking for a blessing. When he saw the child, Jesus, he burst into poetic ecstasy and spoke what has come to be known as the Nunc Dimittis. Also on the same occasion a prophetess, Hannah or Anna, of the tribe of Asher was in the temple. She had been married for seven years. As a widow of eighty-four, she never left the temple, worshiping night and day. She also rejoiced in the birth of the child and announced to all who longed for Jerusalem to be redeemed that the savior had been born. Luke concludes his account of the very early life of Jesus by saying that when the family had finished all that was required by the law, they returned to Galilee and to their hometown of Nazareth. He remarks that Jesus grew and became strong, that he was full of wisdom, and that god's blessing was with him.

Matthew tells a different story about the earliest days in Jesus' life. He does not refer at all to the incidents of Luke's account. Both stories, however, show that the birth of Jesus was not an ordinary event and that the child's life was fraught with divine meaning. According to Matthew, after the Magi had left, an angel appeared to Joseph in a dream, telling him that he should flee to Egypt with his family, for Herod would be looking for the child so that he might kill him. Joseph fled with his family during the night and remained in Egypt until Herod died. Herod was furious when he learned that the visitors from the east had tricked him, and he gave orders that all the boys in and about Bethlehem who were two years or younger should be killed. After Herod's death, an angel again appeared to Joseph in a dream and directed him to return to his native land. So he went back to Nazareth in Galilee. In this story Matthew is seeking to show that the events he describes were the fulfillment of ancient Judaic prophecy. Hosea 11:1 had identified the messiah with Egypt, and Matthew says that according to the prophets he would be called a Nazarene.

Concerning the early years of Jesus' life in Nazareth little is known. It may be that he was a student at a synagogue school. Probably he was a regular participant in the services of worship. He was thoroughly familiar with the Judaic scriptures, for he was aptly able to quote from them to illuminate points of his teaching. Luke provides the one statement of this period which surely indicates how unusually wise in religious matters Jesus was (Luke 2:41-52). He says that every year the parents went to Jerusalem for the Feast of the Passover. On their way back they noticed that Jesus was not with them. Their failure to notice his absence earlier would not necessarily be unusual, for Jews making the journey would travel in fairly large groups as a means of protection from bands of robbers, especially in Samaria. After the third day they found him still in the temple in Jerusalem, where he was sitting with the Jewish teachers, listening to them and asking them questions.

All who heard him were amazed at his intelligent answers. His mother said that they were terribly worried about him and were trying to find him. He declared that they should have known that he had to be in god's house. They took him back to Nazareth, where, the scriptures note, he was obedient to them. Mary treasured all these things in her heart. The story aims to show that Jesus was an exceptional child. He was twelve years old at the time.

In addition to his religious schooling, Jesus also developed a trade, that of carpentry. It was perfectly natural for a boy at that time to adopt the vocation of his father. Also, Jesus grew up in a large family. There were at least six other children, four boys (James, Joses, Simon, and Jude), and sisters, although the number and the names of the sisters is not given.

No sure information is available regarding the next eighteen years of Jesus' life. No references are made in the Gospels to anything that may have happened. During this time his father, Joseph, may have died, for there are no later references to him. It may be that Jesus took over his father's business with the help of his brothers. Some persons surmise that during this time he may have been a carpenter engaged in the rebuilding of Sepphoris, four miles to the north. That city had been burned during the Zealot rebellion of 6 B.C. Others suggest that during this period he was a member of the Qumran community or a similar community. No hard evidence exists for such suppositions.

When Jesus was about thirty years old he underwent a transforming experience that shaped his later career. He became, like Amos, Isaiah, and Jeremiah of the Jewish tradition, a prophet; yet he was regarded by many as more than a prophet; he was the messiah, the lord's anointed one, the Christ. He also founded a new religion.

John the Baptist had a role in this transforming experience of Jesus. John came out of the eastern desert, calling persons to repent, for god's kingdom was at hand. In effect he was announcing the close of the present era and the introduction of a phase of human history in which god's will and righteousness would prevail. He also baptized those who repented and believed. Baptism was a ceremony in which the old life was symbolically washed away, and the person emerged with new purity. But John was not only a visionary concerned with the last days and a ceremonialist who baptized people. He also was a stern moralist. He declared that the man who had two shirts should share one with the man who had none. He called upon tax collectors to be honest and soldiers not to make false charges against people or extort money. He condemned the illegal marriage of Herod Antipas to his brother's wife, Herodias, and for doing so was finally imprisoned and beheaded.

Jesus was caught up with John and his message. For a time he apparently became one of John's company; his baptism by John suggests this. However the experience is to be accounted for, Jesus did become deeply moved religiously and from that time on he devoted himself to doing what he believed to be god's will. Mark records that as Jesus was coming up out of the baptismal water he saw the heavens torn open and the holy spirit coming down like a dove to enter him. Out of the heavens came a voice: "You are my son, my beloved. You are my chosen."

Jesus then retired to the wilderness to contemplate his mission. Tradition says that he stayed forty days, and that during this time Satan tempted him. The temptation involved basically three vital issues. First, should he continue to work or should he devote himself solely to his mission? The answer was that he would do the latter. Second, should he employ miraculous means to attract attention? The answer was that he must put events into the hands of god, shunning mere shows. Third, should he seek to deliver Israel through political and violent means? The answer was that such changes are not lasting, for they are not fundamental enough. When the wilderness experience was over, Jesus was ready to start his prophetic activities. He felt that he was called by god to preach about the coming kingdom, to heal the ill and infirm, and to call persons to a high morality that even superseded the traditional legal requirements. He was to be his own man, under god, not a mere echo of any of the groups with which he was familiar, including that of John the Baptist. He would resolutely preach, heal, and teach.

The ministry of Jesus is too long and detailed to be recounted here comprehensively. Although it covers three years at most, the information regarding his activities makes up most of the Gospels. Only some of its main characteristics may be noted. Galilee was the chief scene of his early ministry. He made Capernaum his headquarters. This city on the northern end of the Lake of Galilee was the locus of a fairly developed culture because of its location on an international trade route. It is said that when he got to the city he entered the synagogue and taught the people, to the astonishment of even the scribes, who were learned scholars in the Jewish law. He gathered four disciples (Simon Peter and his brother Andrew, James and his brother John, the sons of Zebedee, all four of whom were fishermen) and continued his preaching.

The synagogues were too small for his audiences, so he took to the marketplaces and the seashores and the open fields. The Sermon on the Mount (Matt., chs. 5 to 7) and the Sermon on the Plain (Luke 6:20-49) are two versions of his preaching. These probably were not actual sermons, but compendia of bits and pieces that he had included in various sermons. But they well illustrate the kinds of subjects that comprised his message to the people. He also was a master in the use of the parable. Taking apt examples from nature and from human relations, he portrayed situations that his hearers could easily understand, drawing conclusions from them that forcefully advanced his cause. In his preaching, moreover, Jesus taught with authority. Those who heard him were often amazed at his perceptiveness. Often he broke with the traditional wisdom of Judaism. Although he acknowledged that the people may have heard particular views and standards from the past, he did not hesitate to break with these, offering his own teaching as the new norm.

Another key element in his ministry was his healing. Many stories of his cures are provided by the Gospel writers. Sometimes the cures were of persons who were physically impaired, such as the blind, the deaf and dumb, and epileptics. At other times they were of persons who suffered some kind of psychological impairment. The common view in Jesus' time was that such persons, as well as others, were possessed by demons. Jesus exorcised these demons. On one occasion (Matt. 8:28-34), Jesus conversed with the demons, whereupon they left the possessed man and entered into swine. From a current point of view it is very difficult to know how to account for these seeming miracles, although in Jesus' time such unusual events were taken as usual when performed by such a person as Jesus.

There are other miracles that are associated with Jesus that had nothing to do with healing. His feeding of the crowds with a few loaves and fishes is one illustration. His walking on the water is another. But no matter how all these unusual events might be explained adequately to the modern mind, they are made a part of the life of Jesus to show that he was indeed no mere man, but that he possessed the power of god in all realms.

Undoubtedly Jesus became popular throughout Galilee through his teachings and actions. People ran to hear him; they pressed in upon him at the lakeshore, so that he had to take a boat and speak to them from the water; so many gathered to hear him in a house that there was no room to prepare a meal. His cause prospered. In time he gathered twelve men about him as his disciples. They represented a variety of vocations before their calling, their temperaments and abilities were varied, and even their loyalty to Jesus was uneven. But they formed the nucleus of the new religion that would enable it to take root and grow, along with the efforts of such others as Paul, the great missionary and organizer of the early church. Luke also records (Luke 10:1-20) that there were seventy followers who were sent out in groups of two and who were under rather strict injunctions to advance the new faith. Possibly the Lukan account was taken from the standard code for missionaries in the early church and given

Gospel sanction. At any rate, others around Jesus took up his cause and in his lifetime and after his death enabled it to succeed.

But not everyone liked Jesus. The Pharisees and the Sadducees disliked him because he broke the religious law as they understood it. When his disciples picked the heads of the wheat on the Sabbath, the Pharisees objected. But Jesus declared that the Sabbath was made for man, not man for the Sabbath. Probably what irritated the Pharisees and Sadducees even more was the sense of authority in such matters that Jesus assumed. Jesus also offended the Zealots because he would not sanction their acceptance of violence. He declared that those who take the sword will be killed by the sword. They, too, opposed him. Seemingly even the common people lost confidence in him. When he returned to Nazareth, for example, he found that the people of his hometown lacked faith. It is said that even his parents came to visit him in Capernaum to express their concern. The storm of conflict was rising.

Perhaps unsettled and in doubt regarding his mission, Jesus with his disciples went north to the region about Tyre and Sidon, which were in southern Syria. His time there apparently was one of reassessment and of consolidation of his disciples. When he and his disciples had reached Caesarea Philippi, the capital of the tetrarchy of Philip, Jesus asked his disciples who they thought he was. It was Peter who answered: you are the Christ. Upon this confirmation and show of confidence, Jesus asked his disciples to keep the matter secret for the time. Then he said that he and they would be going to Jerusalem, where he must undergo suffering and even death to achieve his mission.

On the journey to Jerusalem, Jesus continued to preach and to heal. He entered the holy city at the time of the Feast of the Passover. Pilate, the Roman procurator, had moved to the city for the occasion from his headquarters at Caesarea. Herod Antipas had also come to Jerusalem from Galilee, in part to show that he was at least a nominal Jew. Entering the city on a borrowed colt, Jesus was well received by the people. They proclaimed him as Jesus, the prophet of Nazareth in Galilee. But his opponents were closing in upon him. His disruption of the temple by overturning the tables of the money changers was badly interpreted. His outright refusal to enjoin against paying the poll tax was not accepted well by the people.

The writers of the Gospels agree that at this time Jesus understood his impending death. He called his disciples together for a last supper in which he initiated a ceremony of remembrance. Later, as he was praying in the garden of Gethsemane, he was betrayed by Judas to a group of men armed with swords and clubs and was taken before the Sanhedrin and condemned to death. The charge was blasphemy against the Jewish law. The Sanhedrin turned Jesus over to Pilate for the execution of the sentence and, after some maneuvering, he was chosen for death over Barabbas, a Zealot insurrectionist who was known to Pilate as a murderer. Jesus was taken to a hill outside Jerusalem about noon. Surrounded by a jeering mob, forsaken by his disciples and others, except for some loyal women, he was crucified. He died asking god how he could have forsaken him. Joseph of Arimathaea, seeking to avoid having the body hang on the cross on the Sabbath, arranged for the use of his own empty tomb.

The resurrection of Jesus is an account unmatched among the founders of the other living religions. According to the Gospels, the disciples were depressed and disorganized by despair over the death of their leader. But some of the women visited the tomb of Jesus on the morning of the third day after his death. They were surprised to find it empty. As they told the story, an angel appeared to them and announced that Jesus was not in the tomb and that he had been resurrected. Although he had been dead, he was alive! Following this, Jesus is said to have appeared to Peter and after that to others in various ways. Jesus had survived death. The resurrection gave revived confidence and hope to the disciples and to others. They went about telling of the miraculous event. They also described how Jesus, having been resurrected, ascended into heaven. A new religion had been born.

In his lifetime Jesus was not respected, admired, or loved by all. Some of his townspeople regarded him as an ordinary carpenter; on one occasion they even tried to assassinate him. Some of his own brothers apparently did not support his role and teachings. Some of his friends questioned his sanity. The Jewish leaders thought him to be a dangerous heretic. He was defamed by some because he associated with worldly and wicked people. He was crucified because it was claimed that he made himself equal with god. But after his death and resurrection, he was acclaimed widely as a well-received preacher and healer, a prophet who taught as no man had ever taught, and as being faultless in character. In the estimate of many, he became a man whose nature was thoroughly imbued with the very spirit of god. Later, in theological review, he became the son of god, the personal incarnation of deity, an emissary of the divine to redeem mankind from evil and to initiate the realm of god in which perfect righteousness would prevail. He was Jesus the Christ, god's anointed, the messiah, the savior of the world. Such an estimate, debated in all details, became the basis for the church in its later development through long centuries in various parts of the world.

Jesus' teachings may be viewed from a theological and an ethical perspective, although these two are interdependent. Jesus brought no rational proofs of the existence of god. He assumed god's existence and his own close relationship to him. But his teachings were appealing for two reasons. First, he asserted that god is a highly personal being, a father, who rules the universe with a moral passion. This god is absolutely committed to righteousness and works through nature, individual lives, and in history to develop his providential ways. Secondly, he asserted that god, despite his sternness, is essentially loving and forgiving. God values human beings highly and is able to express love to them no matter what evil they may practice. Like the father in the parable of the prodigal son, god is always ready to forgive his children's sins and to take them back into his fellowship. Reconciliation with god is the keynote of Jesus' theological awareness.

In his ethics, Jesus was no ascetic. He mingled with people freely and apparently enjoyed social relations greatly. But he did call for the discipline of the self, including the body. Such discipline enabled the person better to follow the straight and narrow path that led to the kingdom of god. The primary principle of his ethics was that of doing the will of god in all activities. The will of god required that love be made the primary rule among all peoples. Love is the basis for the kingdom. Love is inclusive; it includes children, the poor, those who were not Jews, and the sinful. No exceptions were allowed. All of mankind was conceived as a common fellowship, governed by a loving god, in which the golden rule is the measure of faithful religiosity. Religion itself is viewed as a possible barrier to the attainment of the complete rule of love. When it was, Jesus condemned its ritualism, spiritual pride, and outworn beliefs. In place of an externally controlling code of moral principles, he called for the revitalization of the inner spirit of man. The genuine issues of life and love lie, in Jesus' view, in the inner condition of the self.

The new religion gathered strength and converts. Its teachings regarding god and man were greatly appealing. The central source for the unity of the faith came in time to be Jesus himself, both as man and as the son of god. It became a flourishing religion, spreading far from its initial base in the Middle East, contributing as a wellspring to the fundamental character of many diverse peoples and societies.

9

MUHAMMAD
AND
ISLAM

Islam is the third of three religions that have a common historic rootage. Both Christianity and Islam openly acknowledge their historical dependency upon Judaism. Judaism, however, does not recognize either one as a proper development of its tradition. Judaism remains an independent religion. Christianity acknowledges its relationship to Judaism and has incorporated the scriptures of that religion into its own sacred literature. Islam is the only living religion that recognizes two other religions as appropriate and respected predecessors. It too has its own scriptures, although it considers the sacred writings of both Judaism and Christianity as inspired and preliminary to its own. Within Islam, moreover, are found significant traces of both these two religions.

Again, Christianity does not recognize Islam as a suitable outgrowth of itself. The two religions today are just as much rivals as they were in the past. Dante portrays Muhammad with his body split from head to waist, assigned to the twenty-eighth sphere of the Inferno. For Dante, an exemplar of medieval Christianity, Muhammad is foremost among the damned souls, for he was the chief heretic and schismatic. Muhammad's view that Islam was a superior religion that would supersede Christianity has ever been considered false by loyal Christians. Although claiming to be the one, true religion for all mankind, including Christians, Islam acknowledges its relationship with Christianity as a precursor religion.

Islam and Christianity have several characteristics in com-

mon. First, they are both part of the cultural stream that originated in Judaism. Second, both feature personal founders who
have been decisive as originators of their respective religions.
Third, both are monotheistic, believing in a transcendent, personal deity, who is lord over all creation. They are theologically similar in other respects as well. Fourth, both religions
are international, or universal, in their intent and in their operations. Fifth, both have risen comparatively late in history.

Jesus, the founder of Christianity, probably was born in 4
B.C. In terms of the other religions that have been reviewed in
this book, this makes Christianity relatively late in its appearance. But the dates for Muhammad's life are usually given as
A.D. 570-632, making Islam even later. Sikhism is the only religion that was founded later than Islam. Nanak, its founder, is
usually assigned the dates of A.D. 1469-1539.

Like Christianity, Islam is large in terms of the number of
its adherents. Although there is no known way accurately to
compute membership in the various living religions, there are
many indications leading to the conclusion that Islam is one of
the largest; perhaps Christianity, at the present time, is the
largest of all the living religions. Given the present circumstances in China, it is difficult to know what the status of Confucianism is in that land. Assuming the traditional loyalty of
the Chinese people prior to the Communist revolution,
Confucianism may be considered to be the second largest religion. If that claim is in error, then Islam would probably be
the second most populous religion. At any rate, it ranks among
the foremost religions in human history, a great spiritual and
cultural force that has helped shape the lives of millions and
the societies in which they live.

Islam is a fast-growing religion at the present time. It is far
from moribund. Muhammad in his own lifetime succeeded in
bringing a high degree of religious and political unity to the
Arabian peninsula. Following his death, the religion succeeded in winning a large part of the Middle East, and even
beyond. The Islamic empire continued to grow until the
thirteenth century, when it suffered a series of defeats, militar-

ily and otherwise. In that period Jenghis Khan brought his Mongols across the ancient Oxus. After his death his grandson, Hulagu, continued the conquest, capturing Baghdad in A.D. 1258 and putting the petty caliph to death. A number of other reverses took place, until the Islamic and Arabic civilization was subdued. For long centuries, then, the religion of Islam, which had been such a force in human affairs within the area, declined. It has only been in recent decades, especially since the Second World War, that a number of the formerly Arabic nations of the Middle East and elsewhere whose religion traditionally has been Islam were able to gain their independence. There has been in these decades a rebirth of fervid nationalism among these Islamic states with an accompanying revitalization of the religion that historically formed their distinctive civilization. At the present time, in many places, Islam is a revitalized, modernized, and forceful faith.

The fortunes of Islam have waxed and waned. Historically it has been extended west to the Atlantic Ocean and across the northern tier states of Africa along the Mediterranean. One hundred years after the death of Muhammad, Islam also had expanded it influence through Spain into southern France. There, in what has been considered one of the most decisive military battles of all time, the invading Islamic forces were defeated by Charles Martel at the battle of Tours, or Poitiers. The marks of the presence of Islam are seen even today in Spain, for example, by its influence upon Spanish architecture. Similarly its expansion took it into southeastern Europe, the area known as the Balkans.

Islam expanded to the east, as well, and is found in such modern nations as Pakistan, India, Bangladesh, China, Indonesia, and the Philippines. Its mosques, or places of worship, dot the landscape in all these countries.

Islam is known both north and south of the land of its birth. It reaches into the southern steppes of the Soviet Union. It can also be found throughout much of Africa, even to the southern tip of that continent.

Islam is probably distinctive among the living religions for

its use of force in making conversions. It is true that a number
of the living religions have employed violence to that end. In
the chapter on Zoroastrianism, for example, it was seen how
Zoroaster converted the king of Iran and then blessed his military conquest of others in the name of the religion. The employment of force is also apparent in the history of
Christianity. But in none of the other religions was force or
military activity raised to the level of a basic tenet of the faith.
The concept in Islam is usually termed *jihad,* or holy war.
Jihad means striving, and the faithful Muslim is urged even in
his sacred scriptures, the Quran, to strive against unbelievers.
The origin of the holy war derives from the times of Muhammad. Arabian society then was divided into a number of warring tribes; conflict among them was an accepted fact. The
tribes made raids upon each other. Although outright wars
were not unknown, the use of raids was quite prevalent.
Usually one tribe would take a small group of an unfriendly
tribe by surprise. The regular object of the raids was to seize
camels and other animals, sometimes even women. The raiders
usually attacked with overwhelming force, but there would be
little loss of human life. If an unfriendly tribe were to suffer
an accidental killing, it would expect to be reimbursed through
the gift of an appropriate number of camels.

The practice of raids was adopted by Muhammad in his
own lifetime. The first one apparently took place in A.D. 623
when Muhammad sent his uncle Hamzah with a force of
thirty men to attack a Meccan caravan returning from Syria
along the Red Sea coast. But the caravan was said to have
been protected by a group of three hundred men under the
leadership of Abu-Jahl, an opponent of Muhammad. The raid
was unsuccessful and probably no fighting ensued. It is said
that a nomadic chief intervened to keep the peace. This was
merely the first of a number of such expeditions sanctioned by
Muhammad.

On a larger scale, Muhammad and his early followers were
engaged in a variety of military ventures. They had war
waged against them, and they engaged in a number of warlike

efforts to conquer those tribes which resisted them. The battle for Mecca, led by Muhammad late in his life, and its eventual conquest is a significant example of the use of force by the new religion.

In the Quran, Muhammad gives further explicit sanction for warfare. The followers are urged to fight strenuously against unbelievers and hypocrites and to be stern with them. Muhammad declared that god loves those who fight in his cause. He required his followers to fight those who do not believe in Allah, the god of Islam, until they pay tribute by their hands and become as little ones. He stated that fighting is prescribed for the faithful.

Because of the original tribal basis for the religion, Islam has always combined religious identification with political membership. In other religions, such as Christianity, to be a religious person has meant chiefly joining with others of a like mind to worship and to conduct certain other limited activities. For the Muslim, on the other hand, to be religious means something more. It means also belonging to a political entity. Islam makes its claim upon the whole of a person's life. The notion of the tribe gave way to the idea of the *ummah*, or community. The *ummah* was the religiopolitical body of believers that was drawn out of the various tribes and that looked to the new religion as its basic bond. In time it was the *ummah* that became the unit for raids. Gradually "striving" by the *ummah* against the several tribes of unbelievers in the Arabian peninsula was successful. Militarily as well as religiously the *ummah* ruled throughout Saudi Arabia. This was largely accomplished in Muhammad's own lifetime. But the military expansionism did not stop with the consolidation of Muhammad's homeland. As the *ummah* was faced with an ever-expanding border of unbelievers it maintained its basic style of religious and political conquests. The result is described as *jihad*, or holy war. Those who were conquered by force throughout the international sphere associated with the expanding religion became Muslims. Sometimes, however, when they were not converted by forceful conquest, the people were permitted to pay tribute. It is said that the believer who is killed while seeking the forceful conversion of unbelievers would go straight to heaven as a sign and guarantee of god's blessing upon him for his effort. Thus, Islam's expansion throughout various parts of the world has historically relied on the use of violence.

In the West, Islam commonly is called Muhammadanism, after its founder. But the followers of Islam object to this. They claim, for one thing, that they do not follow the faith of a man called Muhammad. To them Muhammad was a great prophet in a long line of prophets extending back to Abraham, but he was merely a prophet. The religion comes directly from god. Muhammad was simply god's messenger, or his instrument of revelation.

In a sense it may be claimed that Muhammad was the only founder of a religion who himself named the religion. The name that he gave to it was Islam, though at the start the new religion had no name. The early Muslims considered themselves to be the followers of Abraham, the *hanif*, the surrendered one. Abraham as the *hanif* refers to the requirement made by god of Abraham that he sacrifice his son in humble obedience. Abraham's willingness to follow god's command was, to the early Muslims, a prime example of man surrendering himself to god—utterly and completely. In Arabic then the *hanif* is the Muslim, the surrendered one. Islam is a verbal noun which corresponds to Muslim, signifying the act of surrendering to god. These meanings are provided within the Quran, the contents of which were given by Muhammad. Sometimes the Quran is called the Koran in the West and Muslim is spelled Moslem. Also, there are variant spellings for Muhammad, the most usual one being Mohammed.

Hanif refers to the basic stance of the believer, but in Muhammad's time it also connoted something of the nature of the god to whom one surrenders. Abraham's god, it is assumed, was the one, transcendent deity. In Muhammad's time many deities were worshiped. Polytheism was the rule among the simpler folk. But Judaism and Christianity were also known to

Muhammad and his followers. The idea behind *hanif* is sur-
render to the one god, Allah by name, who is the one deity
surpassing all others, including the gods of Judaism and Christianity.

The complex world in which Muhammad lived naturally
influenced the religion that he originated. No personally
founded religion is created in a social vacuum. Rather it
reflects, sometimes subtly and indirectly, the life and times in
which it springs up. The founder, moreover, is a part of the
process in the sense that he stands between the past and the
future; he is the channel through which the social situation is
reperceived and reinterpreted. So it was with Muhammad.

Arabia in Muhammad's time was racially mixed. Semites
predominated, but there were various other peoples. From the
south, for example, Ethiopians had crossed the Red Sea and
formed settlements along the coastal plain. A Hamitic influence was felt from those Egyptians who had migrated to the
peninsula. Due to wars and changing circumstances, a number
of peoples came from the north.

The land was largely inhospitable. Vast sections of it consisted of a desert in which nothing would grow. Settlements
were established where there was water for the fields and
flocks and some means of sustaining life for the settlers. Lacking a prosperous basis in nature for a supportive economy, the
Arabs turned to other pursuits. Cities such as Mecca were
known to be centers of commerce as well as of religion.
Mecca, the city where Muhammad was born, was ruled by a
large Arab tribe, the Quraish, which included a number of
smaller clans, such as the Banu Umayyah, and the Banu
Hashim. The leaders of the tribe had established a kind of oli-
garchical republic in which the merchants were dominant.
The city, ruled by a *mala,* or council, was divided into sections
where the richer and the poorer lived.

Mecca was a center through which the seasonal caravans
passed, bringing to the city the excitement from far places and
also the business resulting from that traffic. Usually there were
two seasons for the caravans. In the winter they went south to

Yemen. In the summer they went north to Syria and beyond. The caravans carried silks from China, precious stones from India, incense from Yemen, along with such practical items as cottonseed oil and corn. The caravans were huge operations, involving as many as two or three hundred men and two or three thousand camels. The caravans were a source of income wherever they went.

Mecca also had another source of income. It was a place of the *hajj*, or pilgrimage, long before Islam was born. The object of the pilgrimage was the Kabah (which means cube; the Kabah is a cubelike building with no exterior ornament). Within the Kabah was the holiest object in Arabia, a meteorite that had fallen into the Arabian sands long before the time of Muhammad. References are found to it as early as 60 B.C. Arabic tradition says that the black stone fell from heaven in the time of Adam, although another version dates it to the time of Abraham. The stone was worshiped just as other objects were. But it was an object of special veneration for many tribes throughout Arabia. There they would sacrifice sheep or camels, walk about the stone seven times in a counterclockwise route, and kiss the stone. So would the god's grace be received. In the less central places within the Kabah was the *maqam*, a sacred stone of Abraham, and various images of other deities from near and far. There was also an image of the chief Arabian deity, Hubal. About him but below him in importance were the goddesses: Al-Lat, Al-Manah, and Al-Uzza. These were the main gods in the pantheon. But there was another god, Allah, who was imageless. The word Allah derives from the oldest name for god in the Semitic tradition. It consists of the consonant *l* preceded by smooth breathing, making it in Judaism El. Allah was recognized long before the time of Muhammad as the one, supreme god. It was this god, recognized throughout Arabia, that Muhammad reinterpreted, reasserting his singleness and transcendence to the point of eliminating the need for the lesser deities. Allah was known to those who made the *hajj* to the Kabah at Mecca.

Close to the Kabah was a sacred well, Zamzam, around

which a number of traditions had grown. It was said, for example, that some centuries before Muhammad's time the well had been filled up by a tribe that controlled Mecca before they were expelled by another tribe. Later, when the Quraish tribe came to power in Mecca, Abd-al-Muttalib, Muhammad's grandfather, discovered the well, cleaned it out, and restored it as a religious site. Another tradition, derived from the Jews, concerns the time when Hagar was expelled from Abraham's tent. She brought her son, Ishmael, to the early site of Mecca, a place barren and without water. Hagar went in search of water to quench Ishmael's thirst. But in her absence the child in a fury beat against the ground with his heels, thus creating the well. At any rate, along with the Kabah, Zamzam was held in reverence. It became the basis for the so-called Lesser Pilgrimage in which those making the *hajj* to Mecca and the Kabah would pace back and forth seven times between two hills near the Kabah in imitation of Hagar's frantic search for water. There also was a so-called Greater Pilgrimage which took place during a holy month in which the pilgrims walked for several days among the hills east of Mecca.

The traffic of the caravans and pilgrimages to the black meteorite were the chief sources of income for the Meccans. Both were good reasons why the Quraish tribe required a measure of social control within the city and about it. Religion, from this perspective, had strong economic implications. This fact played its part in the rise of Islam. By Muhammad's time the importance of the caravans decreased at the same time as the importance of the pilgrimages increased. Caravan trading had been greatly weakened by the Egyptian development of water travel through the Red Sea. This obviated the need for land travel. Some of the smaller towns along the caravan routes were lucky to be able to survive through a minimal agriculture. But Mecca was built in a barren valley, and there was no such basis for maintaining its people's income. In Muhammad's time Mecca was in economic decay. Pilgrimages to the holy places, then, became all the more important. The city's ruling group saw that and capitalized on it, resisting any threat to the support of the pilgrimages. It is said that in the very year that Muhammad was born, Mecca faced a dire crisis. The Christian governor of southern Arabia, an Abyssinian, marched with his troops upon the city with the object of destroying what he considered to be its pagan shrines. The time is known as the year of the elephant because the governor's forces were led by a battle elephant, unusual for the time and place. Mecca anticipated its ruin, but the governor was forced to return to his own territory without success. Smallpox broke out among his troops, and the expedition was called off.

Muhammad in his life and teachings was faced with three chief religious traditions. It was in contention with these, along with his own inimitable contribution, that the religion of Islam was formulated. The first of these was the traditional Arabian religion. This religion was complex and was derived from a number of sources. Part of it has already been described. To a major degree Islam was a reaction against that religion. It was essentially animistic in nature. As such it perceived divine forces in various natural objects and events. Gods were assumed to inhabit wells, rocks, trees, and places. Sacred stones were used as altars where sacrifices would be made. The idea of the blood brotherhood was introduced by the practice of worshipers dipping their hands in the blood or licking some of it from the sacred stone. This meant that those who shared in the ceremony were completely bound to each other through their recognition of the god to whom the stone was an embodiment. Muhammad reacted against such practices and beliefs. In the Quran he roundly condemns such worship, calling it the work of Satan and unclean. In the Quran he calls upon the faithful to shun animism. Animals slain at such sacrifices were not to be eaten by Muslims. On the other hand, Islam has preserved the reverence for the black stone of the Kabah. It is stroked or kissed by the faithful making the desirable *hajj.* Muhammad seemed to believe that the power of the god was available through touching, either with the hands or the lips. Muhammad also sought to extirpate other animistic beliefs and practices, although his success, as later times give evidence, was not complete. However, the tradition of the pilgrimage, a part of pre-Islamic religion, was carried over with great fidelity into the new religion.

The second religious tradition with which Muhammad was faced was Judaism. No certain knowledge is available regarding the time and conditions under which Jews first came to Arabia. Some scholars think they may have migrated as early as the eighth century B.C. Others say they may have come in the first and second centuries A.D. as a result of their harsh persecution in Palestine by the Romans. It may be that they entered the peninsula during all those centuries as merchants. It is known that there was a thriving Jewish community in Yemen where at one time even the ruler was a Jew. The Jews of Muhammad's time were largely a prosperous group. They often owned the best land and were engaged in the most successful businesses. As a group they were far more affluent than the Arabs. And they were numerous in some places. In Medina, for example, it is estimated that they numbered about half the population.

It is difficult to evaluate the nature of the influence of Judaism upon Muhammad's own thought. Obviously he must have had some knowledge of Judaism by reason of the existence of the Jews around him. It is thought that Muhammad was unable either to read or write; this is the orthodox view. But in his adult life he was a merchant, and reading and writing may be assumed to be a part of the skills of such a person. His knowledge of the sacred scriptures both of Judaism and Christianity, however, was so faulty that it is possible to conclude that he relied upon oral information regarding these religions. Certainly, in broad outline, his developed views were those of both Judaism and Christianity: the succession of prophets, the idea of a sacred book (the Quran), the notions of revelation, of the resurrection, and of the afterlife, and other features. Later when he came into conflict with the Jews, he rejected them with scorn.

Christianity was the third tradition that faced Muhammad. There were a sizable number of Christians in Mecca. Among them were Syrian physicians, Abyssinian slaves and mercenaries, businessmen, and artisans. Muhammad certainly knew them. It is said that Waraqah, the cousin of Muhammad's wife, Khadijah, had been converted to Christianity. Throughout the Arabian peninsula there were a number of tribes that had been converted, sometimes only nominally. But the Christians were divided into at least three major and conflicting sects: Greek Orthodox, Monophysite or Jacobite, and Nestorian. The Greek Orthodox tradition is well known today. The Monophysites held that Jesus as the Christ had only one nature and that he was the incarnate word of god. The Nestorians believed that Christ was indeed human, a man, but that he was born as god through the virgin Mary. All three movements were active in converting the Arabs, but at the same time they were also fierce rivals. Sometimes their rivalry even took the form of religious warfare. The bitterness continued for centuries.

Muhammad was surely influenced by the Christianity about him. Originally he believed that Jesus was the messiah long prophesied in Judaism. He also accepted the virgin birth of Jesus and the immaculate conception of Mary. His views on the final state of affairs in life and in history were directly derived from Christianity, although he modified these outlooks. He believed in the anti-Christ, the resurrection of the body after death, the final judgment of good and evil, and the vivid reality of eternal life. These ideas he secured probably from oral tradition, since he did not show much precise knowledge of the New Testament. One Islamic tradition says that, prior to his triumph at Mecca, Muhammad wore tunics given him by desert monks. A reliable source also indicates that when he came to Mecca in triumph in A.D. 630, he ordered all the idols and paintings on the inner walls of the Kabah to be destroyed except one painting of Jesus and his mother, Mary. But later his break with Christianity was decisive. He was not a Christian; he was the founder of a new religion—Islam.

Several sources exist for portraying the life of Muhammad. The chief source is the Quran. One hundred and fourteen *suras,* or chapters, make up the book. The first chapter contains a short prayer called the Fatihah. Following it the chapters are arranged according to their length, with the longest first and the shortest last. Some modern versions of the Quran rearrange the chapters to fit the sequence of events that they relate. The Quran is not quite as lengthy as the New Testament. Many references are made in the Quran to the folk religion of Muhammad's time, and to Judaism and Christianity. For example, Jesus is mentioned twenty-five times. The Quran is held by Muslims to be the very revelation that Muhammad received from Allah. In fact, Allah is the main speaker in it. He either speaks directly and generally or directs that Muhammad speak for him. Yet Muhammad probably did not record the Quran. That task was left to his successor, Abu Bakr, who ordered that the teachings of the master be written down from the memories of his disciples. About a dozen years later the caliph Othman ordered that the first edition be destroyed and a more consistent version be created. Practically nothing is known about the first edition of the Quran today.

The Quran comprises the canonical, or authoritative, scriptures of Islam. In addition, however, there are noncanonical writings that also provide information about Muhammad and his religion. The *hadith,* or sayings, and the *sunnah,* or traditions, are valuable in that they consist of various accounts of what was known in early times of the life and preaching of Muhammad. They are chronologically more remote from his lifetime, however, and therefore not so reliable. Also among the noncanonical accounts is the *sirah,* the biographies, which were written by various persons in the eighth century and later. These make use of the Quran and the *hadith,* but their information is arranged in the form of consistent and chronological biographies of the founder. The biography by Ibn Hisham, who died in 834, is one of the oldest and most reliable.

The date of Muhammad's death seems certain: A.D. 632. But the date of his birth is uncertain. It is usually given as 569, 570, or 571. His birth, according to tradition, was preceded by various celestial signs of his importance. One legend says that

Muhammad's grandfather, Abd-al-Muttalib, had a dream before Muhammad's birth in which he saw a tree growing out of his back. The top of the tree reached to the sky and its branches extended far to the east and the west. From the tree came a light that was seven times brighter than the sun and it was worshiped by the Persians and the Arabs. He went to an interpreter of dreams and was told that this predicted that from his family would come one who would be a world ruler and a religious leader.

Muhammad's mother, Aminah, also experienced remarkable signs. She knew none of the limitations of pregnancy until one day, when she was in a state between waking and sleeping, she heard a voice declaring that the son whom she would bear would be a ruler and a prophet of his people. She was advised to wear iron rings about her neck and arms, but after a few days she found that the rings had been broken. Again the voice spoke to her and commanded that her newborn child be named Ahmad. This name has the same meaning as Muhammad—the illustrious one. His real name is not known and that by which he was later known was an honorific title. The use of such titles is not unknown among the other living religions. Muhammad was known also as Abul-Qasim, or *kunyah*, meaning the father of al-Qasim.

It is said that at the hour of his birth a bright light shone throughout the world. Aminah also saw in a vision the palaces of Syria and the necks of camels in Busrah. At his birth, Muhammad was said to have fallen to the ground, picked up some earth, and gazed significantly toward the sky. It is also said that he had no birthmarks, that he was already circumcised, and that his navel cord was already cut. These and other stories, derived from traditions that sprang up long after his death, show the great reverence that was held for him by his followers.

Orthodox Islamic tradition states that Muhammad was born into a distinguished family. It believes that god chose the family Banu Hashim for the prophet. This family was part of the Quraish clan, which in turn was a part of the larger tribe of the Banu Kinana. Banu Hashim, it is said, was a leading citizen of his time. He was responsible for equipping the caravans that made their way north and south. His son, Abd-al-Muttalib, Muhammad's grandfather, was the custodian of the Kabah and, at one time, the virtual head of the Meccan community. He also apportioned the water from Zamzam and was responsible for the feeding of the pilgrims. He had ten sons. They were stately men, with noble profiles. One of these sons was Abdullah, father of the prophet. Aminah derived from the Najjar branch of the Khazraj, a major tribe of Medina. Next to nothing is known about Abdullah, since he apparently died before Muhammad was born. It is said that he left Aminah with an unborn child, an old female slave, and five camels. Little is known about Aminah, except that she died when Muhammad was six years of age. As an orphan, however, Muhammad did not forget his parents. Once he threw himself into a grave and wept, saying that he was weeping for his mother because he had asked Allah to forgive her sins and Allah had refused to do so. A later legend says that Allah later relented and revived Muhammad's father and mother from death so that the prophet might preach to them and convert them.

Nothing much is accurately known about Muhammad's early years. Tradition says that he had a foster mother who cared for him in addition to his real mother (perhaps his mother was ill). The foster mother, Halimah, found that her home was blessed with the child's presence. Once, when Muhammad was in the fields tending the sheep with his foster brothers, two angels came and laid him on the ground, took a drop of black blood from his heart, and washed him within with melted snow that was taken from a golden cup. Then the angel weighed the lad against ten persons, then a hundred, and finally a thousand, but the boy always tipped the scale in his own favor. One of the angels then declared that the weighing should stop because he could be weighed against the whole nation and he still would weigh more. In these and other ways, the early life of Muhammad was seen as potent, eventful, and marvelous.

At the age of six, when his mother died, the child was taken into the family of his grandfather, Abd-al-Muttalib, where, it is said, he was loved more than his grandfather's own children. But this arrangement lasted for only two years, for then his grandfather died. Fortunately his uncle, Abu Talib (his real name was Abu Manaf, Talib being an honorific title), took the boy into his household. Early accounts say that Muhammad was very well received in Abu Talib's family. It is said, for example, that he could not sleep unless Muhammad was at his side and that whenever he went outdoors he wanted the boy to go with him. Various signs indicated to Abu Talib that Muhammad was an unusual person. Even the physical appearance of the prophet made a difference; he always looked as though he had been anointed with eye salve.

No knowledge exists of any formal schooling for Muhammad. His association with his grandfather, however, must have provided an environment in which the growing boy would become familiar with some, though not many, of the facts and values of his time, for his grandfather was a leading citizen of Mecca. Muhammad must have gained his knowledge of the larger world from the caravans that passed through the city. But apparently he secured additional understanding by going on a caravan journey. Some accounts suggest that he made more than one journey. One story says that his uncle took him with a caravan to Syria, where they met a Christian monk, Buhaira, who lived in a hermit's cell. Buhaira possessed esoteric Christian knowledge that had been passed on to him by previous monks. Usually, says the account, he paid no attention to the caravans traveling through. But when Muhammad came by, he went out and invited the whole assemblage to visit with him. He also held a feast to which he invited all. He recounted that he had seen several special signs: a cloud shading Muhammad as he was riding; a tree lowering its branches to shade him as the caravan came to rest. Buhaira inquired of the youth regarding the esoteric knowledge that the monk kept in a book. Muhammad was able to confirm this knowledge. The monk was most impressed and suggested to Abu Talib that he

take special care of the youth, especially against any harm
that might come to him from the Jews. Such a legend aims to
show the hidden, yet potent, character of Islam's founder as a
youth.

Quite possibly Muhammad at the age of twenty-five did
make a caravan journey to Syria. It is said that his uncle declared that he was quite poor and that Khadijah, the widow of
a merchant, was planning the caravan. The widow from all accounts was an attractive, strong person who had developed
business skills to an unusual degree, especially for a woman of
the times. The uncle sent Muhammad to Khadijah to ask if she
would take the young man. She accepted the uncle's request
and arranged that Muhammad receive four camels in payment
for his services instead of the usual two. The incident with the
monk, Buhaira, was later made a part of this caravan trip. The
journey was a success.

Khadijah was appropriately seated in Mecca to receive the
caravan. She noted that two angels kept Muhammad in the
shade as he rode on his donkey. She was impressed with the
young man. Later she sent a messenger to inquire whether he
was thinking of getting married. Muhammad replied that he
was too poor to think of marriage. When the messenger revealed who had made the inquiry, Muhammad was told that
through marriage with the rich widow he would be gaining a
fortune in addition to a wife of beauty and of noble birth.
Khadijah was a member of one of the leading families of the
Quraish tribe. Muhammad accepted the offer. One difficulty
remained: to get her father to accept the lowly Muhammad.
An acceptance was publicly indicated by the father's wearing
of a special garment given by the son-in-law for the wedding
ceremony. Khadijah seemingly did not believe that her father
would accept Muhammad and his proffered ceremonial dress,
so she got her father drunk, a chronicle says, in order for the
marriage to take place.

Muhammad was twenty-five years old at the time of his
marriage, and his bride was fifteen years his senior. From all
accounts the couple had a very happy married life. In time

they had two sons, but both died in infancy. Muhammad was sad all his life at their memory. They also had four daughters, who married leaders of the new religious movement. The third and fourth caliphs in Islam were married to Muhammad's daughters. His daughter Fatimah married Ali, the son of Abu Talib, Muhammad's first cousin. Muhammad had taken Ali into his own household at the death of his uncle. Abu Talib died after Muhammad had received his call from Allah to found the new religion and three years before the prophet fled to Medina. His uncle was greatly devoted to Muhammad, but he did not embrace the new faith. He declared that he was loyal to the faith of Abd-al-Muttalib. But during his life Abu Talib was loyal to the founder and defended him against his enemies.

Khadijah also was very loyal to her husband. Sometime later, when Muhammad had founded his new religion, she stood by his side, defending him against even the members of the Quraish tribe with whom the prophet found himself in conflict. Muhammad's loyalty to his wife is indicated by the fact that so long as she lived she was his only wife. This was unusual in a time when polygamy was widely practiced, especially among the well-to-do. In his lifetime Muhammad married nine women, but Khadijah was by far his favorite. He declared late in life that Khadijah had stood by him when all others were unbelieving; she believed in him when all others were saying that he was a liar.

Muhammad was forty years old when he received his first revelation from Allah. What specific experiences led him to the state of despondency and criticism that preceded his call are not known. His later message indicates some of the factors against which he was reacting. Preceding his call, he probably was irritated by the state of religious affairs. He was critical of the unabashed polytheism of his time. People believed in many gods and had many idols. Religion also had come to support a number of activities that Muhammad frowned upon: excessive drinking, sexual immorality, gambling, dancing, and elaborate ceremonies and fairs. He was depressed by the fighting and strife that were everywhere about. Rivals for leadership among the Quraish, the leading tribe of Mecca, often fought openly for dominance. Throughout Arabia such intertribal warfare was prevalent. It even broke out during the sacred month, Dhu-al-Qadah, when by common agreement everyone was to be respected. The need for stable social conditions was strong; the vision of a purified religion that would lead to improvement in all spheres of life was the touchstone.

Muhammad turned more and more to solitude and silence in his quest for meaning. It is said that as he wandered far from Mecca and onto the hillsides he heard voices that hailed him as Allah's apostle. Regularly he went to mountain caves where he could meditate and be alone. A later account says that in the month of Ramadan (which was to become a sacred month) he went with his family to a cave on Mount Hira, a few miles north of Mecca; perhaps he went alone, since it was upon his return that he told of the remarkable experience he had there. One night as he was sleeping, the angel Gabriel came to him with a cloth and commanded him to recite. Muhammad said that he could not recite. Gabriel took the cloth and choked him with it until Muhammad thought he would die. Then Gabriel released him and asked again that he recite. Muhammad hesitated. Twice more the angel choked him with the cloth and ordered him to recite. Finally Muhammad asked what he should recite. Gabriel commanded that he recite in the name of the lord who was the creator, who created man from clots of blood. Gabriel declared that this lord was a beneficent one, who had taught men to use the pen and who had taught men what they did not know. Muhammad awoke from his sleep, sensing that a message had been written on his heart. He went out of the cave and onto the mountain. There he heard a voice saying that he was indeed Allah's apostle and that the voice that had been speaking with him was indeed Gabriel's. Muhammad looked up and saw Gabriel, who appeared as a man with crossed legs, on the distant horizon. Muhammad remained standing, gazing at Gabriel. Whenever Muhammad turned from looking at Gabriel he found that Gabriel had moved to the new location on the horizon of heaven. In time the angel disappeared and Muhammad returned to Mecca and to his family. The revelation which he received on Mount Hira has become sura 96 of the Quran.

When Muhammad spoke with his wife, following his great vision, he became uncertain about his experience. He told her that he abhorred idols and soothsayers. Now he wondered whether he himself had become a soothsayer. Khadijah, however, assured him that he was no soothsayer and that Allah was indeed speaking to him. He knew that the soothsayers were possessed by *jinns*, or spirits, that directed their evocations. Muhammad wanted no part of them. His wife assured him that he was an honest and sincere man who in reality had been visited by the angel Gabriel and had received a revelation from Allah himself. Khadijah also visited her cousin, Waraqah, who himself had become a Christian. She told him what she knew. Although he remained a Christian, Waraqah recognized Muhammad as a true prophet. He declared that Muhammad was speaking the truth. He surmised that Muhammad's message was the revelation of a new and great law, such as that enunciated by Moses of old. Muhammad was reassured. In sura 53 he expresses his certainty, saying that he did not err and that he was not led astray. He declared that he was not speaking from some mere impulse. One terrible power endued with wisdom taught it to him.

Muhammad's assurance, however, was not permanent. He became greatly downcast, entering another period of uncertainty and anxiety. He wandered about in the hills to seek a reaffirmation of the initial revelation. Once, it is said, he was so despondent that he considered throwing himself off a high hill. But while he was considering his self-destruction he suddenly heard a voice from heaven. He looked and beheld the angel Gabriel again, sitting on a throne between the heavens and the earth. Gabriel announced that Muhammad was indeed the prophet of the lord, in truth, and that he himself was Gabriel. After this experience, Muhammad was comforted in his heart and returned to his own house. Thereafter, revelation followed revelation, creating the contents of the Quran. Muhammad had concluded that he was truly a *nabi*, a prophet who was fulfilling the line of prophets that had begun in ancient Judaism. He also thought of himself as a *rasul*, or an apostle, a person who has been selected by god to act as his messenger. The gods of Judaism and Christianity, and other religions as well, who were called by a variety of names, had come to Muhammad and had selected him to be the prophetic messenger.

Fortunately for Muhammad there were some who accepted his divine mandate, but they were few in number. First and foremost was his wife, Khadijah, who early and late in their marriage was an unfailing source of acceptance and encouragement. Tradition says that the first male Muslim was Ali, Muhammad's cousin, the son of Muhammad's uncle Abu Talib. Muhammad took the child into his own household when his uncle died. When Muhammad received his great revelation, however, Ali was a boy of perhaps nine or ten years of age. Zaid ibn-Harithah was the third convert. Apparently Zaid had come to Mecca as a slave. Muhammad and Khadijah were attracted to him, bought him, and set him free. Zaid became as a son to the couple, their own sons having died. Zaid greatly respected Muhammad and was ready, at the age of about thirty, to adopt the new religion.

The most important early convert, however, was Abu Bakr. Perhaps two years younger than Muhammad, he had been a friend of the prophet for many years. He too was a merchant, although he probably operated on a scale much smaller than Muhammad and Khadijah. Abu Bakr was the one who introduced Muhammad to five men who became the chief supporters of Muhammad in the later years of governmental administration. It is not clear when Abu Bakr became a believer, but it is known that by the time Muhammad left Medina for Mecca he was the most trusted follower. It was Abu Bakr who became the official successor to Muhammad at his death.

Some evidence suggests that these early followers were able

to convert fifty others in the Meccan community. Probably they did not come from the leading families, because, as Muhammad early discovered, they were opposed to his claims. They had the most to lose from following him. The early followers were young men of the middle and lower classes who could afford to break with tradition, although undoubtedly some persons of position also were converted. One of the arguments raised against him by the Meccans was that he was being followed only by the most abject in their midst.

Tradition says that for three years Muhammad preached his message quietly to his family and friends. In this period he did not seem to challenge openly the religious tradition. He won relatively few converts. But then he began to preach openly and critically. At first he seemed to be tolerant of the polytheism of his time. Then he boldly attacked the many gods, asserting that only Allah was god. This offended the people. He also preached that those who did not accept the faith he taught were lost eternally. Those who did not believe were offended. They scoffed at his teaching of the resurrection of the body and his vivid description of life after death. Muhammad was also a stern moralist who spoke against the behavioral practices of his time. Like the prophets before him, he proclaimed god's distaste for the lack of justice and charity. The idea of an impending judgment by Allah was heard increasingly. He proclaimed that the Quraish should repent, reform, become believers in the one, true god, and thus be saved. Many of the people hated him for this preachment. In addition to being a *nabi*, or prophet, and a *rasul*, or messenger, he became a *nadhir*, or warner. Increasingly and fervently he warned against the impending doom that hovered over the people.

The early Muslims were ridiculed at first. Muhammad's preaching at the Kabah was drowned out by coarse songs and shouts. Once a hearer spat on his face. Again, a hearer threw a sheep's placenta around his neck as he was praying at the Kabah, but the prophet simply got his daughter to wash it off. In time the opposition became more intense, and other charges were raised against him. He was accused of being a sorcerer who derived his message from disreputable sources. He also was accused of fraud, because, it was said, he was passing off as a revelation from Allah those teachings which he had gotten from Jews and Christians. The greatest opposition, however, came from the aristocrats of the Quraish tribe who readily perceived that Muhammad's teachings would potentially undermine the Meccan religious system, which had become a main economic support for the city. The oligarchs could see the handwriting on the wall. Moreover, Muhammad's preaching of social justice was essentially directed against the privileged, and they resented it.

As a result of the rising persecution of the new movement, a number of events took place. The leaders of the Quraish decided that each family within the tribe should take steps, sometimes harsh steps, to suppress the heretical faith. In this regard Muhammad fared well because he was protected by Abu Talib, his uncle, who, although he did not convert to Muhammad's religion, used his prestige and power within the community on behalf of his nephew. Tradition indicates that Muhammad was approached by another uncle, Utbah, with a delegation. If he would give up his new religion, they would gather a fortune for him, they said, larger than any possessed by anyone in the community. They would make him their chief, or if he wished, their king, and bring physicians to heal him of the demons that possessed him. Muhammad refused the offer.

Muhammad and some of his followers were able to resist the pressures of the Meccans. For those who could not, Muhammad advised that they migrate to Christian Abyssinia. From eleven to fifteen families, in A.D. 615, left Mecca for Abyssinia, where they were well received by the ruler. Later, eighty-three others migrated to Abyssinia.

At one point, however, Muhammad seemed to compromise with the hostile Meccans. One day as he was speaking near the Kabah, perhaps in a moment of weakness, he referred favorably to the three female deities, Al-Lat, Al-Manah, and

Al-Uzza, saying that their intercession was to be hoped for. Those who heard were pleased with this concession, although they were unwilling to accept the rest of Muhammad's teachings. Later Muhammad was rebuked by Gabriel in a revelation. He was told that this teaching was not from Allah, for Allah does not recognize male and female deities. Only Allah is god. The names of the female gods are merely names that had been created by the people of Arabia. The erroneous verses were expunged from the Quran.

The year A.D. 620 is called the year of grief in the later Muslim tradition. Both Muhammad's wife and his uncle died in that year. He was despondent over the loss of his wife. But the death of Abu Talib brought changes that led to his having to leave Mecca. Abu Talib had protected Muhammad from various oppositions, including the boycotting by the Hashimites. At his death the headship of the Hashimite clan was assumed by Abu Lahab, who had been part of the opposition. At first he promised protection to Muhammad, but later he also turned against him. Muhammad's bitterness toward Abu Lahab (and his wife) is shown in sura 111 of the Quran. Muhammad had to leave Mecca for his own safety and that of his followers.

Muhammad moved to Taif, a town about forty miles east of Mecca. At one time Taif had been a rival in trade with Mecca, but now it was a haven for the richer Meccans. He entered into negotiations with the leading citizens of Taif, seeking to persuade them of the revelations that he had been receiving from Allah. Obviously he also sought their protection, perhaps believing that they were discontented with what was going on in Mecca. But after a month in Taif, Muhammad met with no success. The leaders of Taif rejected him, and the townspeople threw stones at him as he left. On the way back to Mecca, despite the rejection at Taif, Muhammad is said to have preached to a company of *jinns* on the way, converting them. He also was said to have made a miraculous journey to Jerusalem and even to each of the seven heavens.

Somehow, Muhammad was able to stay in Mecca for two

years more. Protection must have been provided by some clan leader; perhaps Abu Lahab worked out a compromise with him. During this time he met with six pilgrims from Medina, then known by its ancient name of Yathrib. They were impressed with him and thought that he might help their own city with its problems. In the summer of A.D. 621 five of these six returned to Mecca and brought along seven others. They represented two of the leading tribes of Medina that had been feuding: the Khazraj and the Aws. Two of them were adherents of the folk religion of the times, but ten of them were Jews. The Jewish delegates surmised, when they heard Muhammad, that he might be the longed-for messiah. The twelve showed increased interest in the new religion and its prophet, and they pledged themselves to him.

After this Muhammad sent a trusted emissary to Medina to preach the new message and to size up the general situation in the city. The emissary found success. Many converts were made. By the summer of A.D. 622 a group of seventy-five converts, including two women, came to Mecca and met with the prophet secretly by night. They pledged that they would accept Muhammad as Allah's true prophet and that they would even fight on behalf of Allah against all foes. With this show of support, Muhammad, along with about one hundred families of the faithful, left Mecca for Medina, where they were eagerly received. It is said that the Meccans sought to kill Muhammad at this time, but in the company of Ali and Abu Bakr he eluded them and made his way by a roundabout route to Medina. The date of his arrival was September 24, 622. The migration from Mecca to Medina is often called a *hijra* (known also as the hegira). The date became the first year of the Muslim calendar, or 1 A.H. To loyal Muslims it marks the start of a new era in human history, the Muslim era.

After Muhammad consolidated his position there, the ancient city of Yathrib became known as Medina, or the city of the prophet. It was in Medina that the new religion found its first great success. Here Muhammad combined his religious message with the exercise of governmental power. Islam became a religion with complex, manifold, encompassing secular implications. Medina, about two hundred and fifty miles north of Mecca, was quite different from Muhammad's birthplace. It was primarily agricultural, being based on an oasis of about twenty square miles. There were some businesses in the city and some dependency upon the caravans, but Medina did not rank with Mecca in these functions. When Muhammad and his followers arrived, Medina was composed of about a dozen clans, each vying with the other for power in the community. Three of the larger clans were Jewish. But there had been much intermarriage between the Jews and the Arabs, and it was hard to distinguish between them. At one time the Jews had political control of the city. Various groups were in constant and violent conflict with each other. Sometimes this conflict was between two clans, but at other times it took place between blocs of clans.

Muhammad did not become the political chief of Medina immediately upon his arrival. He was the leader of the Muslims, but they were members of the various clans. Probably the early Muslims in Medina comprised yet another group, along with the various clans. But those who came to Mecca to request that Muhammad come to Medina pledged that they would defend him. They wished him to become an arbiter among the warring clans. Such a role was a well-accepted feature of Arabic tradition, so this role was not novel for the prophet. It was through this role that Muhammad became the head of the community. Islam was the primary basis for communal unity. Once in control, Muhammad established the faith as the religion for all and took steps to quash the worship of idols. He spoke on many subjects with the voice of divine authority. Many of the most clear and forceful suras of the Quran come from this era. A year or two after he arrived he composed a charter which added the force of law and reason to all social relations. The charter bound all together through a common allegiance to Islam. Thus a kind of theocracy was created. In addition to his other roles of prophet and messenger, he became a lawgiver and a statesman.

Firmly in control in Medina, Muhammad looked to other worlds to conquer. In the spring of A.D. 624 he sought to raid a large caravan of the Quraish with a force of about three hundred Muslims. The caravan was led by Abu Sufian and was a rich prize. But Abu Sufian was warned before they came to the valley of Badr, where the battle finally took place. He called for help and about a thousand Quraishites came to his rescue, nearly all mounted for battle. The Muslims were greatly outnumbered. But they lacked nothing in fervor and bravery. Goaded by the prophet and the idea that Allah looked with favor upon their cause, they fought extremely well. Abu Sufian and his forces were routed. The victory belonged to Muhammad and his followers; they assigned it to Allah. Muhammad was now also a successful military commander. The people of Medina, impressed with the victory, rallied about the prophet. After a revelation he declared that one fifth of the booty would be his, so that he could meet the needs of his family, the poor, and the army. The *jihad,* or killing in the way of Allah, was established. The Meccans had been humbled.

In the next years Muhammad often engaged in military ventures. After the battle of Badr the Quraish of Mecca, under Abu Sufian, the city's political head, struck back at the battle of Uhud. Muhammad was almost killed in this battle; his forces were greatly outnumbered. But the Quraish failed to capitalize upon their victory and returned to Mecca. The Jewish clans in Medina became discontented. Although they earlier had confidence in Muhammad and his new religion, in time they came to see that it was not the Judaism to which they were committed. They failed to be reconciled to the new faith, and a military confrontation was inevitable.

In A.D. 626 Muhammad laid siege to a stronghold of the Jews, the Banu Nadir clan, and after fifteen days the Jews gave up. Muhammad permitted them to leave Medina with whatever property they could take. But their land and other property was confiscated as the spoils of holy war. This property was given to the Muslim community. Other conflicts with the Jews of the region took place and gradually the new faith found itself in sharp opposition on every front, including the religious, with the Jews of the time. Military conflicts with various other groups also took place, and generally the Muslims were the victors.

Mecca, however, remained. Having conquered the tribes that surrounded Mecca, in A.D. 628 Muhammad took fourteen hundred followers on a pilgrimage to Mecca. They were met on the way by a force of the Quraish which sought to prevent their entry into the city. Instead of another battle, a peaceful solution was established under which Muhammad was assured that he and his followers would be permitted to make the pilgrimage the next year. On his side, Muhammad accepted a ten-year truce with the Quraishites. In the ensuing year, Muhammad further consolidated his rule in Medina and continued his conquests beyond the city.

In A.D. 629 Muhammad returned to Mecca with two thousand of his followers, according to the agreement. The city was vacated of its inhabitants during the three-day visit and all went well. The pilgrimage completed, the Muslims returned to Medina. Conflicts, however, continued. Muhammad, for example, sent out a force of three thousand men to avenge the death of an envoy whom he had sent to try to convert the Ghassanid Arabs. The move turned out to be disastrous, for the Muslims were roundly defeated and Muhammad's adopted son, Zaid, was killed. The Muslims were kept from utter annihilation by the clever retreat of the Muslim commander, Khalid, who followed Zaid.

Muhammad still had not conquered Mecca. So, on January 1, 630, along with a force of about ten thousand men, he set out to accomplish that goal. When he was a day's distance from the city, he was met by a delegation of the Quraish, led by Abu Sufian, who, it must be remembered, was married to Muhammad's daughter. Abu Sufian agreed to submit to the new religion and to place himself and his people under Muhammad's rule. A battle was avoided. The Muslims entered the city in peace. The victor was magnanimous toward the

Meccans. He executed only four persons who were adjudged to be criminals; all others were granted amnesty. Muhammad went to the Kabah, where it is said that he destroyed three hundred and sixty idols with his staff, declaring that god is great, truth has come, and falsehood has vanished. He also declared that the Kabah was the central shrine of Allah, and so it has remained to this day. Then he preached further to the people. He called upon them to fear Allah so that they might receive his mercy. He said that all believers were brethren; peace should be the norm among brothers. The people of the city, seeing Muhammad's triumph and the incapacity of their own idols, were converted in large numbers. The faith had come finally and fully to the prophet's birthplace, from which he earlier had been expelled, the city that was the crown of Arabian civilization.

Following the enshrining of Islam in Mecca, Muhammad sent emissaries to various parts of Arabia. The year A.D. 631 has become known as the year of delegations. Taif, which had rebuffed him before, rebuffed him again but was conquered. Others received the delegates and submitted to the new faith and its leader. Some did not wait, but sent their own delegates to the prophet in submission. Almost everywhere the people praised the new leader. They joined his military forces, paid their taxes to a central power (a novel experience for them), and benefited from the sense of belonging to a successful, appealing faith and its concomitant sacred community. Arabia had never before been unified; it now was. In ten years (from his first revelations to his triumph in Mecca), despite many setbacks, Muhammad had succeeded in establishing a new religion and in creating a new social order that flowed from it. The ties of faith had supplanted the ties of blood. A universal religion was proposed that would make of all mankind one brotherhood in submission to Allah, the one god.

Now Muhammad's end was drawing near. In A.D. 632 he made his last pilgrimage to Mecca, along with a large contingent of followers. When the ceremonies were completed, he went to the top of Mount Arafat, near Mecca, and addressed his followers, calling upon them to hearken to his words. Saying that he thought he might not have another year to live, he called upon the faithful to keep their lives and property sacred and inviolable. He reminded them that they would all face the last judgment and would be required to give an account of their moral actions. He reminded them that all Muslims are brothers and that it is sinful to act unjustly toward one's brothers. Shun injustice, he said. Finally he declared that he had finished his task and had fulfilled his message. He called upon Allah to bear witness to the fact.

He was sixty-two years old. His last days were spent with a favorite wife, Aishah, the youngest daughter of Abu Bakr, his successor. He was feeble and weak, but he managed to maintain public prayers until the last three days before his death. In one of his last statements he begged that if he had wronged any Muslim, he was ready to make amends. He said that all that he possessed belonged to them. He reminded his hearers that all he sought to do was to make lawful that which Allah had ordained through the Quran. Disclaiming any power to save others, he turned finally to his daughter Fatimah and to his aunt Safiyah and instructed them to work on their own to gain favor with Allah. Returning to Aishah's house, then, he died in her arms a few hours later. It was June 8, 632. He was buried in the house. Later a mosque was erected on the spot. To Abu Bakr fell the task of announcing the death. He told those assembled that if any among them had been worshiping Muhammad, he really was dead. But if he really was worshiping Allah, he should know that Muhammad was living and that he would never die.

In his lifetime Muhammad did not claim to possess any special virtues, except that he had been chosen by Allah to receive revelations and to speak for him. He admitted wrongdoing and the need for Allah's forgiveness. Certainly there is no doctrine in Islam that makes the founder a son of god in a unique sense. Orthodox Muslims believe that Muhammad was not a part of the godhead, but a prophet, a messenger, a warner. After Muhammad's death, he began to be looked upon as a very outstanding person, one whose spiritual and secular leadership was unmatched throughout the world and throughout time. He was viewed as having had an existence prior to his birth. Indeed, he is said to have lived even before the creation of the world. Those who admired him later advanced the idea that he was sinless in his life. Other Muslims concluded that there is saving power and grace in the mere repetition of his name. As is true of the several religions, Islam's history achieved no unity as to how the founder should be regarded. A variety of sectarian movements within its history confirms the seeming inevitability of large numbers of believers to disagree in their perceptions of the nature and worth of the founder.

The developed religion of Islam contains a number of beliefs and practices that need to be mentioned. Central to Islam is the belief in a supreme being—Allah. A number of names are used in the Quran to describe him: the provider, the merciful, the king, the powerful, the one, the avenger, the loving, the dominator, the slayer, the compassionate, and the forgiving. Allah also is a stern moralist. He rewards those who are submissive to him and punishes those who are wicked. He stands for justice and charity and requires that all believers follow his decrees in this regard. There are no other gods in the whole universe. Allah is one; he is supreme.

Allah, however, is not alone in the supraterrestrial realm. He has peopled this realm with angels and spirits. Eight angels support the throne of Allah. Nineteen guard hell. The angels are divided into two classes. First, there are those who simply maintain a constant sovereignty. These may be called archangels; they include: Gabriel, Michael, Asrael, Malik (the steward of hell), and Ridvan (the gatekeeper of paradise). Second, there are angels of lesser stature who obediently act at the direction of Allah and the archangels. Another group of spiritual beings also exist in Islam: the *jinns*. They appear to have a status between men and the angels. They are also both good and bad. One of them is Satan, according to the Quran.

The Quran is held to be an indispensable authority of the

religion. Among the sacred scriptures of the world's living religions it is perhaps distinctive in that Muslims believe their founder, Muhammad, wrote (or spoke) every word of it. It literally consists of the very words of Allah which Muhammad received directly and then faithfully passed on to his followers. Muhammad is called the seal of the prophets. This means that the religion recognizes the sacred scriptures of Judaism and Christianity as precursors of the divine teachings of Muhammad as contained in the Quran. But Muhammad is the last of the prophets. The Quran is the final revelation from god.

Islam also teaches of a last judgment at which Allah will weigh carefully and to the minutest detail the ethical behavior of every person. No one can escape this judgment. It will occur at the end of the world and will feature the resurrection of the dead. Those who stand the test at the last judgment will enter paradise. Paradise is a place in which the sensual pleasures are abundantly satisfied. It is basically a male paradise. There the pious will live in verdant gardens, reclining on couches in rows, eating and drinking with good digestion, having fruit and flesh as they like, enjoying the flowing wine, suffering no headaches, and taking pleasure from bright and large-eyed maids. Those who are adjudged to be evil will be sent to hell. There the unfaithful will know no rest, suffering from sheets of fire that will encompass them. When they cry for help, they will be given water like molten brass that will scald their faces. The similarities of these beliefs to those in later Judaism, in Zoroastrianism, and in Christianity appear to be more than coincidental.

Islam also prescribes five essential, religious duties. These are called the five pillars of Islam. First, every Muslim is required to repeat the *kalimah,* or confession of faith, every day in the original Arabic. The *kalimah* is: There is no god but Allah, and Muhammad is the prophet of Allah. This confession is a daily sign that the believer is submissive, the hallmark of the religion. Second, every Muslim must practice prayer at least three times a day: at daybreak, at noon, and at night. The minaret of the mosque is the place where the call goes out to remind the faithful of this obligation. No matter where a person may be or what he may be doing, he prostrates himself in the direction of the most sacred Kabah in Mecca and prays.

Third, almsgiving is a duty for all Muslims. In the early years of the religion almsgiving was considered as a loan to Allah and was directed toward the poor, the needy, beggars, slaves, and others who could benefit. It was collected by the religious leaders, sometimes called *imams,* placed in a common treasury to be used for the poor and others, and for the upkeep of mosques and for other purposes. Today it is less a tax and more a voluntary offering which the Muslim makes as a prescribed duty. Fourth, fasting during the month of Ramadan is obligatory. Except for those who are ill, fasting begins at daybreak, when the believer can distinguish a white thread from a black one, and continues until evening, when the threads are used again to set the time when the fast may be broken. Fifth, every Muslim is expected, unless there are extenuating circumstances, to make a pilgrimage to Mecca during his lifetime. In earlier times this pilgrimage was often accomplished under very difficult conditions. Today, however, with modern means of transportation, it is less difficult, although it may be expensive for the average believer. The ceremonies at the Kabah and its environs are complex. In part the pilgrims start at the black stone and run about the Kabah seven times, three times fast and four times slowly, stopping each time to kiss or to touch the stone. Other parts of the ceremonies make it a reverential and joyous experience of worship. In addition to the five pillars of Islam the religion enjoins various ethical requirements that enable the religion to permeate almost every sector of the believer's life.

Islam, then, founded by Muhammad, is a strong, vital religion, which has succeeded over the centuries and in many lands to appeal to many millions of believers. Advocating submission to the one, true god, Allah, it provides guidelines for the believer's life, both in its religious and its secular dimensions.

SELECTED BIBLIOGRAPHY

Chapter 1. INTRODUCTION

Bouquet, A. C. (ed.), *Sacred Books of the World.* Barnes & Noble, Inc., 1963.

Braden, Charles S., *The World's Religions: A Short History,* rev. ed. Abingdon Press, 1954.

Gaer, Joseph, *How the Great Religions Began,* rev. ed. Dodd, Mead & Company, Inc., 1963.

Noss, John B., *Man's Religions,* 5th ed. The Macmillan Company, 1974.

Smart, Ninian, *The Religious Experience of Mankind.* Charles Scribner's Sons, 1969.

Smith, Wilfred Cantwell, *The Meaning and the End of Religion: A New Approach to the Religious Traditions of Mankind.* The Macmillan Company, 1963.

Zaehner, Robert C. (ed.), *The Concise Encyclopedia of Living Faiths.* Beacon Press, Inc., 1967.

Chapter 2. VARDHAMANA AND JAINISM

Basham, Arthur L., *The Wonder That Was India: A Survey of the History and Culture of the Indian Sub-Continent Before the Coming of the Muslims,* 3d rev. ed. Taplinger Publishing Company, Inc., 1968.

Jacobi, Hermann (tr.), *Jaina Sutras,* 2 vols. Dover Publications, Inc., 1968.

Stevenson, Mrs. Sinclair, *The Heart of Jainism*. New York, 1915.

Stroup, Herbert, *Four Religions of Asia*. Harper & Row, Publishers, Inc., 1968.

—— *Like a Great River: An Introduction to Hinduism*. Harper & Row, Publishers, Inc., 1972.

Chapter 3. GAUTAMA AND BUDDHISM

Bahm, Archie J., *Philosophy of the Buddha*. Collier Books, 1962.

Burtt, Edwin A. (ed. and commentator), *The Teachings of the Compassionate Buddha: Early Discourses, the Dhammapada, and Later Basic Writings*. The New American Library of World Literature, Inc., 1955.

Conze, Edward (selector and translator), *Buddhist Scriptures*. Penguin Books, Inc., 1959.

Fox, Douglas A., *The Vagrant Lotus: An Introduction to Buddhist Philosophy*. The Westminster Press, 1973.

Kelen, Betty, *Gautama Buddha in Life and Legend*. Lothrop, Lee & Shepard Company, 1967.

Morgan, Kenneth W. (ed.), *The Path of the Buddha: Buddhism Interpreted by Buddhists*. Ronald Press, 1956.

Rhys-Davids, T. W. (tr.), *Buddhist Birth-Stories: Jataka Tales*. Leiden, 1973.

Chapter 4. NANAK AND SIKHISM

Archer, John Clark, *The Sikhs in Relation to Hindus, Moslems, Christians, and Ahmadiyyas*. Princeton University Press, 1946.

McLeod, W. H., *Guru Nanak and the Sikh Religion*. Oxford University Press, Inc., 1968.

Singh, Gopal, *The Religion of the Sikhs*. Asia Publishing House, Inc., 1971.

Singh, Sir Jogendra, *Thus Spoke Guru Nanak*. Oxford University Press, Inc., 1934.

Singh, Khushwant, *A History of the Sikhs,* Vol. I: 1469–1839. Princeton University Press, 1963.

Chapter 5. LAO-TZU AND TAOISM

Blakney, R. B. (tr.), *The Way of Life: Tao Te Ching, Lao Tzu. A New Translation of the Tao Te Ching*. The New American Library of World Literature, Inc., 1955.

McNaughton, William, *The Taoist Vision*. University of Michigan Press, 1971.

Smith, D. Howard, *Chinese Religions: From 1000 B.C. to the Present Day*. Holt, Rinehart and Winston, Inc., 1971.

Van Over, Raymond (ed.), *Taoist Tales: The First Mystical Writings of Mankind's Religious Consciousness*. The New American Library, Inc., 1973.

Waley, Arthur (ed. and tr.), *The Way and Its Power: A Study of the Tao Te Ching and Its Place in Chinese Thought, by Lao-tzu*. Grove Press, 1958.

Welch, Holmes, *The Parting of the Way: Lao Tzu and the Taoist Movement*. Beacon Press, Inc., 1957.

Chapter 6. CONFUCIUS AND CONFUCIANISM

Bahm, Archie J., *The Heart of Confucius*. Walker & Co., 1969.

Creel, H. G., *Confucius and the Chinese Way*. Harper & Brothers, 1960.

de Bary, W. Theodore, and others (comps.), *Sources of Chinese Tradition*. Columbia University Press, 1960.

Smith, D. Howard, *Confucius*. Charles Scribner's Sons, 1973.

Ware, James R. (tr.), *The Sayings of Confucius*. The New American Library of World Literature, Inc., 1955.

Yutang, Lin (ed. and tr.), *The Wisdom of Confucius*. Modern Library, Inc., 1938.

Chapter 7. ZOROASTER AND ZOROASTRIANISM

Bausani, Alessandro, *The Persians: From the Earliest Days to the Twentieth Century*, tr. from the Italian by J. B. Donne. St. Martin's Press, Inc., 1971.

Duchesne-Guillemin, Jacques, *Zoroastrianism: Symbols and Values*. Harper & Row, Publishers, Inc., 1970.

Masani, Rustom, *Zoroastrianism: The Religion of the Good Life*. The Macmillan Company, 1968.

Moulton, James Hope, *The Treasure of the Magi*. London, 1913.

Zaehner, Robert C., *The Dawn and Twilight of Zoroastrianism*. G. P. Putnam's Sons, 1961.

Chapter 8. JESUS AND CHRISTIANITY

Braden, Charles, *Jesus Compared: A Study of Jesus and Other Great Founders of Religions*. Prentice-Hall, Inc., 1957.

Bultmann, Rudolf, *Primitive Christianity in Its Contemporary Setting*, tr. by R. H. Fuller. Meridian Books, 1956.

Burrows, Millar, *The Dead Sea Scrolls*. The Viking Press, Inc., 1955.

Grant, Frederick C., *The Gospels: Their Origin and Their Growth*. Harper & Brothers, 1957.

Pfeiffer, Robert H., *History of New Testament Times: With an Introduction to the Apocrypha*. Harper & Brothers, 1949.

Schweitzer, Albert, *The Quest of the Historical Jesus*, tr. by W. Montgomery. The Macmillan Company, 1961.

Trocmé, Etienne, *Jesus as Seen by His Contemporaries*, tr. by R. A. Wilson. The Westminster Press, 1973.

Chapter 9. MUHAMMAD AND ISLAM

Andrae, Tor, *Mohammad, The Man and His Faith*, tr. by Theophil Menzel. Harper & Brothers, 1960.

Cragg, Kenneth, *The Call of the Minaret*. Oxford University Press, Inc., 1964.

Dawood, N. J. (tr.), *The Koran*. Penguin Books, Inc., 1956.

Guillaume, Alfred, *Islam*. Penguin Books, Inc., 1954.

Patai, Raphael, *The Arab Mind*. Charles Scribner's Sons, 1973.

Schuon, Frithjof, *Understanding Islam*, tr. from the French by D. M. Matheson. Penguin Books, Inc., 1972.

INDEX AND GLOSSARY